The New Authentics

Artists of the Post-Jewish Generation

by Staci Boris

Foreword by Rhoda Rosen
Essay by Stephen J. Whitfield
Excerpt from *The History of Love* by Nicole Krauss
Artist essays by Sarah Giller Nelson and Lori Waxman

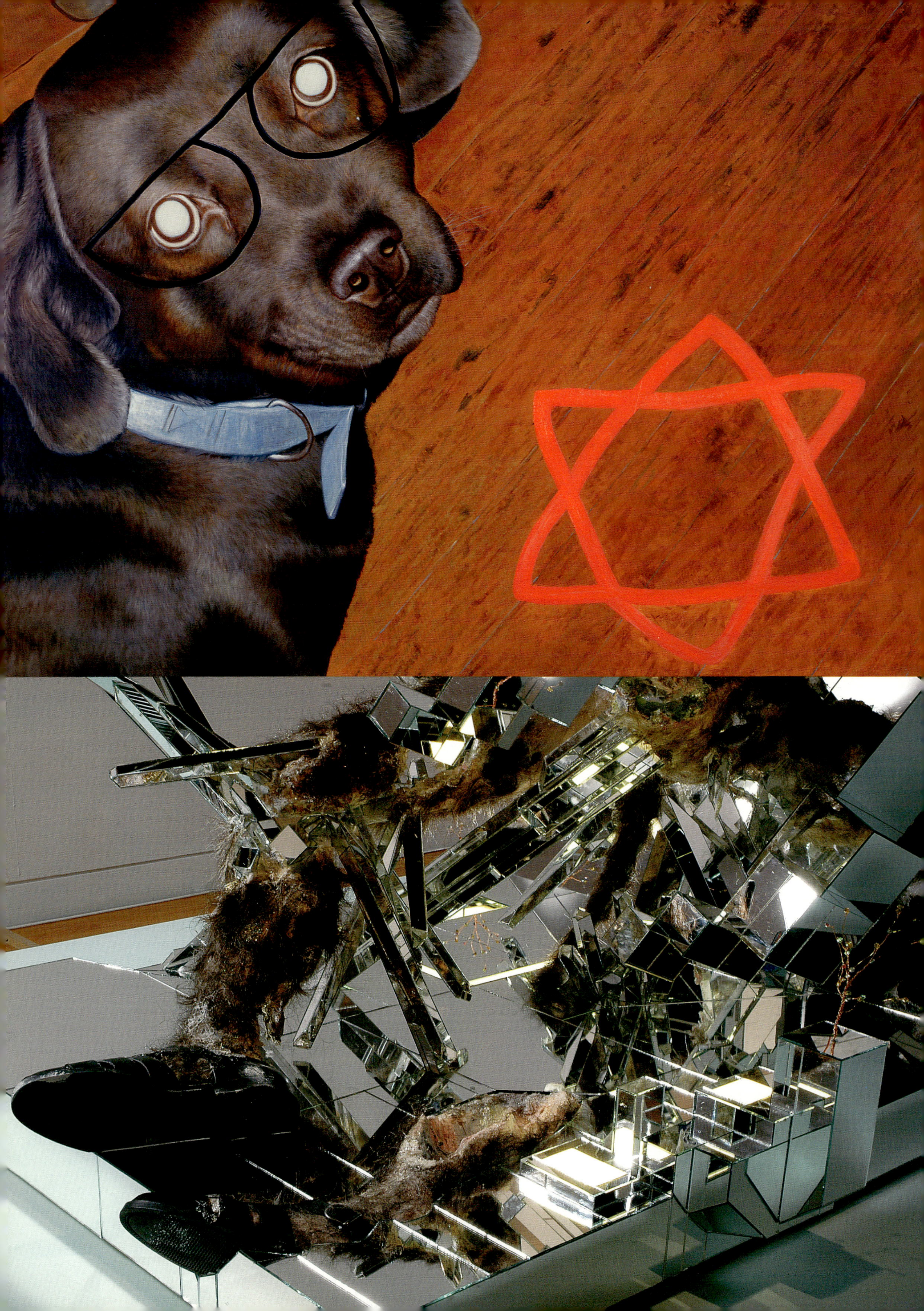

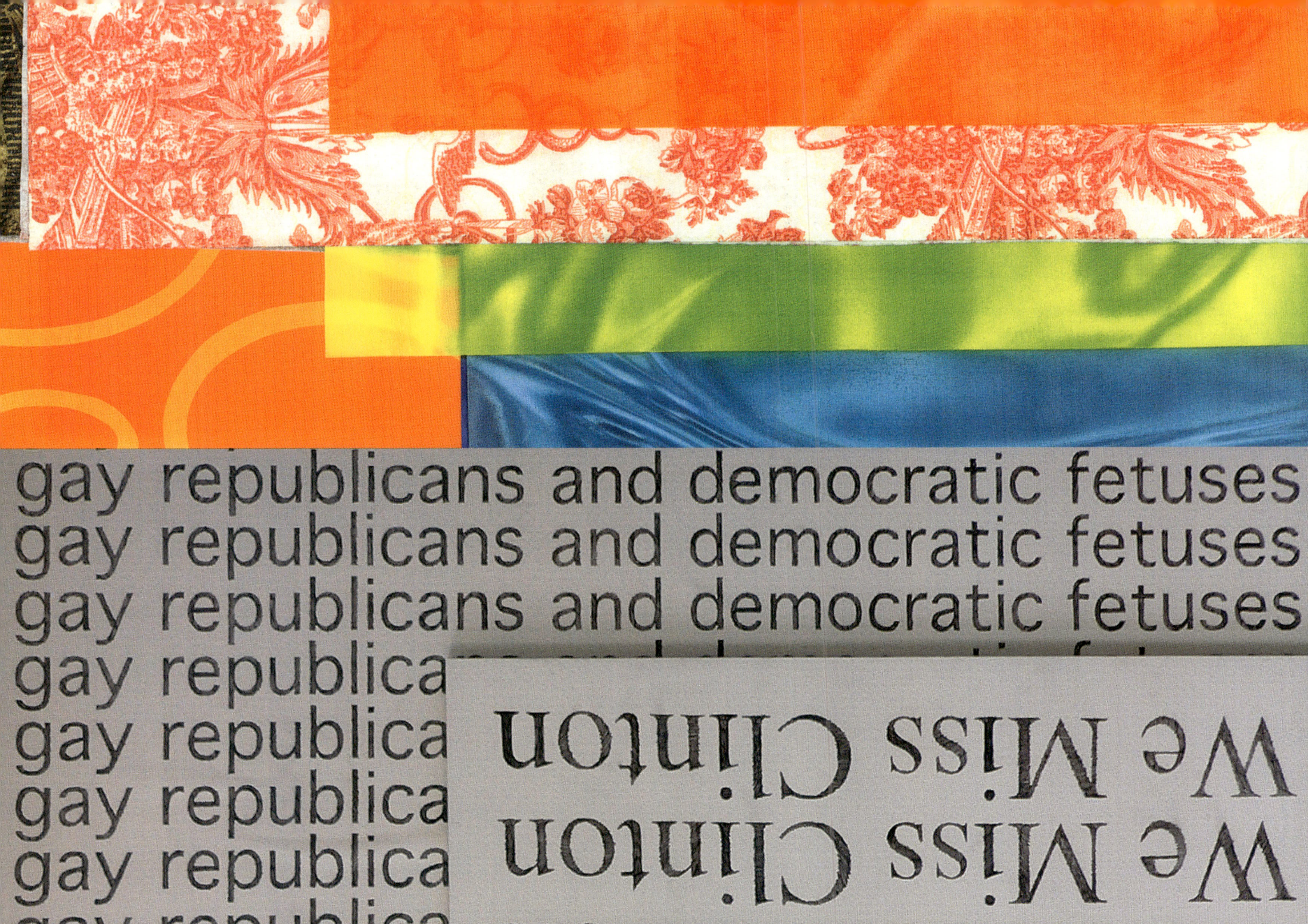

gay republicans and democratic fetuses
gay republicans and democratic fetuses
gay republicans and democratic fetuses
gay republicans and democratic fetuses
gay republicans
gay republica
gay republica
gay republica
gay republica
We Miss Clinton
We Miss Clinton

The New Authentics

Artists of the Post

Spertus Museum
Spertus Institute of Jewish Studies

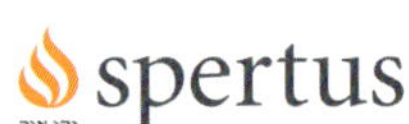

David Altmejd
Cheselyn Amato
Johanna Bresnick
Shoshana Dentz
Lilah Freedland
Matthew Girson
Karl Haendel
Laura Kina
Fawn Krieger
Jin Meyerson
Collier Schorr
Mindy Rose Schwartz
Ludwig Schwarz
Joel Tauber
Shoshanna Weinberger
Jennifer Zackin

ewish Generation

Curated by Staci Boris

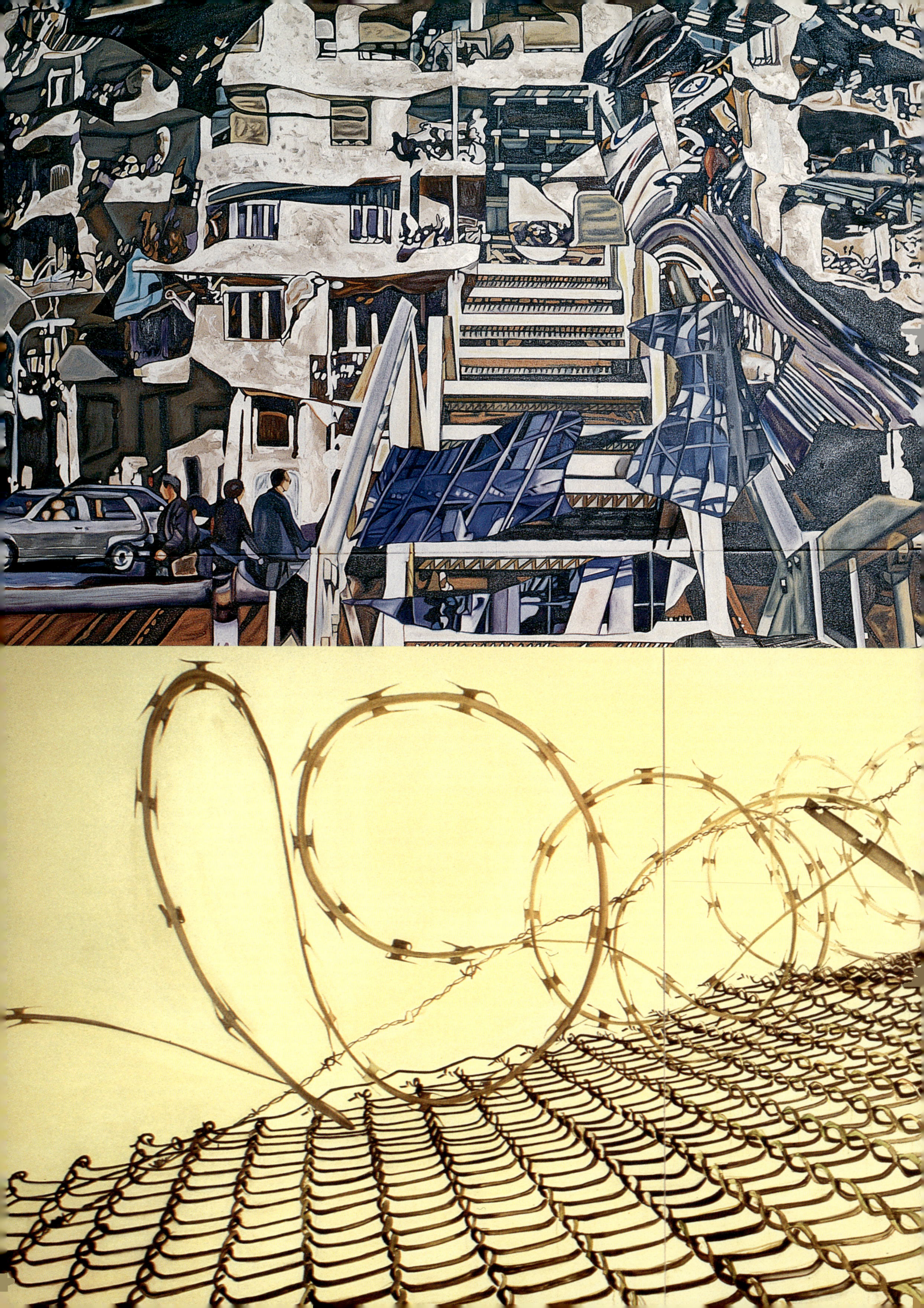

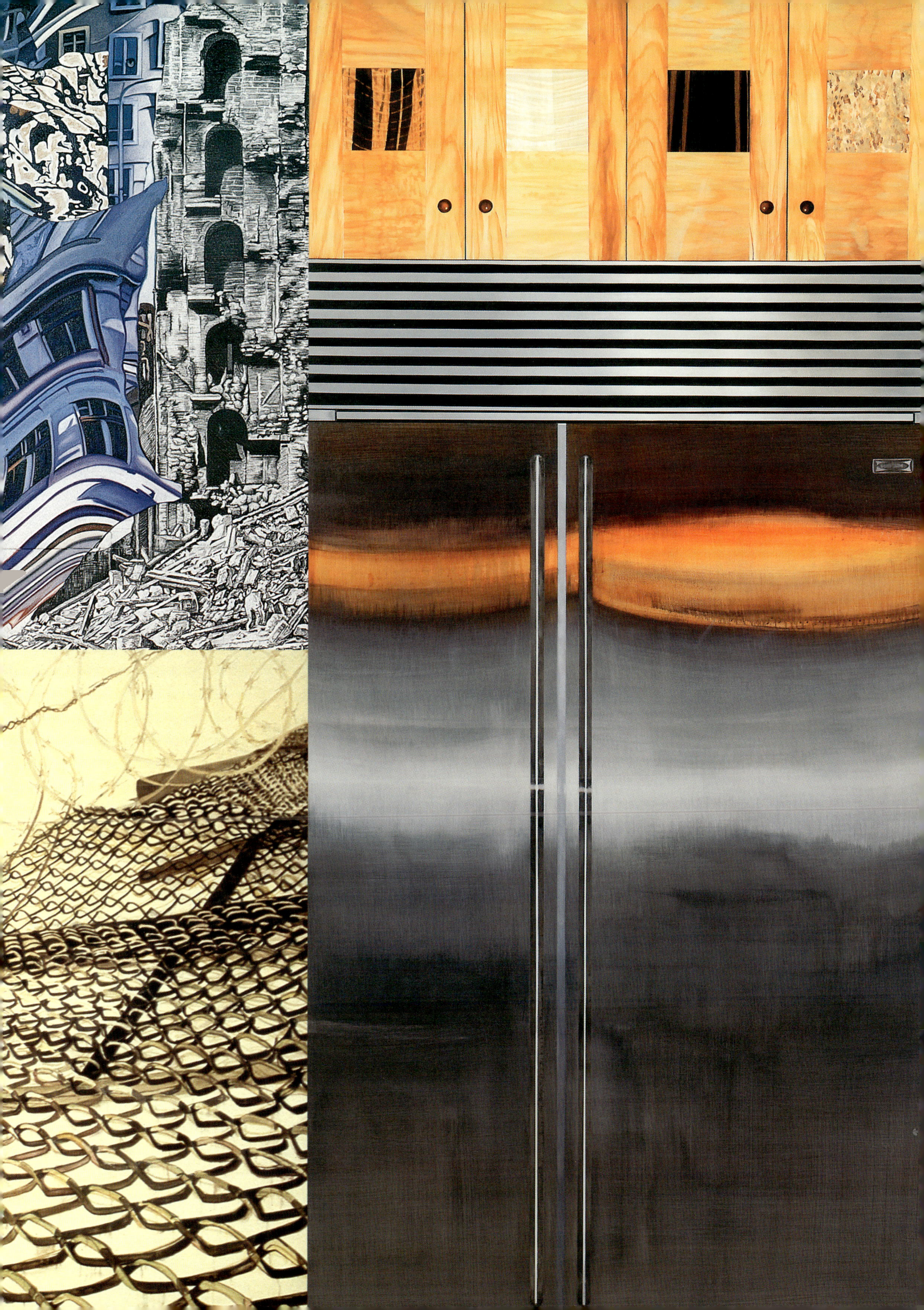

This book has been published in conjunction with the exhibition
The New Authentics: Artists of the Post-Jewish Generation, organized by Spertus Museum.

SPERTUS MUSEUM, CHICAGO
November 30, 2007–April 13, 2008

THE ROSE ART MUSEUM, BRANDEIS UNIVERSITY, WALTHAM, MA
May 9–July 27, 2008

Spertus Press Chicago
Copyright © 2007 by Spertus Institute of Jewish Studies, Chicago.
All rights reserved. No part of this publication may be reproduced without written permission of:
Spertus Institute of Jewish Studies
610 S. Michigan Avenue
Chicago, IL 60605

Spertus Institute of Jewish Studies is a partner in serving our community,
supported by the JUF/Jewish Federation.

ISBN-13: 978-0-935-98265-7

Library of Congress Control Number: 2007923149

Curator and author: Staci Boris
Editor: Jennifer Liese
Designer: JNL Graphic Design, Chicago
Printer: Everbest, Hong Kong

Excerpt from *The History of Love* by Nicole Krauss is used by permission of
W. W. Norton & Company, Inc. Copyright © 2005 by Nicole Krauss.

Cover image:
Lilah Freedland, *dream as though you'll live forever, live as though you'll die today*, 2003, c-print, 24 x 20".

MADE IN CHINA

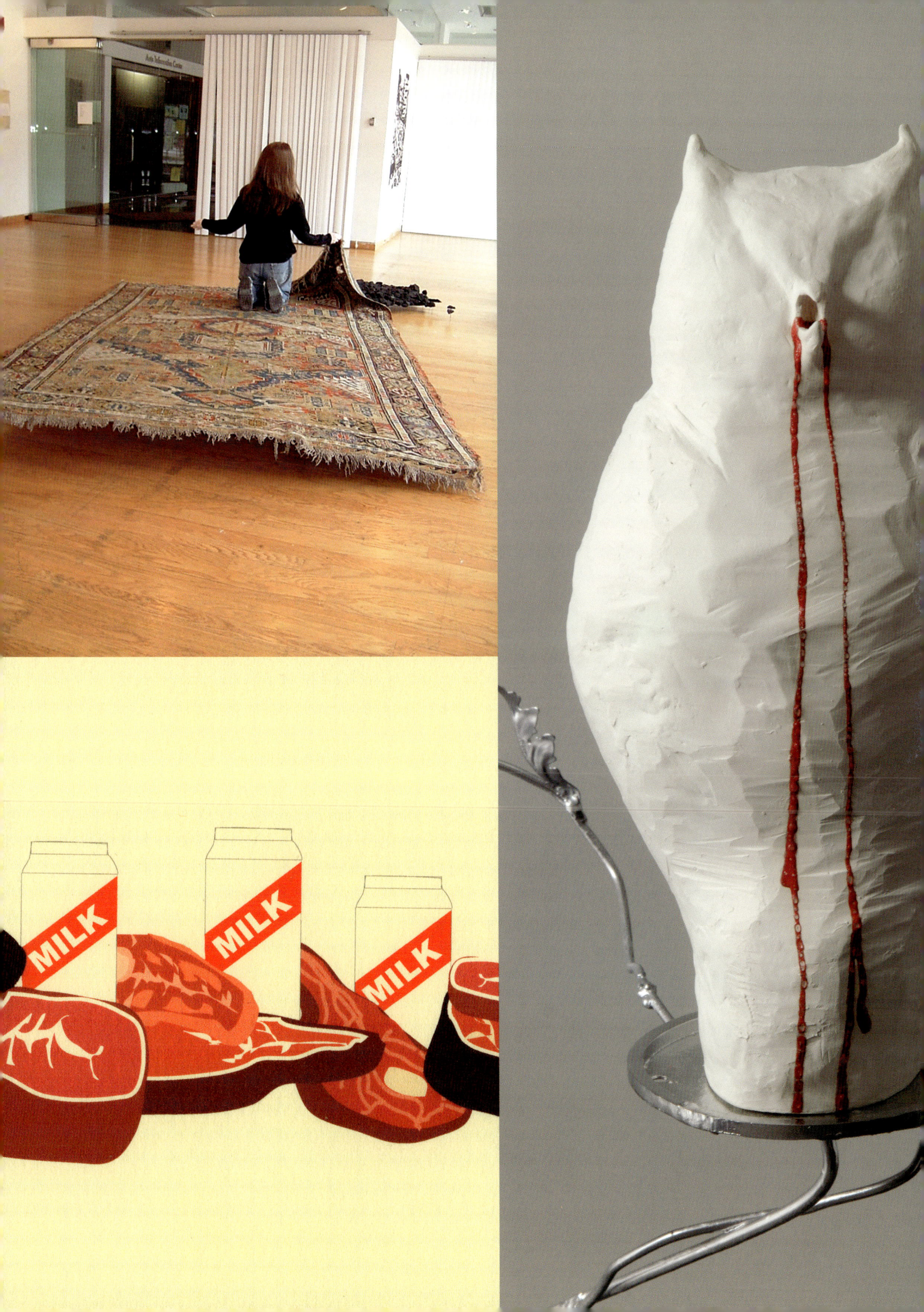

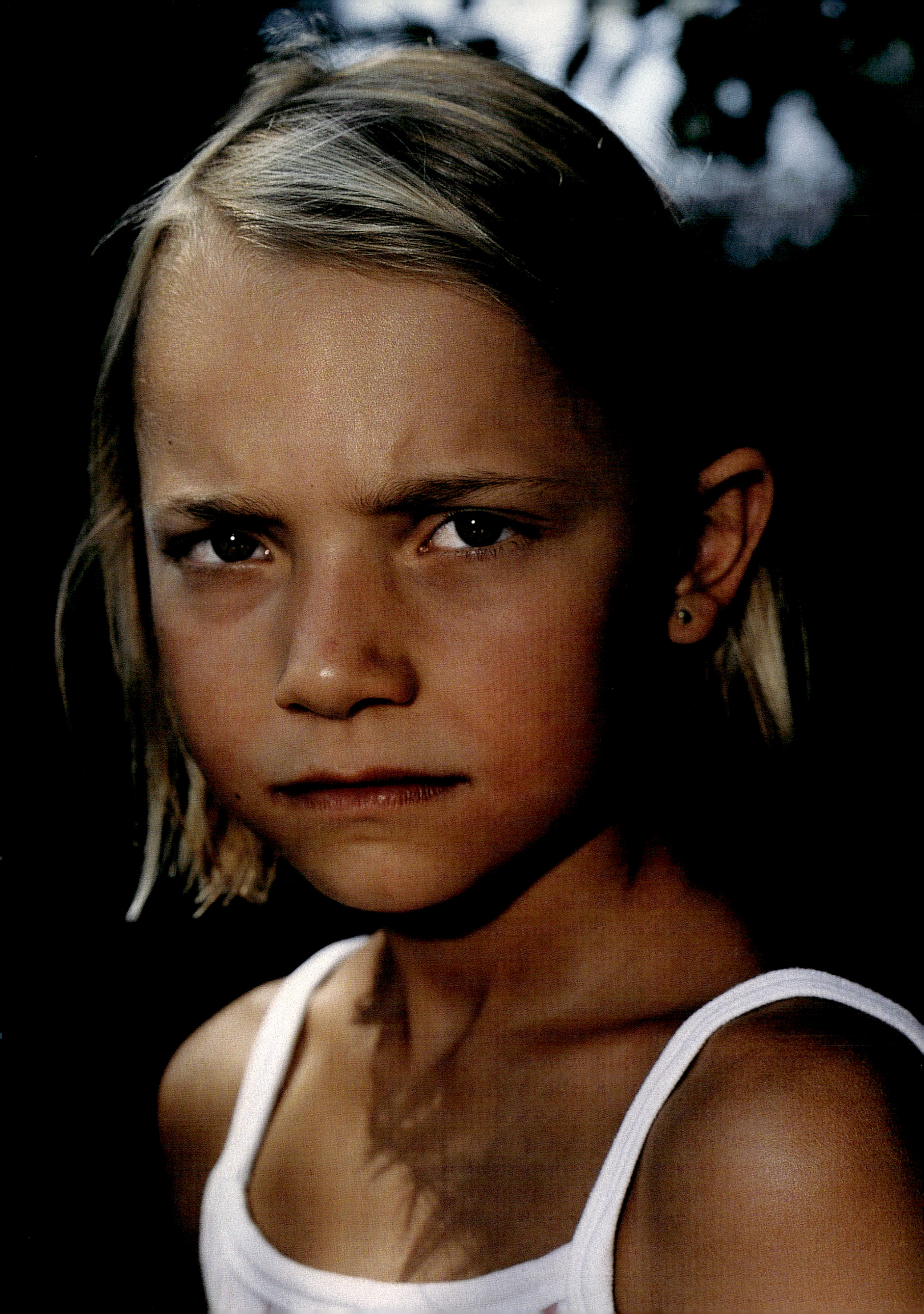

Contents

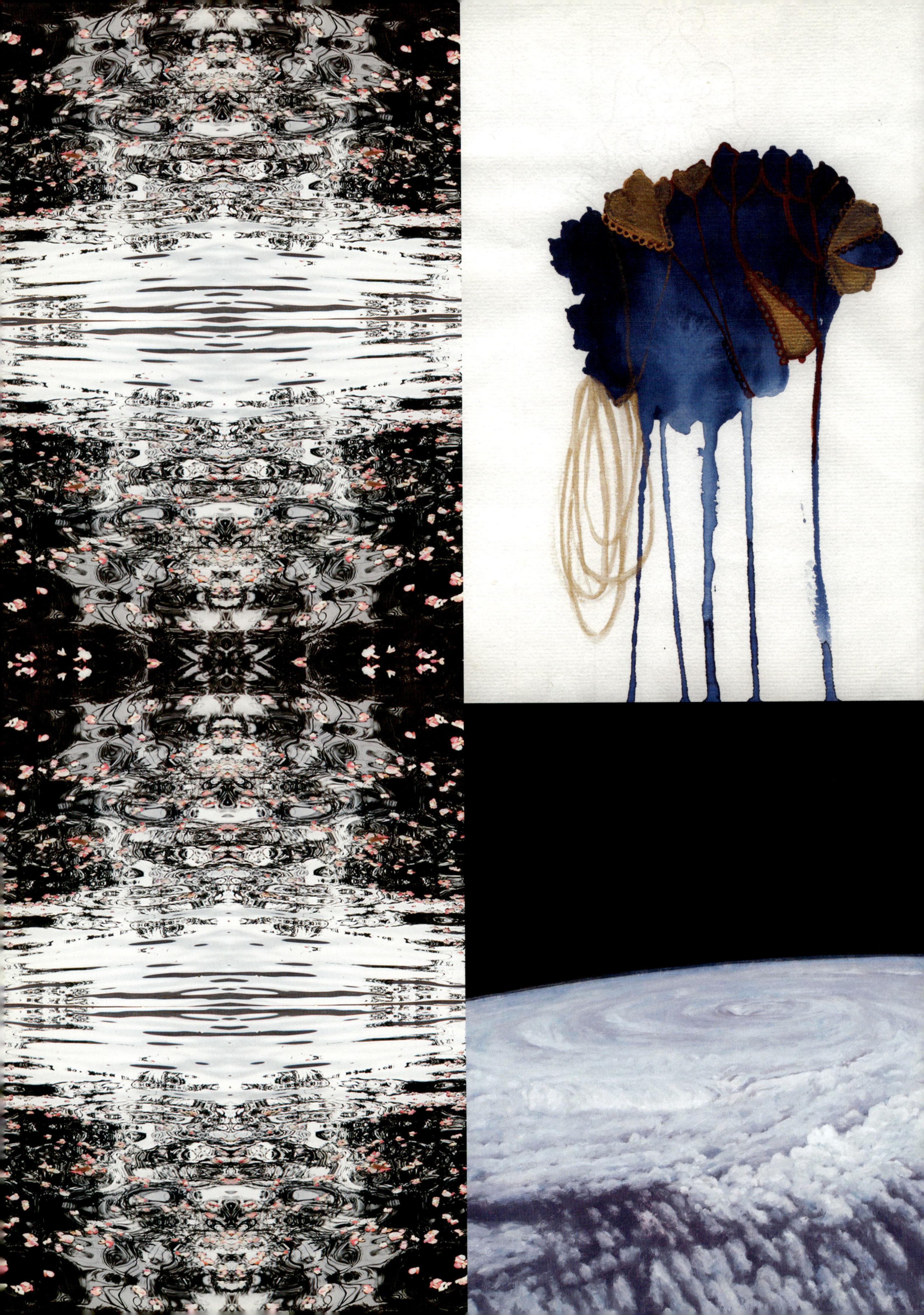

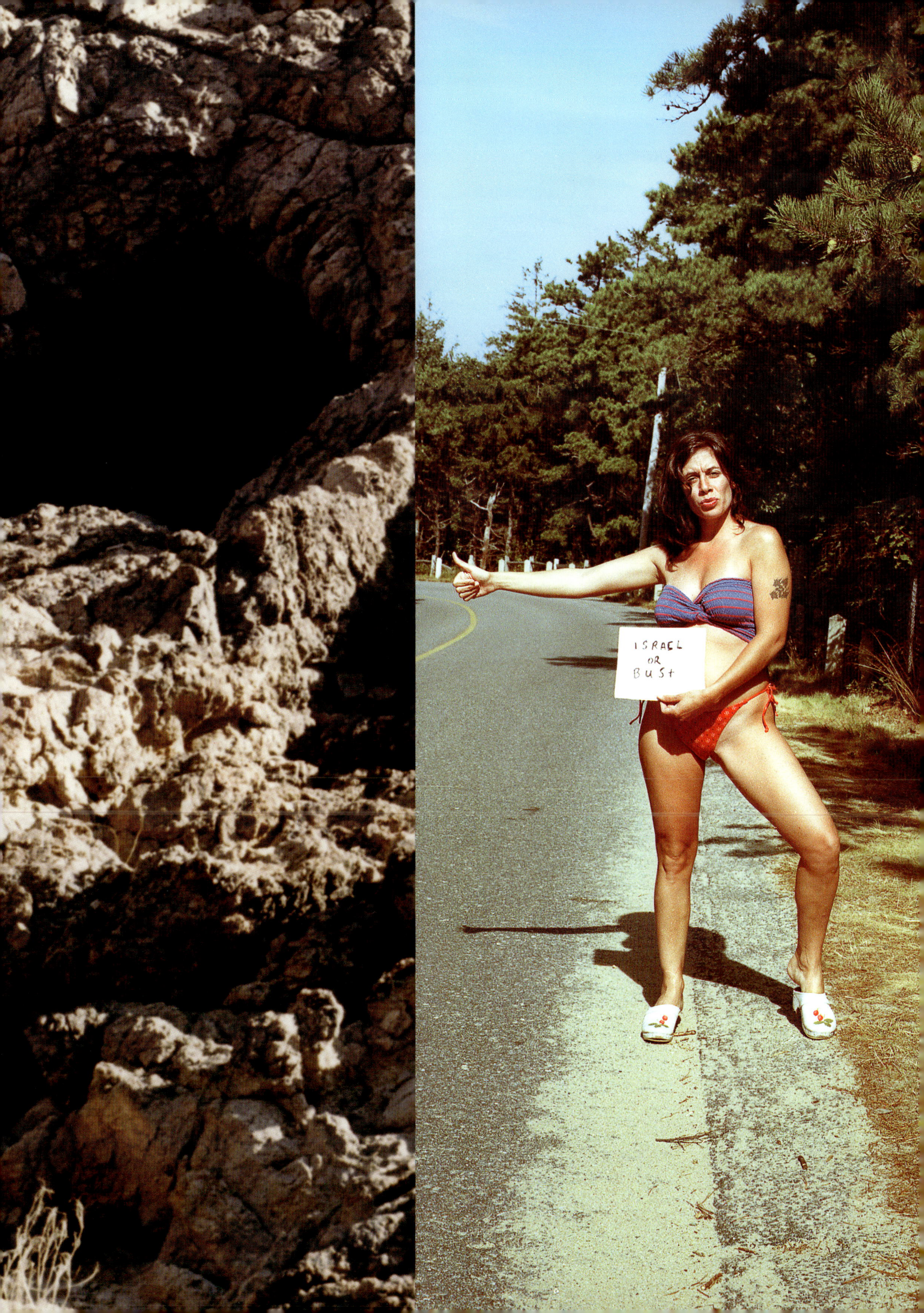
ISRAEL
OR
BUSt

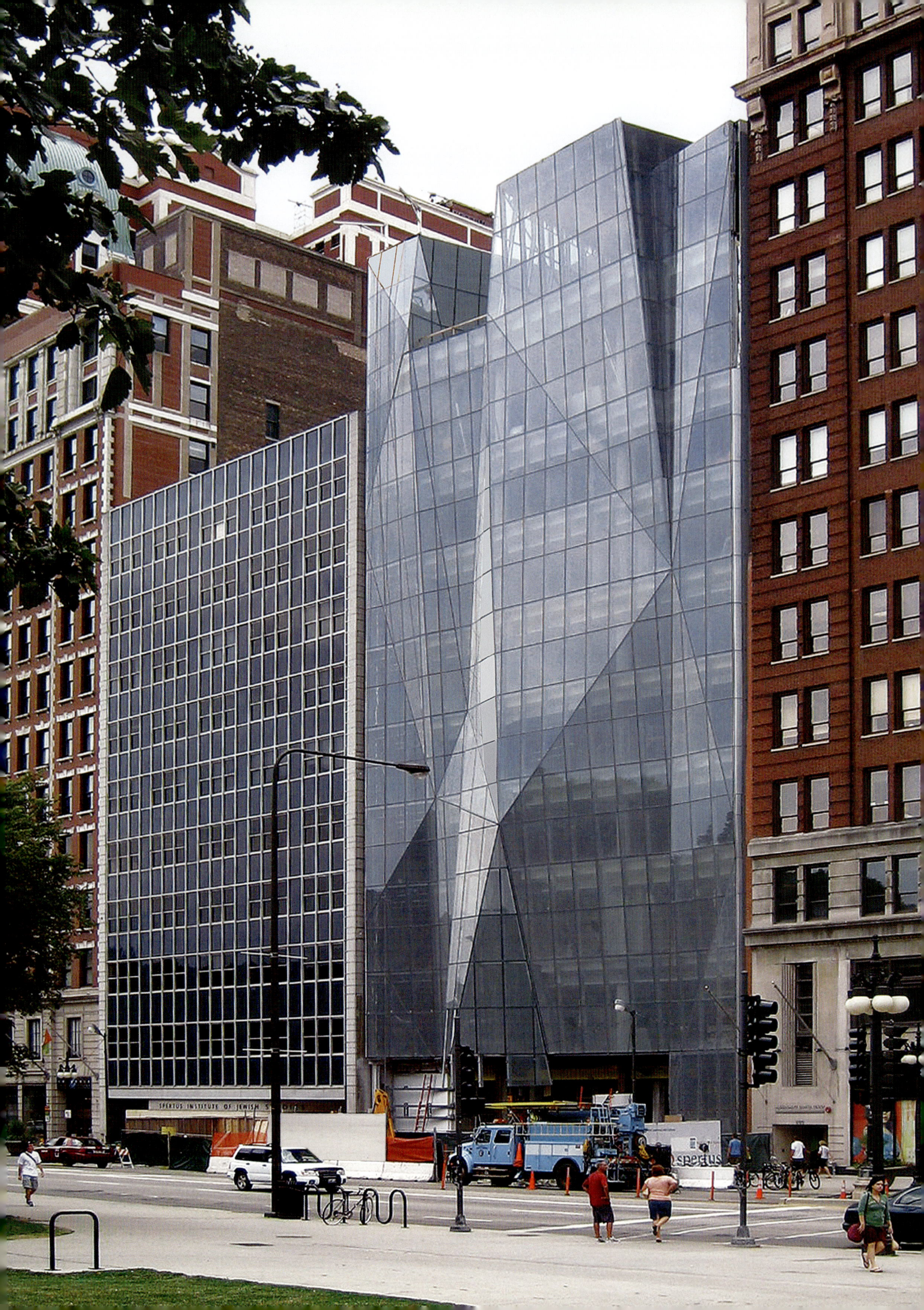

Director's Foreword

by Rhoda Rosen

The New Authentics: Artists of the Post-Jewish Generation

is both an inaugural and a culminating moment. With this Spertus Museum exhibition we initiate a bold new space on Chicago's Michigan Avenue. The only contemporary building in a city-designated historic district, this state-of-the-art facility features a daring glass facade. Bathed in light by day and illuminating Grant Park at night, the faceted facade bravely reinterprets the historic street wall, while subtly and sensitively responding to the majestic, historic buildings surrounding it. In addition to its architectural accomplishment, the building heralds Spertus' new place among the great public institutions stretching from Millennium Park to the Museum Campus. The design is open and embracing, a gift of both architectural and civic significance to the City of Chicago.

Along with the depot, our collection-based display, *The New Authentics* lays out our museum staff's intellectual vision and our sense of the scope of what a Jewish museum might be. Together, they represent the conclusion of a five-year, rigorous and thrilling intellectual journey, spearheaded by a small team of women: Dr. Felicitas Heimann-Jelinek, senior Judaica curator, Staci Boris, senior curator, and myself. Along the way, we have clarified and reinforced our position with regard to the responsibilities of stewarding a collection held in trust for the public, an initiative for which we are indebted to Spertus registrar and collections manager Arielle Weininger. Further, we have reenvisioned the way in which the young visitor engages with Jewish knowledge. Our dramatic children's display is the product of an ongoing partnership forged with Jim Lasko, artistic director of Redmoon Theater, and his collaborators. The unique merging of Redmoon's spectacle theater and museum display, with a curriculum developed by Spertus Museum veteran Susan Bass Marcus, is a visionary new model for urban arts education.

When Krueck & Sexton Architects conceived the new Spertus Museum galleries, which are located on the top two floors of the new ten-story building, they dreamt of an open, light-filled experience that would mesh with the lake and horizon beyond. Their design suggests both that the Jew can be at one with the city and that the Jew is finally transparent. The intellectual project of the museum explores the limits of this dream. Our mission examines the particular nature of Jewish experience, while it also crosses and smudges lines of demarcation: our object research, our depot (which straddles exhibition and storage functions), and new collecting plan, for example, target the seam where Jewish and broader culture meet; our commitment to provenance research, similarly, takes aim at the boundaries of ownership; our collection-based display questions the limits of permanence, the borders of ritual and context, the field of museological practice, and the definition of aesthetics. Likewise, *The New Authentics* pursues the ever shifting, hazy, indistinct, yet so often assumed boundaries of Jewish identity, but nevertheless finds that American Jewish identity is not synonymous with mainstream American identity. Indeed, at Spertus Museum the Jew is no longer considered a stable and single ethnic, religious, or cultural category of analysis. Although the Jew was never really reduced to these classifications, this is the historical moment in which the complexities of being Jewish are more evident than ever.

The freedom to weigh and prioritize one's Jewishness naturally leads to differing perspectives on significant issues that perhaps at one time seemed clear-cut. This dynamic is demonstrated in Spertus Museum's decision not to include one of artist Karl Haendel's drawings, with his consent, in *The New Authentics* when, during exhibition planning, it came to our attention that the work was part of the controversial collection of Friedrich Christian Flick. Flick is the heir and grandson of Friedrich Flick, a Nazi industrialist (and convicted war criminal) who employed thousands of slave laborers and profited from the seizure of Jewish-owned businesses during World War II. Both the sale of this work to Flick and the refusal to exhibit it here are viable American Jewish stances. Because the ethics of collecting and presenting art, Judaica, and material culture is a central and ongoing subject of attention and debate at Spertus Museum, we felt that within the context of this large-scale, opening exhibition, the Flick controversy could not be effectively addressed. Haendel agreed to make a new version of the drawing to replace the one in question for the exhibition.

At Spertus Museum we spotlight Jewish cultural interaction with the broader community because we believe these cultures have always been mutually constitutive of one another. We are establishing our new vision and programming at an historical juncture in America, when the multiculturalism of the late twentieth century, which encouraged respect for assumed circumscribed groups and singular identities, is being replaced by an understanding that identity has neither essential qualities nor clear boundaries but rather is permeable and constantly on the move. As the essays in this catalogue make clear, identity is performative and self-renewing. Like all identities, Jewish identity is now seen as having many iterations within an increasingly global context. In keeping with these shifts in our conception of identity, *The New Authentics* and other programming at the new Spertus Museum offer no grand historical or cultural narrative, but rather an invitation to question some of the central problems facing historians and historiographers today.[1] The museum embraces Jewish identity as a contradictory, dislocated, ever changing, voluntary affiliation, respectful of historical legacies, but not reduced to these. For us, identity is not given, but constructed. Rather than becoming transparent and part of wider culture, choosing to put on the various mantles of Jewish identities marks contemporary Jewish difference. The impact of choosing to be visible rather than transparent is, as postcolonial scholars have taught us, still a radical challenge to the post-Enlightenment, secular national subject. At Spertus Museum we embrace and explore the place where national culture and specific culture rub against one another. It is fitting that against the beautiful, transparent facade implying a seamlessness with broader culture, the organizing principle of the gallery in which *The New Authentics* is installed is the deep, wide opening to the atrium below. A lack and absence at the very heart of the question of identity, this opening suggests a visual refusal to seamlessness.

Unlike many European Jewish museums, Spertus Museum is not built on the site of a Jewish tragedy, nor in the shadow of Jewish tragedy. Neither are our collections representative of the immigrant communities that came to Chicago. Our collection, like that of many other Jewish museums in America, is a collection of material culture. It is a collectors' collection, and this dissociation of objects from their contexts offers us the opportunity to question the rifts and fissures in the Jewish narrative rather than pretend to mend historical rupture to provide a semblance of continuity. *Post-Jewish* is a term we adopt following the brave lead of other communities that have explored the constructed nature of identity. In keeping with terms such as *post-black*, *postcolonial*, and *postethnic*, *post-Jewish* does not imply "after Jewish," but rather a vigilance and challenge to assumed cultural categories. Our project, in speaking to occlusions, aims to resist amnesia and to honor what geographer Derek Gregory, in characterizing Walter Benjamin's philosophy, calls "a conception of history that could accommodate the spasmodic irruptions of multiple pasts into a condensed present."[2] We at Spertus Museum look forward to addressing this condensed present, to stewarding and providing access to a fine collection, to positioning ourselves as a research hub and training ground for mentoring future museum professionals and, as *The New Authentics* demonstrates, to presenting exhibitions that take the difficult path of challenging assumptions.

---

1. Among those contemporary scholars of Jewish identity following in the lineage of multicultural and postcolonial scholars, such as Leela Ghandi and Dipesh Chakrabarty, to whom we owe a debt are David Hollinger, Jonathan and Daniel Boyarin, David Biale, and Stephen J. Whitfield (a contributor to this catalogue). Their influence has gone beyond the world of academia to impact Jewish American youth, institutional leaders, and programs like our own.

2. Derek Gregory, *Colonial Present: Afghanistan, Palestine, Iraq* (Oxford: Blackwell Publishing, 2004), 7.

Jews are an ethnic group, but
not an ethnic group traditionally
conceived. Neither are they
characterized by uniform
religious practice or beliefs.
The instability of and multiplicity
of Jewish identity, which has
a long history going back to the
Bible itself, has become even
more true today. In a free society
all Jews are "Jews by choice."

David Biale[1]

This openness and fluidity of
personal religious identity
is an exceptionally compelling
idea, making it clear
to Jews and other groups in
America that there are no
firm boundaries, existential,
psychological, or concrete,
within which one lives.
The doors are open; one may
enter and exit as one pleases.

Roberta Rosenberg Farber
and Chaim I. Waxman[2]

In America, one can be
Jewish in several, different,
equally valid ways, and no
one, regardless of his or her
ancestry, can be told by
this or that authority, that
he or she is, or is not, a Jew.

David A. Hollinger[3]

The New Authentics:
Artists of the
Post-Jewish Generation

by Staci Boris

INSTABILITY, MULTIPLICITY, CHOICE, OPENNESS, FLUIDITY—SUCH BOUNDLESS TERMS
pervade contemporary scholarship not only on Jewish identity formation but on identities of all
sorts, whether based on ethnicity, nationality, religion, gender, or sexuality. The effort to define
(or complicate) a particular self or group is a vital pursuit that reflects social circumstances,
challenges preconceived notions, and moves a culture forward, and there is no shortage of
writings addressing modern Jewish identity, particularly American Jewish identity in the late
twentieth and early twenty-first centuries. Examples range from academic articles to mainstream anthologies to personal postings on the Internet, which shows that grappling with this
issue is widespread among academics and laypeople alike. In fact, the grappling itself is at
the heart of the process, as cultural critic Vincent Brook describes: "What may be the most
defining characteristic of postmodern American Jewish culture and identity is the increasing
inability, yet persistent necessity, to define it. The 'knowledge of not knowing,' as Freud posited
early in the last century and as the postmodern age appears to affirm, lies at the core of what
it means to be a Jew."[4]

So this is the conundrum—we constantly pursue an answer knowing full well that there may
not be one, or that there will be many. Maybe it is the love of the game, the journey, not the destin-
ation, that is most valuable. If "Jewish" is an undefinable category, then how does one negotiate
membership? This is where *post-Jewish* can come into play. The term is found sporadically in a few
texts written in the past two decades, from John Updike's 1998 novel *Bech at Bay*, in which the
aging, Jewish American writer Henry Bech's new girlfriend is loosely described as "twenty-six,
post-Jewish, frizzy big hair, figure on the short and solid side,"[5] to titles of journalistic and scholarly
articles about Jewish identity by the likes of famed literary critic Leslie Fiedler or more recently
Vincent Brook.[6] Toward elaborating it, we can invoke historian David Hollinger's concept of *postethnicity*, which does not reject the past, but welcomes adaptation and refinement. In keeping
with Hollinger's notion, a post-Jewish perspective would emphasize "voluntary over involuntary

affiliations," a balanced "appreciation for communities of descent with a determination to make room for new communities," the recognition of "multiple identities," the "dynamic and changing character of many groups," and the "potential for creating new cultural combinations."[7]

Post-Jewish also takes its cue from postmodernism—a pervasive if highly contested state of cultural affairs in which all notions of purity and certainty (modernism's key values) are rejected in favor of hybridity and relativity. It is also indebted to the term *post-black*, as it was applied to the work of twenty-eight emerging African American artists in The Studio Museum in Harlem's 2001 exhibition *Freestyle*. Curator Thelma Golden defined the description as having "ideological and chronological dimensions and repercussions; it is characterized by artists who were adamant about not being labeled as 'black' artists, though their work was steeped, in fact deeply interested, in redefining complex notions of blackness."[8] In her positioning, Golden was careful not to claim that there is such a thing as "African American art," an art with a cohesive set of formal or conceptual characteristics, but she didn't deny that race plays a role in these artists' work. Offered up as an ironic yet serious provocation, the post-black concept has been widely discussed and understood as a watershed in identity politics.

In the past five years a number of ethnic-specific art exhibitions, like *The New Authentics*, have taken this indeterminate approach in positioning artists and art. Regarding a 2005 exhibition of contemporary art by Latino artists, *The New York Times* critic Holland Cotter used the phrase "beyond category," noting that "elements once virtually defined as 'Latino' may seem absent, but are actually present in new ways. Far from taking the 'Latino' out of art, much of the work simply presents it sotto voce, as a subliminal, oblique, even optional content."[9] Likewise, the Museum of Modern Art's 2006 exhibition *Without Boundary: Seventeen Ways of Looking*, which focused on work by artists from Islamic countries, emphasized the diversity rather than the commonality of the artists. Such curatorial projects speak to an apparent easing of the predicament of minority artists who have long been pressured—implicitly or explicitly—to work within certain thematic or stylistic parameters in order to be welcomed by the mainstream art world. After decades of consciousness-raising identity politics, African American artists, for instance, no longer need reference the color of their skin or their presumed heritage in their work. Women artists, too, are free to concentrate on everyone's issues, not just "women's issues." This freedom, however, does not require that these concerns be forgotten or omitted in producing artwork. Rather it demonstrates that decisions now lie with individual artists, as they respond to varied personal circumstances, influences, and social forces. As viewers and interpreters, we too have choices: we can evaluate art with *and* without an identity context. Cultural production can and should be understood in multiple ways (with the caveat, of course, that our analyses are always partial and provisional).

At the dawn of the twenty-first century, as Jews are integrated into American society and have the luxury of what has been called a "unique insider/outsider" status, rendering them simultaneously "part of the American majority yet also a self-chosen minority,"[10] contemporary artists are engaging in various ways with Jewishness. An early take on this engagement can be found in *Too Jewish? Challenging Traditional Identities*, an exhibition organized by New York's Jewish Museum in 1996 that inserted Jewish artists into the decade's discussion of multiculturalism and the politics of difference, exploring the resurgence of ethnic consciousness among artists from Deborah Kass and Cary Leibowitz to Art Spiegelman and Rona Pondick. Issues of representation and cultural stereotyping were at the fore in *Too Jewish?*, with the questions "Who represents us? How are we represented? How do we represent ourselves?" inscribed right on the exhibition's entry wall. Complex responses to ethnic "passing," big noses, Jewish princesses, exclusionary traditions, contemporary rituals, and notions of victimization and outsider status were suggested in the show's diverse and often humorous artwork.

Today, eleven years later, in sync with the larger cultural shifts in identification described in this essay's epigraphs, the conversation continues along a slightly shifted path. In recent years, many commentators have debated the benefits of multiculturalism.[11] While acknowledging the cultural and social advances brought by ethnic consciousness in the United States, some have advocated for alternative, flexible perspectives, like Hollinger's *postethnicity*, to challenge the authority of descent-defined (biological rather than constructed) categories. Others have argued for increased cultural specificity (Chinese rather than Asian, or Jewish rather than white) to offset how multiculturalism "play[s] down religion, region, class, ethnicity, and similar divisions," narrowing difference to broad categories.[12] Furthermore, as one scholar has noted, "Jewish insistence on representation in the multiculture is inevitably interpreted as a bid for the status of victim."[13] No longer self-identifying as victims or "others," the post-Jewish generation focuses on self-definition and on balancing lived experience and heritage in intellectual and daily practice. The struggle against how the "dominant culture" defines a Jew has been replaced by an internal, highly personal consciousness as to how one connects with Jewishness today.

It is into this conversation that the "New Authentics" insert their voices. Sixteen artists with varying degrees of Jewish affiliation, diverse backgrounds, and all but one raised in the United States, most do not define themselves as Jews first and foremost, and many do not prominently assert their Jewish identity in all of their work. What one might consider Jewish subject matter or motifs, from the memory of the Holocaust or commentary on the Middle East to the inclusion of a Jewish symbol or allusion to a ritual, appear only on occasion, and the Jewish experience seems only sometimes to influence the artists' choices and points of view. Finally, only a few have formal religious educations and were raised in traditional or observant environments. Nonetheless, all of these artists identify themselves as Jewish and, given their participation in this exhibition, presumably consider it worthwhile to partake in conversations about how this perspective affects their art. In fact, one could even speculate that it is through their art that these artists most profoundly connect with and express their Jewishness.

Born in the 1960s and '70s and raised in North America, these artists have shared histories. Most spent their formative years under the same governments, the same social influences, and in the same media-saturated environment. Though the emphasis in this exhibition is on individual artists, their collective work represents the concerns of their generation (roughly, for lack of a better designation, Generation X). They are as media-savvy, independent, tolerant, and adaptable as so-called Generation Y, but they also lived through Watergate, Iran Contra, the emergence of AIDS, the war on drugs, and soaring divorce rates. According to a recent book on generational collision, "Xers" are marked by skepticism; they call every major institution, from government to corporations to marriage, into question.[14] It is not a great leap to presume these cohorts would apply their feelings of suspicion, uncertainty, or outright rejection to institutionalized religion as well. Indeed, for younger American Jews it seems that "the conflict is less with gentile society than with the Jewish old guard,"[15] and over the past twenty years or so, Jewish organizations across the country have lamented lower membership in synagogues as well as high rates of intermarriage. Yet in interviews with a cross-section of "moderately affiliated" American Jews in the late 1990s, scholars Steven M. Cohen and Arnold M. Eisen found that their subjects "care deeply about their Jewishness—even when, or perhaps especially when, they are rejecting it. Indifference concerning Jewish identity was nonexistent." They also found that the "Jewishness the individuals defined no longer centered on denominational boundaries, concern for the state of Israel, or anxiety over anti-Semitism." Instead, they propose, affiliation is marked by both "passion and ambivalence," and "Judaism [is] constructed and performed one individual at a time."[16]

In recent years this shift has manifested itself through the growth of cultural organizations and outlets, which are providing something of a stage on which young secular American Jews are invited to "construct and perform" their individual Jewish selves. These venues range from hip and irreverent magazines like *Heeb* ("The New Jew Review") to multimedia community arts and culture centers like New York's Makor, where concerts, lectures, classes, and family programming are geared toward twenty- and thirty-somethings, to Reboot, a non-profit network dedicated to providing "an open space for participants to question, explore, and reclaim identity and community on their own terms."[17] In *Lost Tribe: Jewish Fiction from the Edge*, editor Paul Zakrzewski gathered together "edgy" writing by a new generation of young Jewish authors including Myla Goldberg, Jonathan Safran Foer, and Gary Shteyngart. He called these writers the post-Roth generation (a nice parallel to post-Jewish), for their inclination to articulate controversial and topical debates about sex and sexuality, materialism, assimilation, religious intolerance, and the legacy of the Holocaust. These are the sorts of sites into which one dips in and out, exercising Jewishness at will. The way in which the "New Authentics" approach their work is similarly episodic, with Jewish subjects or references surfacing and receding at various points in their practice. And of course *The New Authentics* is another example of the remarkable proliferation of new Jewish cultural expressions.

Art historian Matthew Baigell, in his ambitious and insightful 2006 book *American Artists, Jewish Images*, surveys fifteen artists of the twentieth century whose works feature Jewish subject matter.[18] He chose a roster of artists (ranging from Max Weber to Barnett Newman to R. B. Kitaj) for whom he felt being Jewish formed the crux of their work as well as their individual identities. The book traces the evolution of Jewish subject matter over the century, demonstrating that one generation's Jewishness might be another generation's nostalgia. To riff on Baigell's title, this exhibition could have been called *Jewish Artists, American Images*, as its multidimensional works demonstrate how personal associations with Jewishness intermingle with so many other facets of contemporary life: popular culture, history, gender, sexuality, class, politics, and nationality among them. *The New Authentics* exhibition and publication include artists of a specific place and time, representing the wide contours of both American Jewish identity and American art now, while posing the following questions: How do contemporary Jewish artists operate within a larger relational context? If an artist chooses to incorporate a Jewish subject, a Jewish image, or a Jewish symbol, how and why does she do it and what can it mean? What are today's Jewish artists' particular perspectives and obsessions, and, given their diversity, can they all be called "authentic?"

In philosophy the notion of authenticity describes a person's connection to his or her true internal spirit or character vis-à-vis the external world. It is about maintaining individual consciousness without falling prey to imposed dictates, self-centeredness, or, more perilously, to insistence on "purity." It is non-dictatorial. To connect this back to Jewishness, it is worth repeating Hollinger's crucial observation: "In America, one can be Jewish in several, different, equally valid ways, and no one, regardless of his or her ancestry, can be told by this or that authority, that he or she is, or is not, a Jew."[19] An authentic identity is therefore either nowhere, or, just as easily, everywhere. By this measure, the "New Authentics" (and by extension all who claim Jewishness) are "authentic" Jews of the twenty-first century—as much as they want to be, that is. As

Fig. 1 **Ludwig Schwarz**, *Untitled (Wiggles #2)*, 2003, oil on canvas, edition 1/4 (painted in China), 60 x 84".
Private Collection.

Fig. 2 **Johanna Bresnick**, *Ohne Lebensraum*, 2004, rug, mannequin, wood, foam,
and latex paint, 40 x 92 x 140".

historian David Biale puts it, "We may not be able to choose our grandparents, but we can choose the extent to which we affirm our connection to this or that grandparent."[20] While this may seem like an ideal state of free will, the task of locating one's identity without a set of preconditions can be bewildering. Vincent J. Cheng, a Chinese-born scholar who is married to a Jewish woman and raising their adopted Taiwanese son as a Jew, asks, "What is Jewishness? Is it a race/ethnicity, religion, culture/history, nation? Since it is hard to pin down what each of these terms actually means, and since Jewishness as a category of identity keeps slipping and sliding . . . it is no wonder that it is so difficult to know what Jewishness means."[21] Indeed, this state of uncertainty has an authenticity all its own, and charges much of the work in this exhibition.

Take, for example, Ludwig Schwarz's portrait of his dog, Wiggles, or Johanna Bresnick's self-portrait, both of which address the complexities of identity stemming from each artist's biography. Schwarz's bespectacled dog (brought into the family by his wife, a converted Jew), captured next to a Star of David on the floor (a chew toy?), seems to be contemplating the very question perplexing Cheng and others: What does it mean to be a Jew? Part of an ongoing series of paintings that Schwarz had fabricated by traditional painters in China, *Untitled (Wiggles #2)*, 2003 (fig. 1), in both subject and mode of production, plays with notions of value, truth, substance, and authenticity in the art world and beyond. In *Ohne Lebensraum*, 2004 (fig. 2), Bresnick portrays herself in sculptural form atop a "flying carpet," facing an unknown future. The title, which translates to "without living space," references Hitler's plan for territorial expansion and also the predicament the artist's grandparents faced in Germany, as, according to family lore, they used the very rug in the installation as their transient home throughout World War II. Thus Bresnick's installation speaks to unresolved concepts of identity, history, and representation, precariously balancing the identity she has chosen with the heritage she has been given, as suggested by her figure's revealing (or hiding) the coal under the carpet.

Memory, legacy, and the inheritance of both personal and collective Jewish histories play significant roles in works by several of the "New Authentics." Despite the passage of time, American Jews still wrestle with the repercussions of one of the defining events of the twentieth century—the Holocaust. How does one remember and comprehend the mass murder of six millions Jews and at the same time move beyond it? Where past generations of artists have attempted to directly portray the unthinkable horror of the tragedy, today's artists, further removed from the events and wary of couching their Jewishness in terms of victimhood, often use Holocaust-related imagery as source material in the service of raising broader issues, from universal humanitarian concerns to aesthetic challenges. For these artists the Holocaust has global implications as well as personal meaning and becomes part of a larger discourse on the ways in which history and identity are transmitted, constructed, and interwoven.

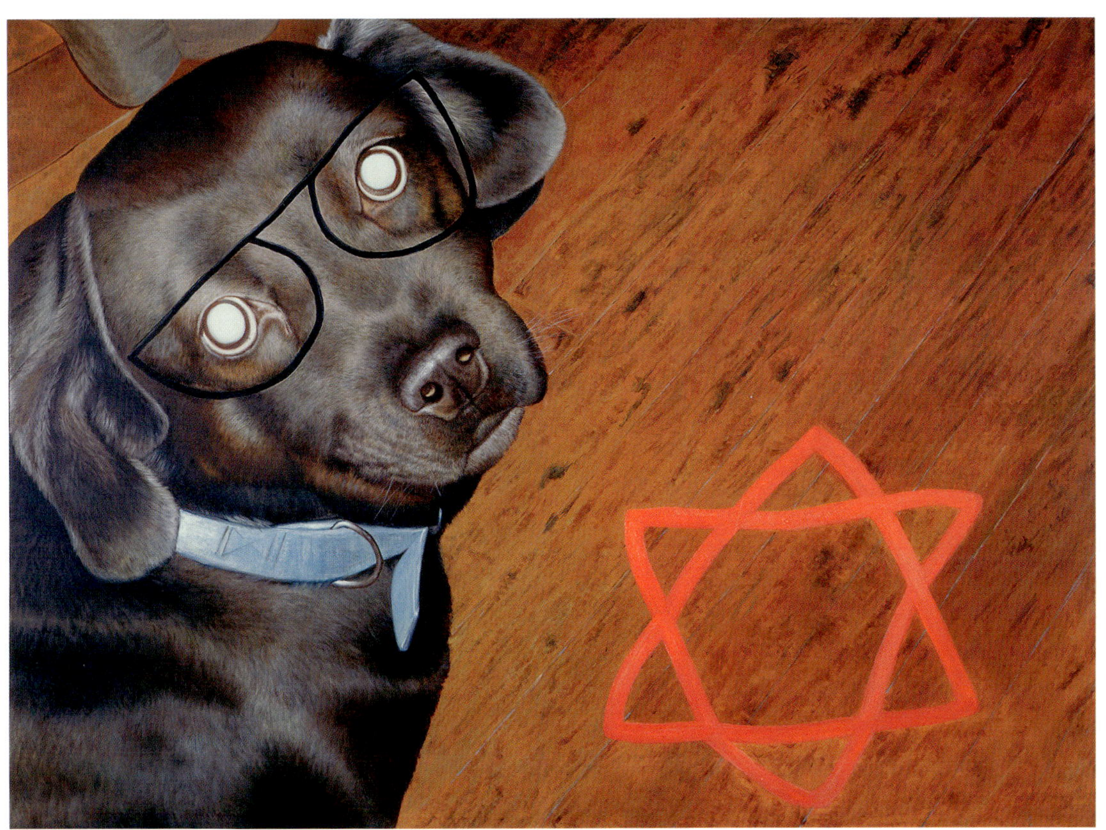

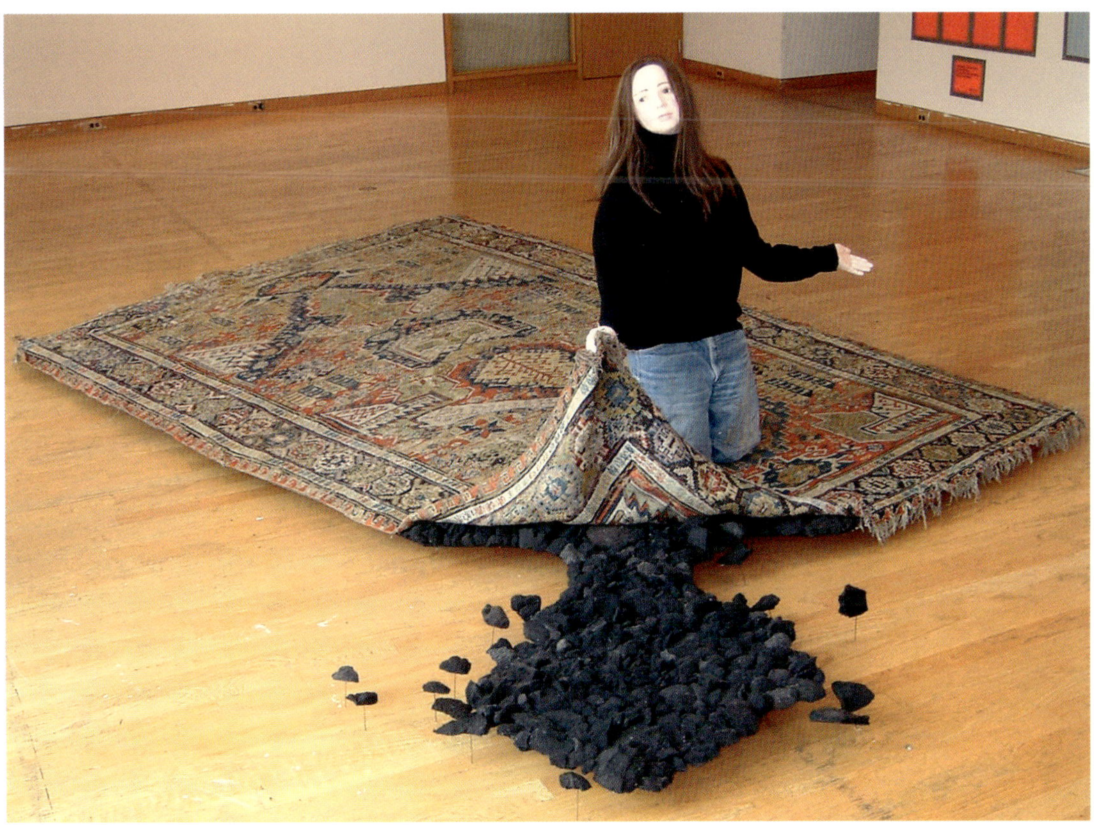

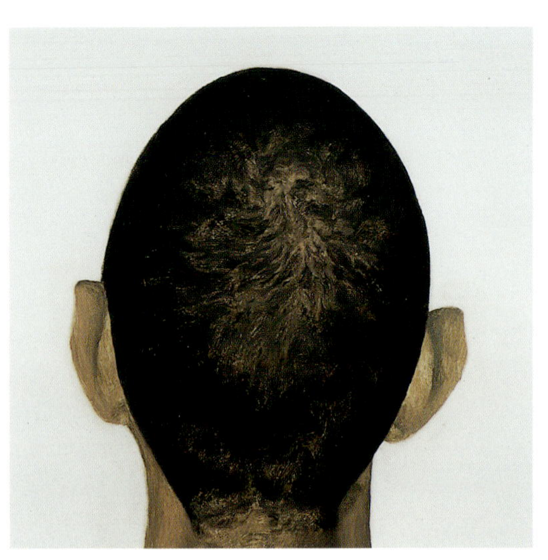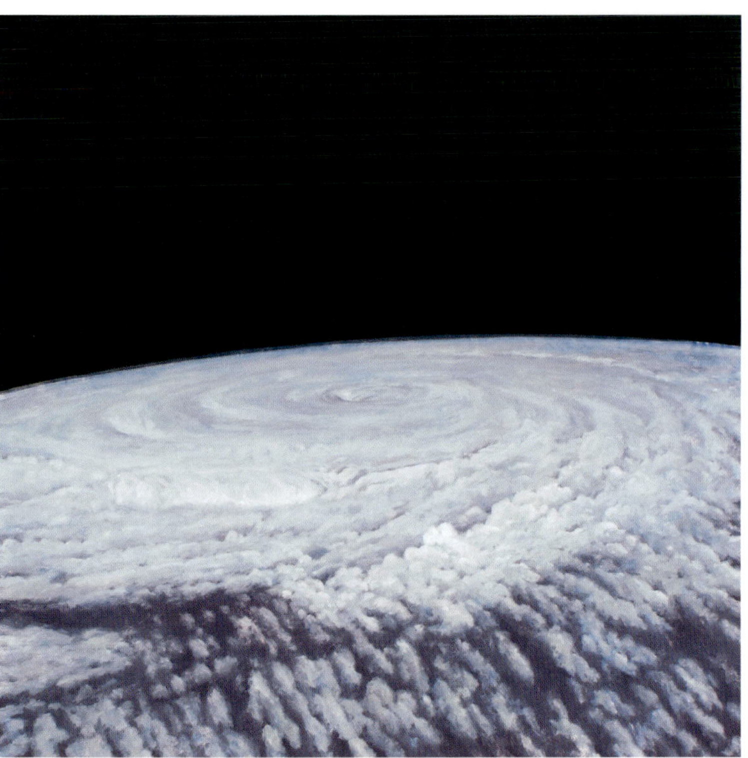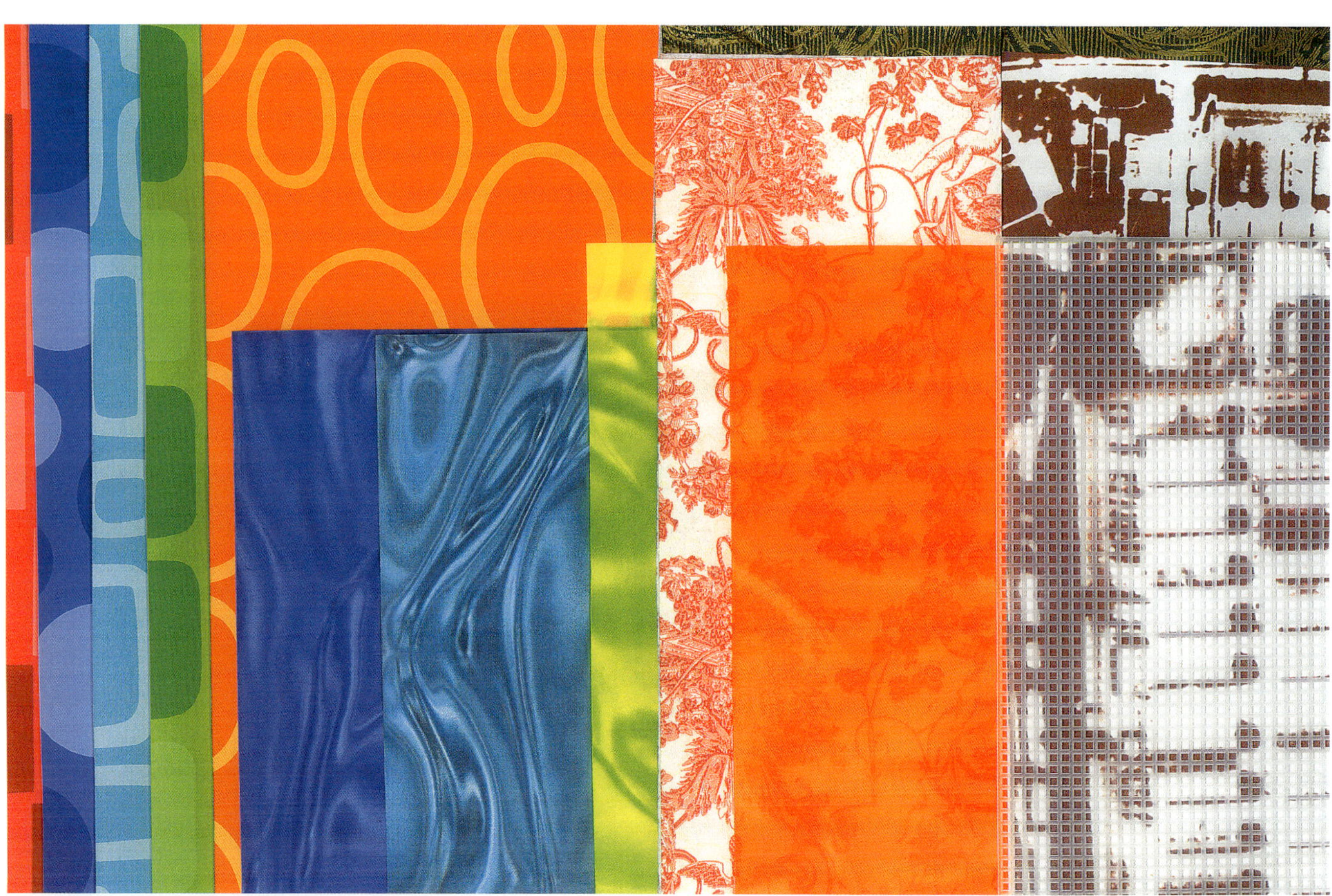

Fig. 5 **Cheselyn Amato**, *Fabric Collage (Placemats, Napkins, & Deathcamps)*, 2004, inkjet print, 22 x 34".

Fig. 3 **Matthew Girson**, *Dizzy Heights V*, 2005, oil on canvas, 20 x 20".

Fig. 4 **Matthew Girson**, *Satellite View #2*, 2006, oil on canvas, 63 x 63".

Artists Matthew Girson, Cheselyn Amato, and Collier Schorr approach the subject of the Holocaust introspectively—their artwork reflecting how each has absorbed and processed the knowledge of trauma in different ways. Girson, whose past work draws directly on the landscape of postwar Germany, today makes paintings that more obliquely explore the limits of representation evoked by the Holocaust. A white square superimposed onto the surface of his landscapes is a recurring motif, expressing emptiness as a metaphor for loss. In the series "Dizzy Heights," 2005 (see fig. 3), this void becomes a backdrop for small paintings of the artist's own head. Shown alongside the series "Satellite View," 2005–2006 (see figs. 4 and 62), large-scale paintings based on aerial views of hurricane patterns, these works suggest the artist's internal struggle to understand and depict a world laden with such beauty and such destruction. In short, Girson's work answers historian Saul Friedlander's "call for an aesthetics that devotes itself primarily to the dilemmas of representation, an anti-redemptory history of the Holocaust that resists closure, sustains uncertainty, and allows us to live without full understanding."[22]

Amato's digitally printed *Fabric Collage (Placemats, Napkins, & Deathcamps)*, 2004 (fig. 5), juxtaposes symbols of "civilized" society—funky, boldly colored table linens—with an aerial photograph of a concentration camp. Once this image comes into focus, the attractive composition fragments into chaos, illustrating literary critic Leon Wieseltier's blunt description of the contemporary American Jewish condition: "We are the luckiest Jews who ever lived. We are even the spoiled brats of Jewish history. And so the disparity between the picture of Jewish life that has been bequeathed to us and the picture of Jewish life that is before our eyes casts us into an uneasy sensation of dissonance."[23] As the events of the Holocaust transition from memory to history, Amato's receding image of a camp among layers of cheery textiles exemplifies the lure of moving on.

Schorr's photographs demonstrate her generation's willingness to establish new relationships with German history, culture, and citizens, however ambivalently. For more than a decade the artist, who lives part-time in a small town in southern Germany, has photographed the landscape as well as her nephews and their friends, whom she occasionally outfits in military surplus. Schorr has explained: "Germany has such a hold when you're a Jew. . . . I wanted to not

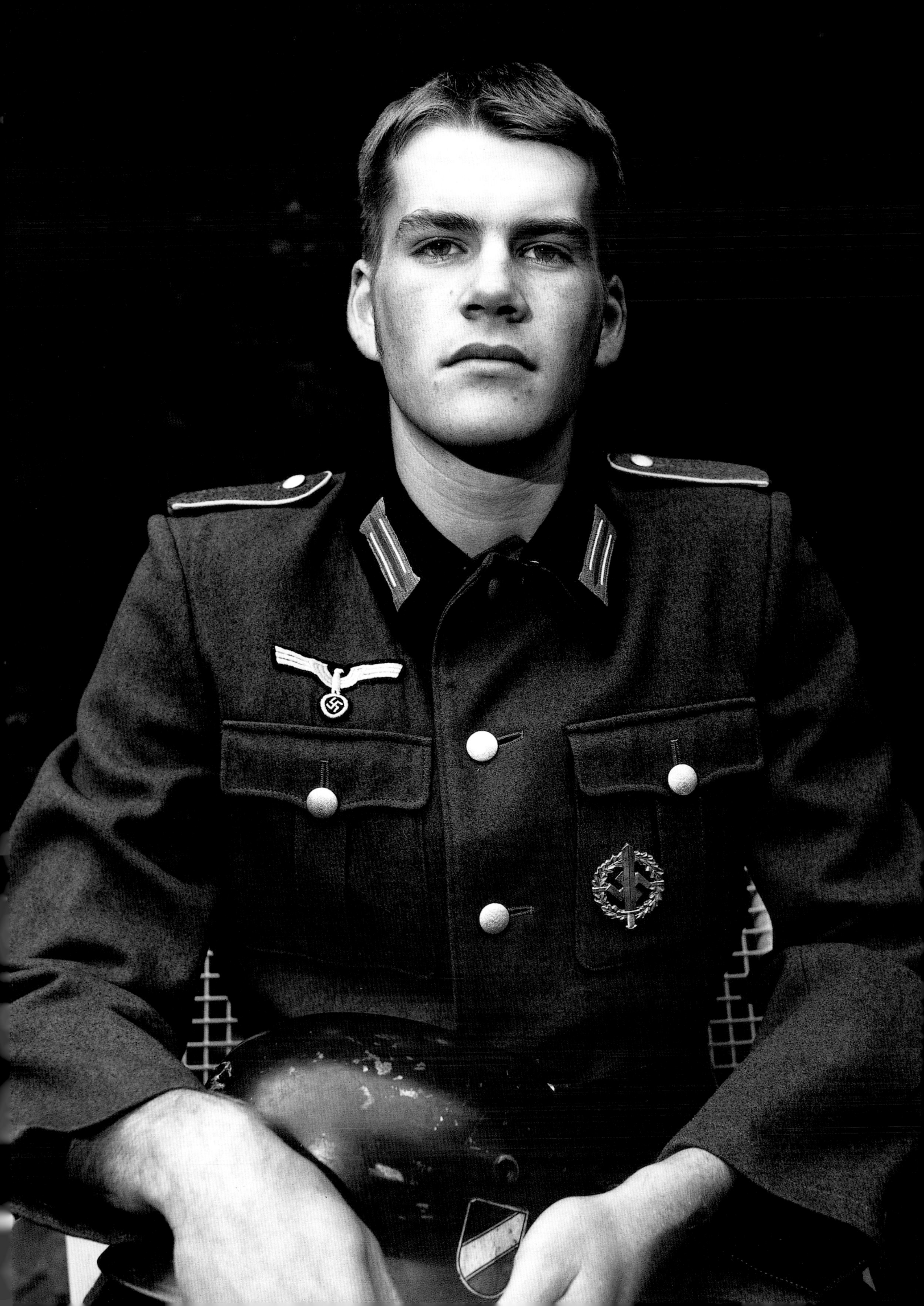

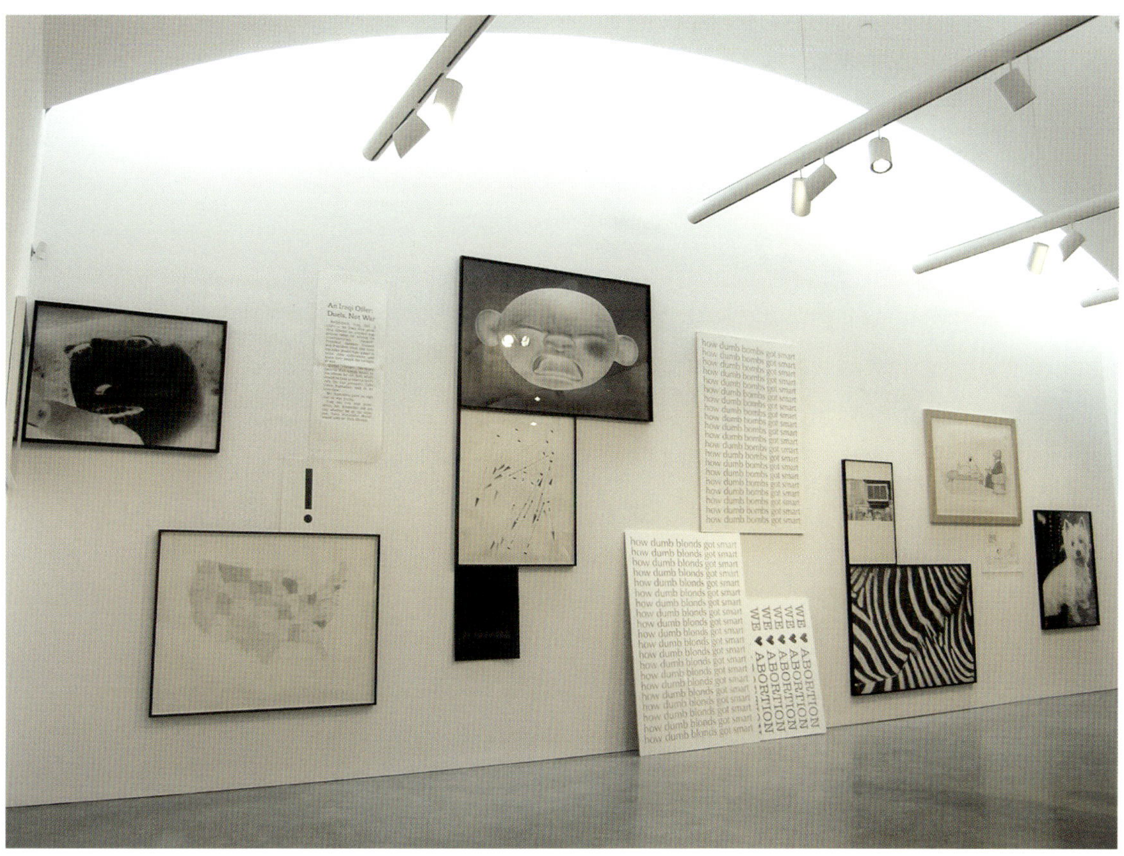

stand in its shoes, but to sort of see it from all sides. I always saw it from the side of the Jew who felt victimized, or the Jew who felt oppressed. And I was very comfortable in that role for many years. But by being in Germany for a longer amount of time, my experience changed and my relationship changed to the country. And my curiosity about what it was like from the other side opened me up."[24] Schorr's images, such as *Steffen, Barbarostrasse, Garden*, 2001 (fig. 6), a black-and-white close-up of a young man in a replica SS uniform, blend artifice and realism, the past and the present, while inquiring into a history that is often repressed in German life. Shattering taboos on both sides, Schorr, as both insider and outsider, makes "work that Germans would make about Germany if they were American."[25]

Karl Haendel makes work about America that is thoroughly American. Blatantly critical of "the rampant hypocrisy" that he feels is "running and ruining the world,"[26] he borrows, redraws, and juxtaposes imagery from American consumer culture, the popular media, and art history to suggest injustices and incongruities. Into vast groupings of drawings and photographs (see fig. 7), he occasionally inserts imagery that self-consciously mocks, yet marks, his almost stereotypically over-educated, New York–born, Democratic, liberal Jewish leanings (from *New Yorker* cartoons to pages of Art Spiegelman's *Maus* to drawings dedicated to his favorite Democratic senators). Though an atheist, Haendel partially attributes his value system and his insistence on truth to

Fig. 6 **Collier Schorr**, *Steffen, Barbarostrasse, Garden*, 2001, gelatin silver print, 37 x 28 ½".
Collection of Jay Dandy and Melissa Weber, Chicago, IL.

Fig. 7 **Karl Haendel**, *Untitled*, 2005. Installation view, *Uncertain States of America: American Art in the 3rd Millennium*,
Center for Curatorial Studies, Bard College, Annandale-on-Hudson, NY, 2005.

Fig. 8 **Shoshana Dentz**, *home lands #13*, 2004, oil and gouache on canvas, 70 x 140".

Fig. 9 **Fawn Krieger**, left to right: *DAWNING 1* (detail), 2006, fabric, stuffing, and thread with wood base, 69½ x 28 x 4"; *DAWNING 4* (detail), 2006, fabric, stuffing, and thread with wood base, 63 ½ x 20 x 4".

the "old school rules" he absorbed through his Jewish upbringing: "[about] treating people respectfully and honestly, about humility, about charity. About the value of an education, the value of learning, the value of discourse, of interpretation, of everyone getting their turn to speak . . . these values are shared by most religions, but they seem to me to be particularly stressed in Judaism."[27]

Shoshana Dentz's works are political and personal, and, like Haendel's, they question ideologies. "home lands," an ongoing series of paintings and drawings begun in 2003 (see fig. 8), features dramatically skewed fences that allude to both psychological and political borders, containment, and power. Drawn from areas near her Brooklyn home, the countryside, and news images, Dentz's renderings of barriers depict transparency—the negative space between the chain links rather than the links themselves—suggesting the possibility of "seeing through" to the other side. Raised in an Orthodox Jewish environment and instilled with values from which her own politics began to diverge over time, Dentz reexamines these inherited viewpoints in her paintings, making art a site for debate. Her past use of the keffiyeh pattern as well as the

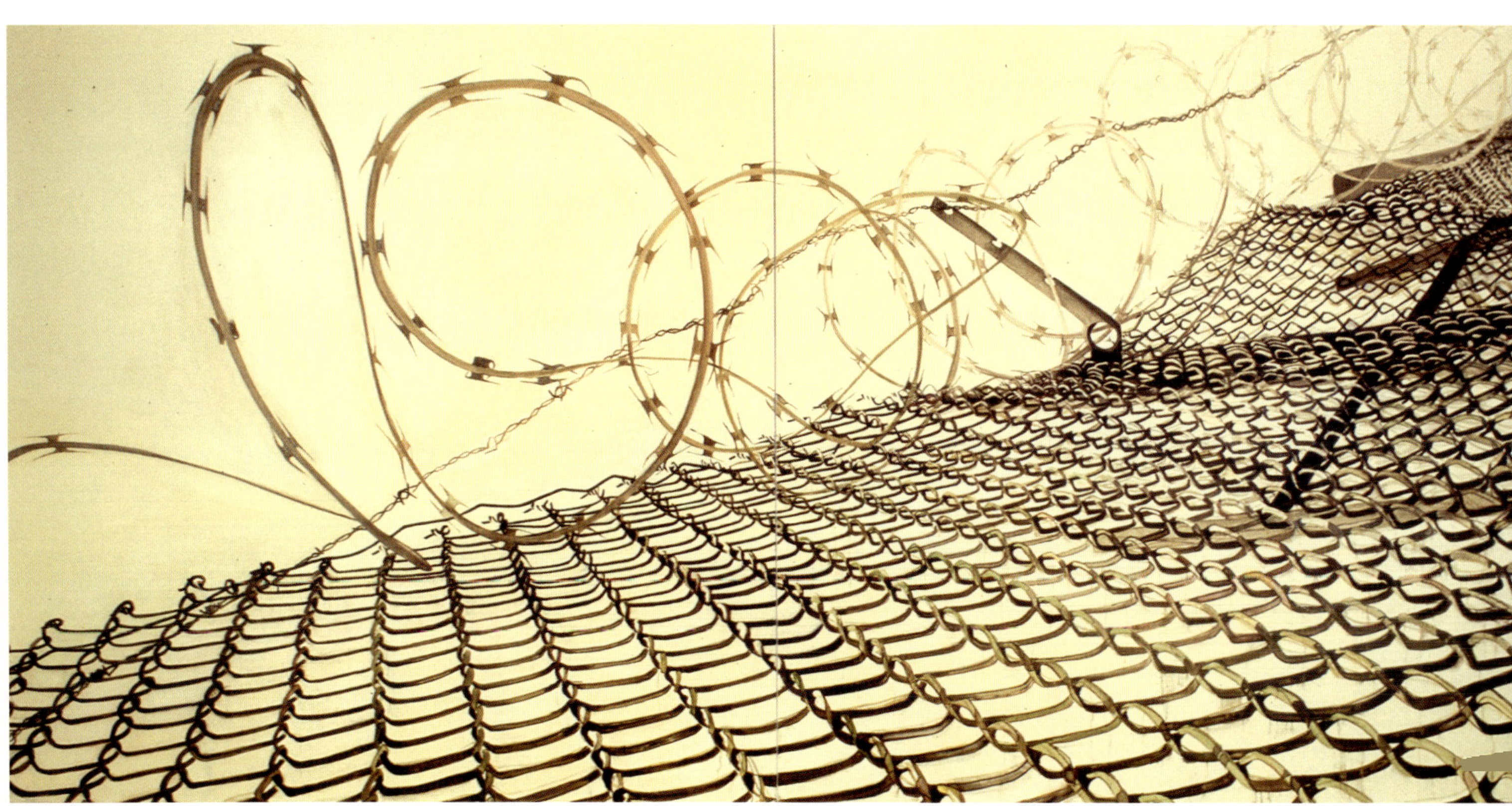

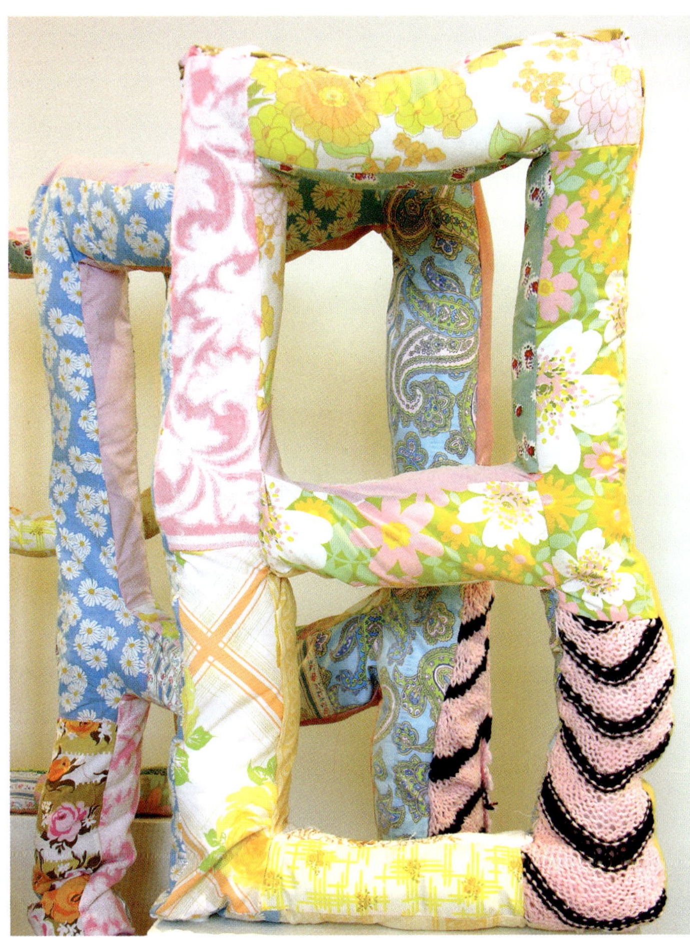

fences hints at the Israeli-Palestinian conflict as a central point of reference. Dentz's gestures, both painterly and conceptual, suggest both the inherent difficulties and the endless possibilities of understanding the presumed "other," while complicating the relationship between home and territory.

Idiosyncratic considerations of home—physical and psychological, sentimental and fraught— also appear in works by Fawn Krieger, Mindy Rose Schwartz, and David Altmejd. Though a new generation of American Jews has been called post-diasporic (settled in to the United States, they no longer yearn for or are defined by an ancestral homeland[28]), home on a personal level is variously defined and expressed by the "New Authentics." Krieger's soft sculptures depicting windows in the series "DAWNING," 2006 (see figs. 9 and 83), for instance, are sewn from bed linens from her grandparents' former summer home on Fawn Lake in Pennsylvania and allude to emotional and physical connections between body and home, presence and absence, inside and outside. The artist's processes of tearing, mending, stuffing, and folding her family textiles further materialize the past. As she writes, "The tattered family linens remember traces of histories of exile and of freedom because they were imprinted by the bodies that they held. These fabrics frame a site that is available to occupation, interruption, fantasy, projection, as much as absence, disappearance, and erasure."[29]

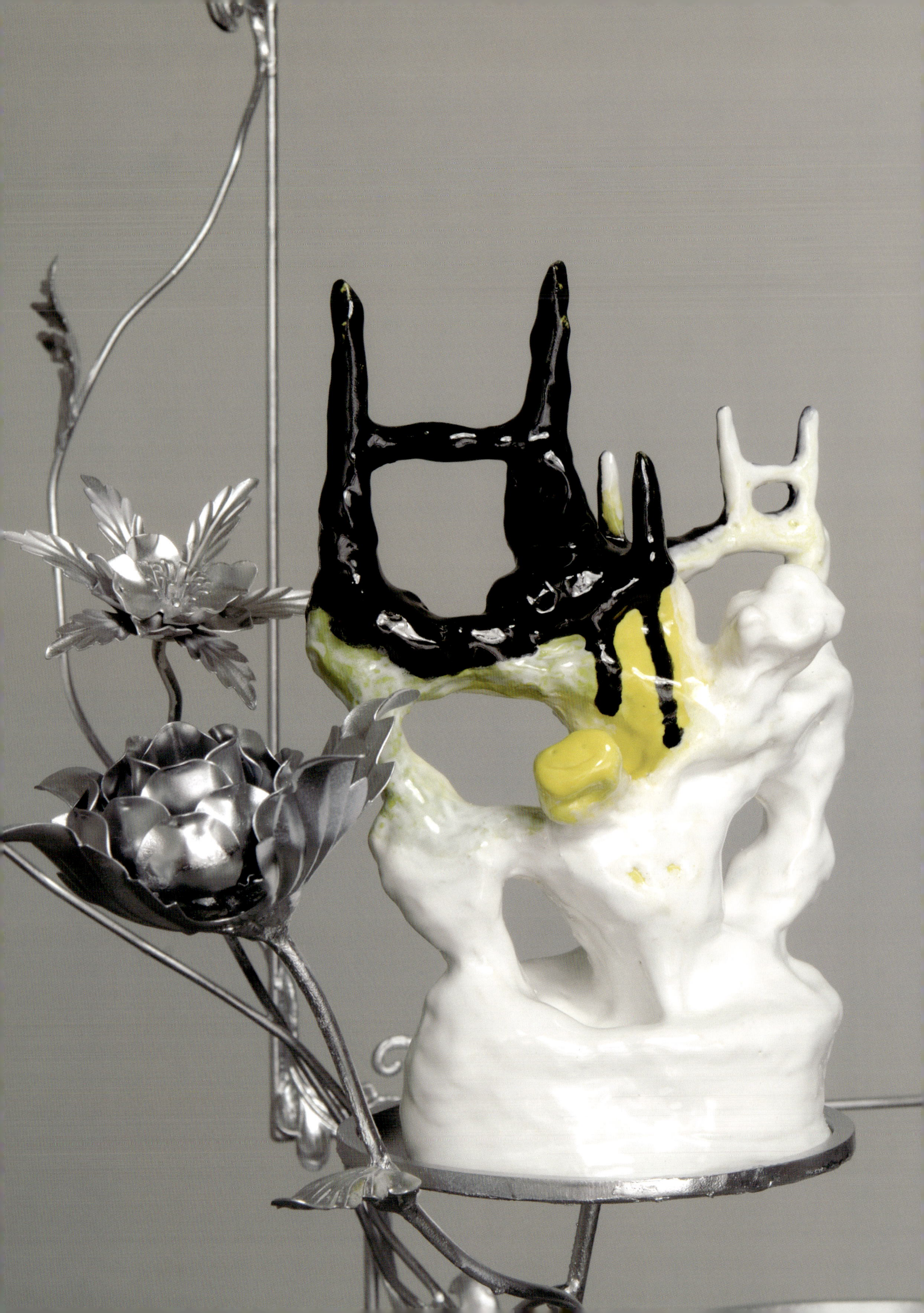

Fig. 10 **Mindy Rose Schwartz**, *Untitled (The River)* (detail), 2007, steel, rope, rocks, wood, foam, wire, resin, crystals, plaster, paint, clay, glaze, glue, pencil, ink, mulberry paper, fabric, and artificial plants, dimensions variable.

Schwartz also borrows materials from a childhood home. Informed by the decor of her family's middle-class suburban residence in Skokie, Illinois, she inventively meshes mass-produced collectibles and curious decorative elements to generate hybrid forms that are part furniture, part decoration, and part craft (see fig. 10). Her recent work, such as *Untitled (The River)*, 2007, made especially for *The New Authentics*, alludes to everything from Chinese painting to 1950s and '60s interior design to 1970s feminist art to the do-it-yourself home-improvement fad of the present day. As in previous works, Schwartz uses strands of macramé (a "gendered" skill she learned at Jewish summer camp) to connect her sculptures and found objects to their new sites, highlighting strange relationships between objects, their environment, and the emotional memories they may hold.

Likewise, Altmejd's elaborate sculptures suggest connections between form, often the human form, and space, and seem part house, part tomb, and part decorative object. His startling array of materials and the jarring way in which he combines them contribute to the dazzling uncertainty and fluidity of his inventions. *The Settler*, 2005 (fig. 11), features a prone and decaying hairy figure out of which mirrored fragments erupt and almost envelop the body. What looks like a corpse seems to be attempting to generate new life, accentuating processes of transformation rather than stagnation. Altmejd's vision of metamorphosis, coupled with the title of this sculpture, suggest a reference to immigration and movement (Altmejd's Jewish father emigrated from Poland to Canada in the late 1960s and the artist, after living in Montreal for most of his life, now lives in New York and London), hinting at the complexities of seeking and establishing a home.

Jennifer Zackin often dispenses with the homing instinct altogether, immersing herself in cultures far from her East Coast residence in search of moments when "the contemporary and the ancient, the east and west, the macro and micro intersect and transform."[30] Interested in Jewish culture and tradition yet unmoved by what she recalls as a prescribed religious practice in the suburban synagogue of her youth, Zackin engages performance, repetition, and pattern in a practice influenced by the rituals of indigenous cultures and their engagement with nature.

Fig. 11 **David Altmejd**, *The Settler*, 2005, wood, paint, Plexiglas, mirror, foam, resin, synthetic hair, ▶ lighting system, shoes, wire, beads, and glitter, 40 x 46 3/8 x 90 5/8 ".

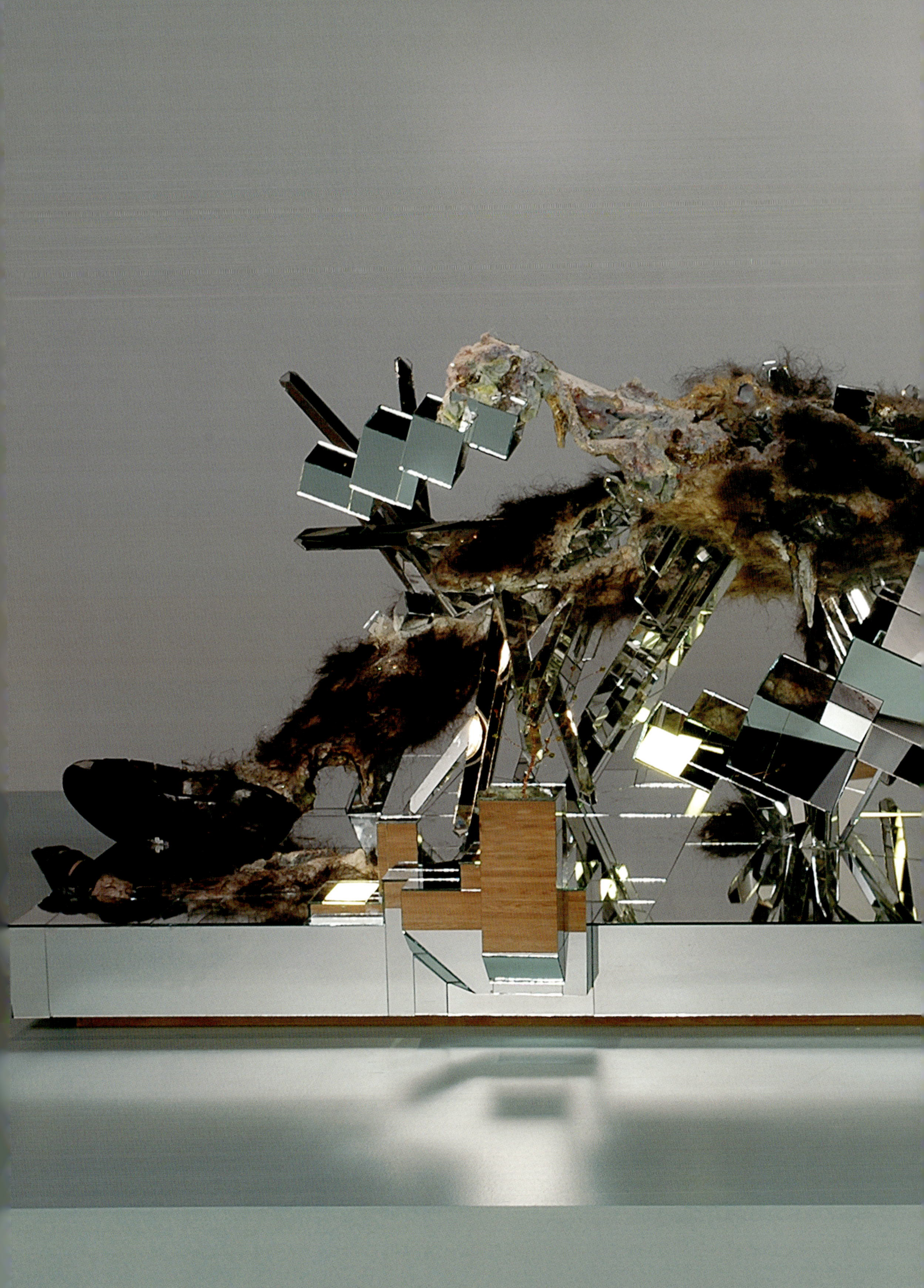

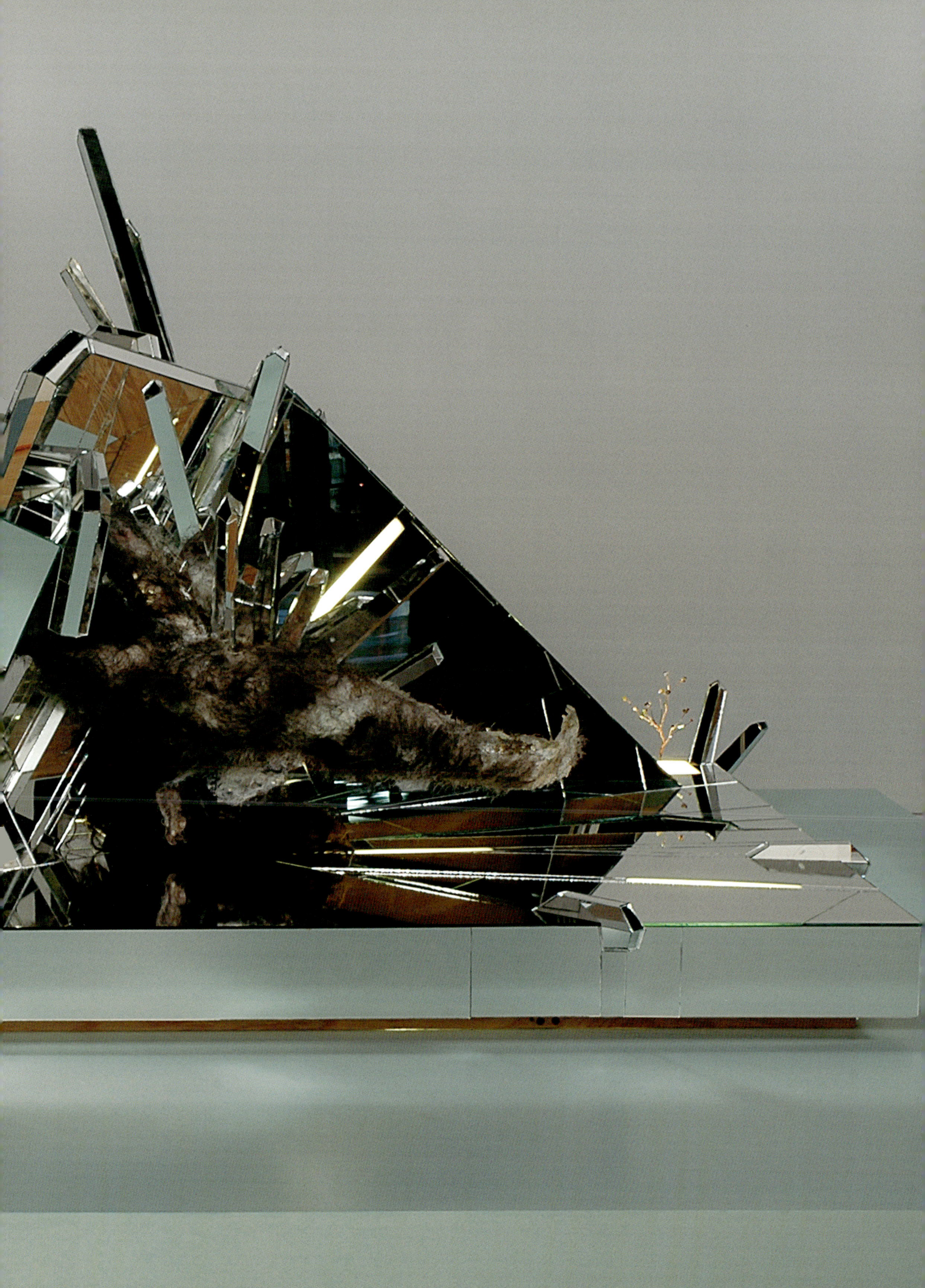

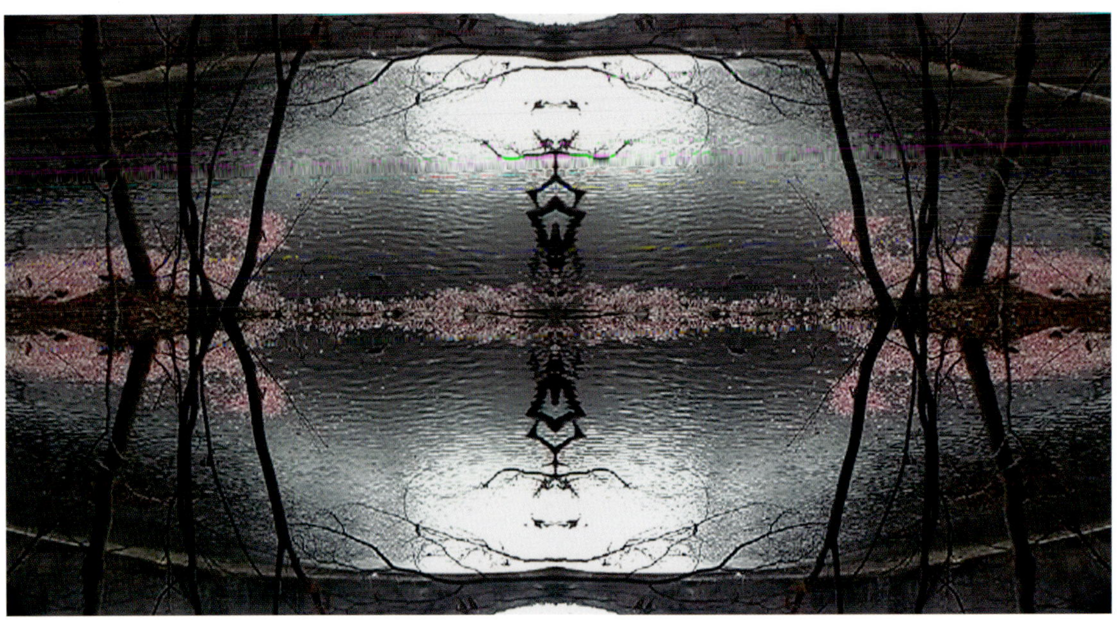

For *Lake Rescue*, 2007 (fig. 12), she applied these motifs from far away to a site back home. The source of this shimmering image, which reads something like a video painting, is a project for which Zackin offered thousands of rose petals into Lake Rescue in Plymouth, Vermont, where she grew up. In a moment of synergy (courtesy the miracle of video editing), a short video clip, replicated four times to fill the screen with Rorschach-like pairs, morphs into a contemporary icon that hovers over a picturesque space of reflection.

Joel Tauber also communes with nature to create private rituals as alternatives to those of his formal yeshiva education. His practice consists of eccentric attempts to experience transcendence through interactions with the West Coast landscape, an inclination that came out of his "realization that [he] could no longer rely on Jewish rituals and Talmudic law for ethical and spiritual guidance."[31] Working outside the confines of organized religion, Tauber imagines a physical yet meditative process, carries it out, and then digests and chronicles it for others. *Seven Attempts to Make a Ritual*, 2000–2001 (see fig. 13), for instance, is a video documenting the artist inserting himself into holes in the earth in hope of establishing a divine connection. As Tauber describes, "I feel that the idea of searching for a ritual to relate to God is taboo among the intellectual elite in our postmodern world. It is precisely because of its lack of 'coolness' that I feel that it is critical to tell the story."[32]

Using art as their medium of enlightenment, Zackin and Tauber rework traditions to suit individual spirituality, acknowledging that what might be moving, powerful, or useful for one person won't necessarily be for another, which makes cultivating flexibility and invention within spiritual practice a logical choice. Further, Tauber's particular sense of spiritual taboo—and a strong desire to overcome it—mirrors a shift in the general culture. These days, communing with God is no longer the sole concern of the observant, it's fashionable. Alongside the celebrity

Fig. 12 **Jennifer Zackin**, *Lake Rescue*, 2007, still from a single-channel video, 3 minute loop.

Fig. 13 **Joel Tauber**, *Untitled Image from Hole #1*, 2000, production still from the video
Seven Attempts to Make a Ritual, 2000–2001.

craze for kabbalah and a wave of popular television shows with spiritual themes (*Heroes*, *Battlestar Galactica*, and *Lost*, to name a few), the art world has embraced God. One case in point: the 2004–2006 international traveling exhibition *100 Artists See God*, curated by artists John Baldessari and Meg Cranston, in which spiritual attitudes ran the gamut from earnest to irreverent.

Lilah Freedland spans this very range with cheeky portrayals of contemporary Jewish customs. Flirting with the sacred and the profane, Freedland dedicated the series "Hebrew School Pin-Ups," 2001–2005, to the pubescent boys with whom she attended Hebrew school,

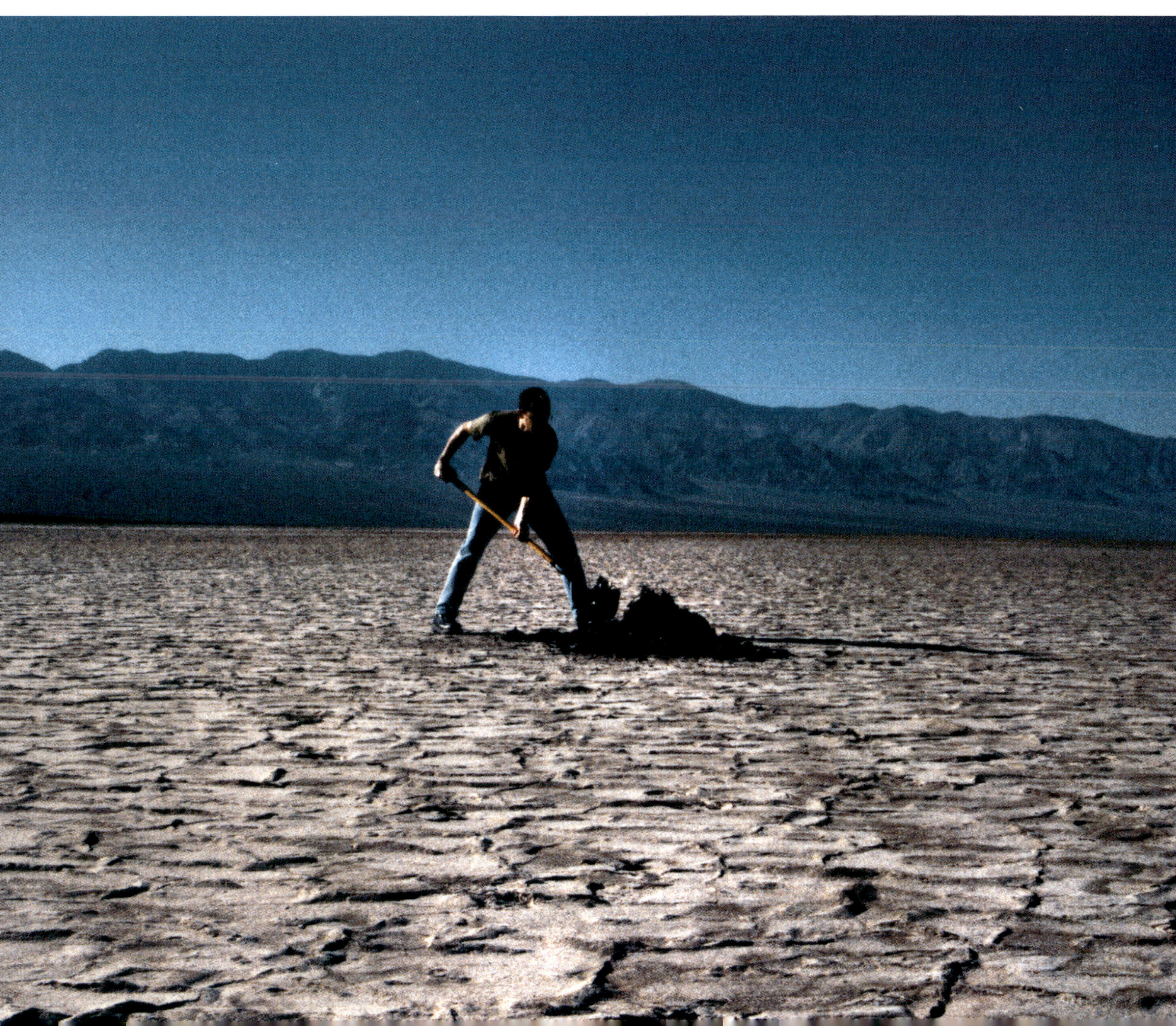

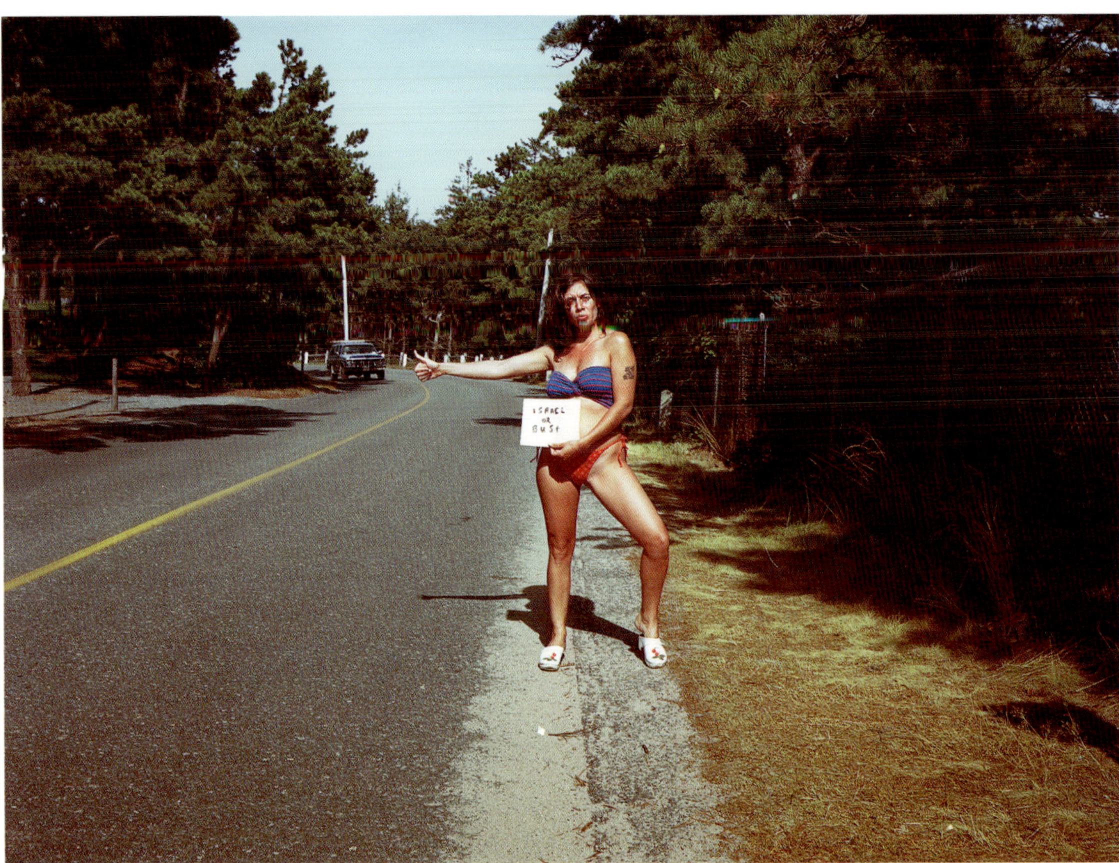

an American Jewish rite of passage that is as much social as it is religious. Photographs such as *next year in the holy land*, 2002 (fig. 14), and *dip ya karpas*, 2001 (fig. 53), with their alluring Jewesses enticing the male gaze, resemble Madonna's *Sex* pictures more than confirmation portraits. These over-the-top images of the female body as the source of erotic desire replace stereotypes of the repressed Jewish American princess, overbearing Jewish wife, or self-sacrificing Jewish mother with a post-feminist Jewess who knows her own sexual power.

Sexuality and notions of beauty related to ethnic identity also inform the work of Shoshanna Weinberger, who calls herself a "Jamaican Jew." Weinberger's dual heritage (gentile/Jewish and black/white) further complicates the post-Jewish condition. The (hybrid) mules, (black-and-white) zebras, and amorphous corporeal forms that populate her gouaches and collages reflect a constantly shifting sense of self, less sure of her prowess, let's say, than Freedland's femme fatales. The title of one of Weinberger's works, *Strange Fruit*, 2005 (fig. 15), named after a 1930s anti-lynching song written by Jewish schoolteacher Abel Meeropol and sung by Billie Holiday, mirrors her dual lineage, and her works, all forms of self-portraiture, personify her travels between two cultures yet her membership to neither.

Living with multiple identities is common to the postmodern condition, and many American Jews, already hybrid, have ties to other ethnicities and religions as well. With intermarriage, adoption, conversion, heightened awareness of Jews from non-European cultures, and the embrace of Jews of partial descent, the character of the American Jewish population is becoming increasingly diverse. Those of mixed heritage are often called hybrids, implying that out of a

Fig. 14 Lilah Freedland, next year in the holy land, 2002, c-print, 20 x 24".

mixture of different things comes something entirely new, but, as Biale posits, the concept of multiplicity is more apt: "As opposed to the melting pot in which a new identity emerges or the cultural pluralism model in which only one ethnic identity remains primary, this is the sort of identity in which one might retain at least two different cultural legacies at once."[33]

Such cultural multiplicity informs the work of artists Jin Meyerson and Laura Kina, both Jews of Asian descent. About the title of his 2004 exhibition *Social Distortion*, Meyerson wrote,

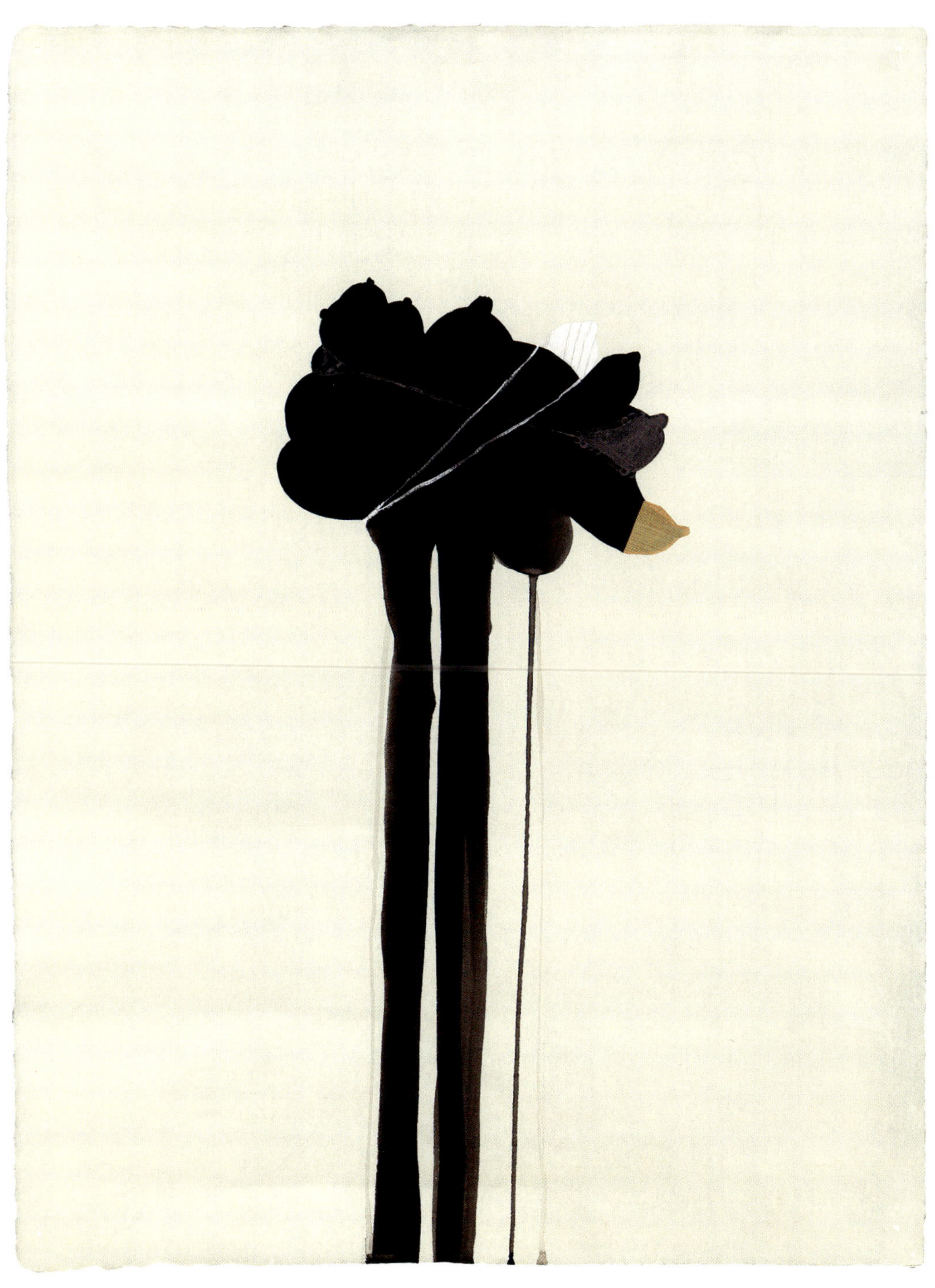

Fig. 15 **Shoshanna Weinberger**, *Strange Fruit*, 2005, gouache and collage on paper, 24 x 18".

Fig. 16 **Jin Meyerson**, *Tower* (detail), 2005, oil and acrylic on canvas, 139 x 144".
Ostrow Family Collection.

"I am that Inchon city orphan korean born, small town american raised adopted by a Jewish New Yorker and Swedish Minnesotan combination. The paintings have always been created with this twisted perception of american culture."[34] Jarring, distorted, overwhelming, loud, layered, slippery, and shifting, Meyerson's monumental canvases reflect this sense of chaotic multiplicity. *Tower*, 2005 (figs.16 and 94), whose layered imagery is culled from different time periods and disparate histories, alludes to the biblical story of the Tower of Babel, which refers to a multilingual and multicultural world and also admonishes against hubris—a fitting symbol for the confusion that fuels Meyerson's practice.

Kina's worldview and artistic practice are informed by her mixture of Japanese, American, and Spanish heritage as well as her conversion to Judaism. Her oeuvre brings visibility to the multiethnic experience and underscores that this seemingly glamorous or exotic condition (think Keanu Reeves, Tiger Woods, and presidential hopeful Barack Obama) is becoming all the more common, yet certainly no less complicated. Kina's early paintings present domestic spaces or appliances as stand-ins for the ethnic body. Her three paintings of refrigerators from 2001, *The Aronsons* (fig. 17), *The Rosenfelds* (fig. 81), and *The Kina-Aronsons* (fig. 82), completed shortly after her conversion, for example, represent Jewish households of not only different ethnicities,

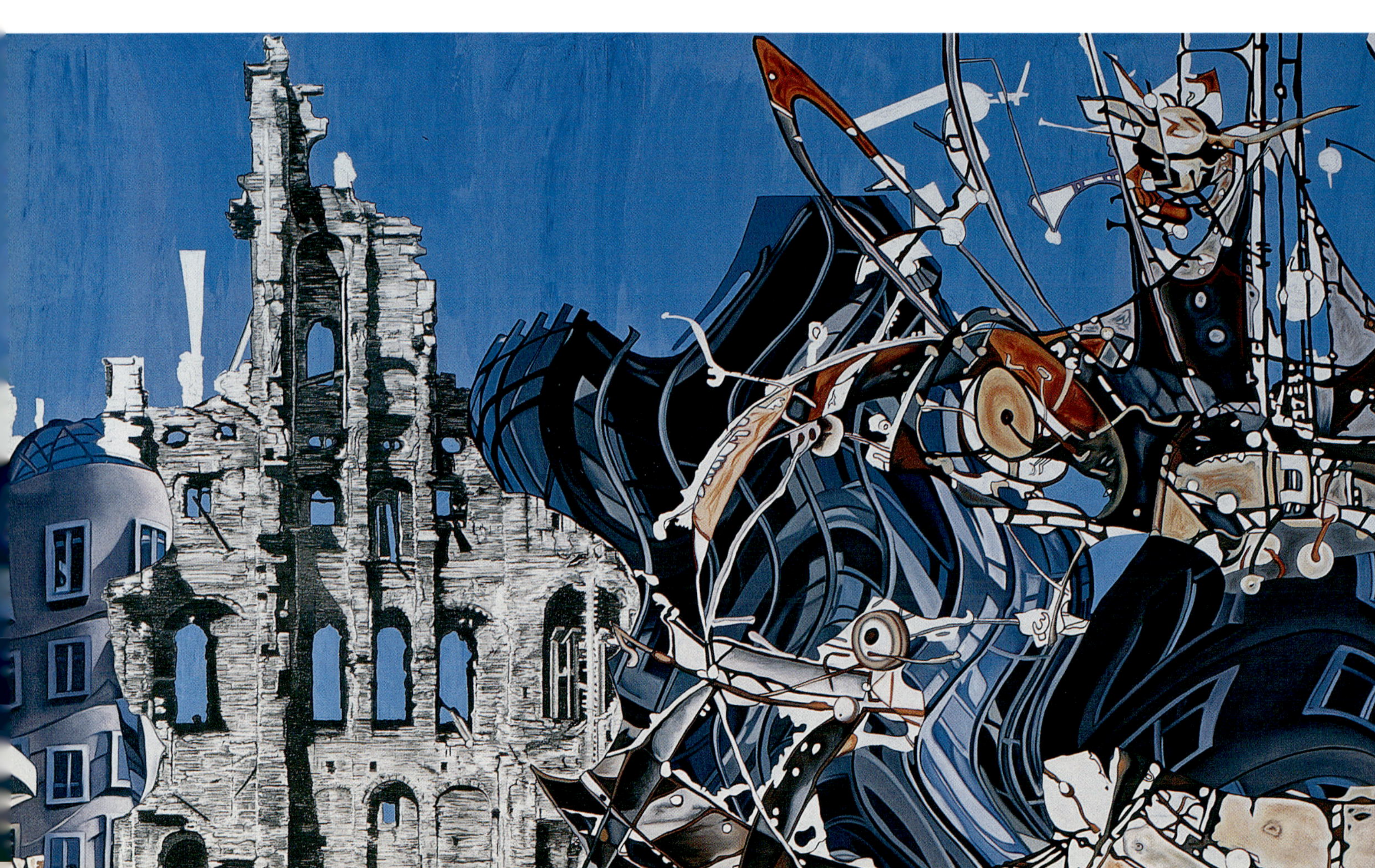

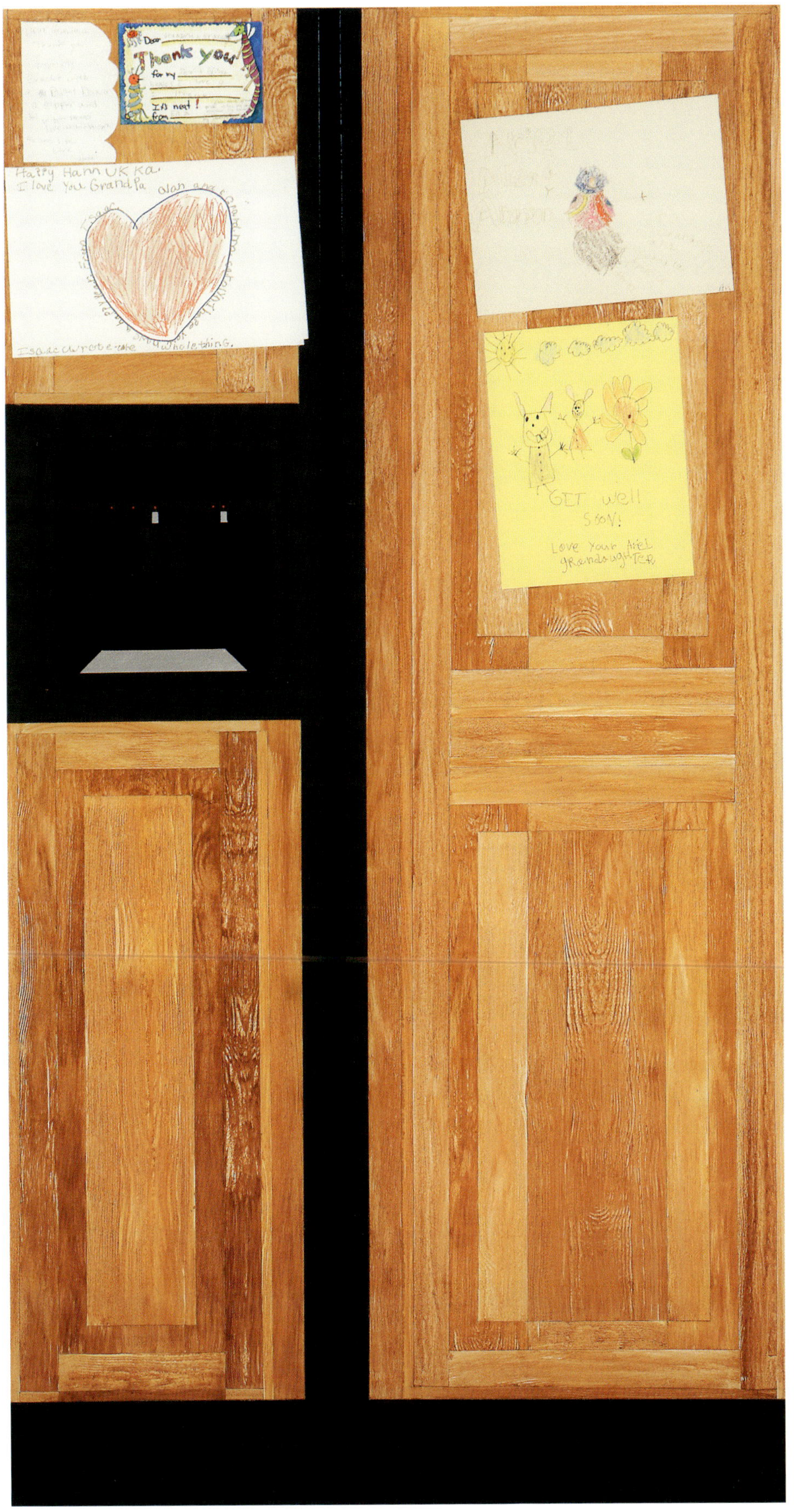

Fig. 17 **Laura Kina**, *The Aronsons*, 2001, acrylic, pen, and crayon on canvas, 70 x 36".

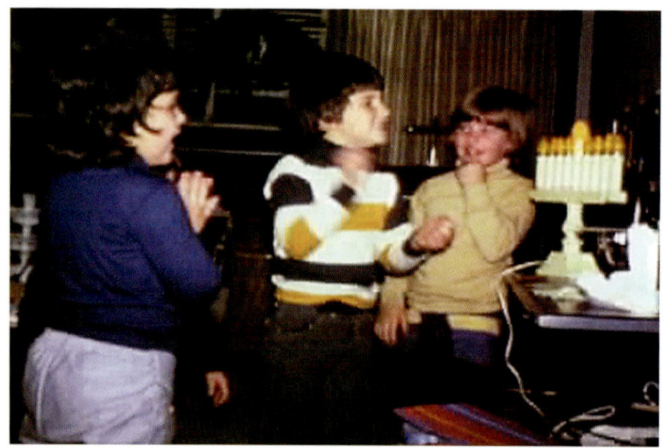 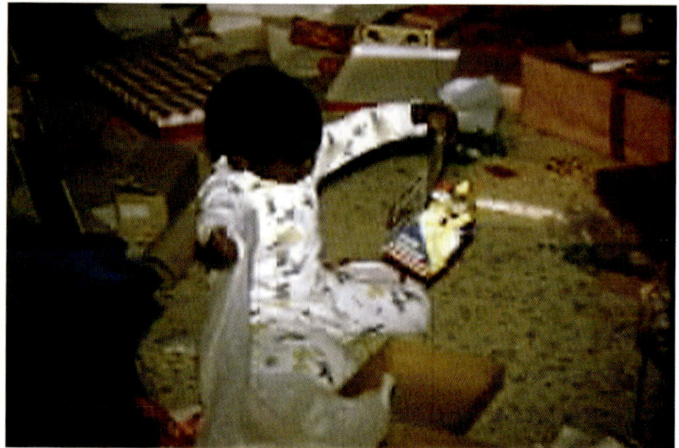

but differing socioeconomic standings. Kina's own cluttered, standard white fridge contrasts with the high-end appliances of her extended family, perhaps representing her own sense of difference, class and otherwise, as she attempted to build a new identity as a "mixed-race Asian American Jew by choice."[35]

As a final expression of the "New Authentics," consider Zackin and Sanford Biggers's video installation *a small world . . .*, 1999–2001 (fig. 18), in which home movies of each artist's family— one Jewish American, one African American—display nearly identical rituals. Watching these paired 1970s suburban birthday parties, piano lessons, trips to Disney World, holiday celebrations, and backyard barbecues, we are left to wonder: Did the artists select a representative survey of their histories, or were scenes that distinguish these histories left on the cutting room floor? In other words, does the scenes' homogeneity dispel the very notion of categorization and difference, or are we witnessing a Disneyesque ideal? In keeping with the diversity and dynamism of the post-Jewish experience, the artists provide no easy answers, only opportunities to ponder the possibilities for anyone willing to stop and take a look, whether they are Jewish, non-Jewish, part Jewish, post-Jewish, or all of the above.

1. David Biale, "The Melting Pot and Beyond," in *Insider/Outsider: American Jews and Multiculturalism*, eds. David Biale, Michael Galchinsky, and Susan Heschel (Berkeley, CA: University of California Press, 1998), 31.

2. Roberta Rosenberg Farber and Chaim I. Waxman, "Constructing a Modern Jewish Identity," in *Jews in America: A Contemporary Reader*, eds. Roberta Rosenberg Farber and Chaim I. Waxman (Hanover, NH: University Press of New England for Brandeis University Press, 1999), 193.

3. David A. Hollinger, "Jewish Identity, Assimilation and Multiculturalism," in *Creating American Jews: Historical Conversations about Identity*, ed. Karen Mittelman (Philadelphia: National Museum of American Jewish History; and Waltham, MA: Brandeis University, 1998), 52.

4. Vincent Brook, *You Should See Yourself: Jewish Identity in Postmodern American Culture* (New Brunswick, NJ: Rutgers University Press, 2006), 6.

5. John Updike, *Bech at Bay* (New York: Alfred A. Knopf, 1998), 152.

6. Leslie A. Fiedler, "Growing Up Post-Jewish," in *Fiedler on the Roof: Essays on Literature and Jewish Identity* (Boston: David R. Godine, 1991), 117; and Vincent Brook, "Post-Jewishness? The Third Phase of the Jewish Sitcom Trend," in *Something Ain't Kosher Here: The Rise of the "Jewish" Sitcom* (New Brunswick, NJ: Rutgers University Press, 2003), 148.

7. David A. Hollinger, *Postethnic America: Beyond Multiculturalism* (New York: Basic Books, 2000), 3–4.

8. Thelma Golden, *Freestyle*, exh. cat. (New York: The Studio Museum in Harlem, 2001), 14.

9. Holland Cotter, "Latino Art, and Beyond Category," *The New York Times*, September 2, 2005. Cotter was reviewing El Museo del Barrio's exhibition *The (S) Files / The Selected Files 2005*.

10. Biale, "Melting Pot," 32.

11. See Cheryl Greenberg, "Pluralism and Its Discontents: The Case of Blacks and Jews," in *Insider/Outsider*, 55–87.

12. Ibid., 78

13. Naomi Seidman, "Fag-Hags and Bu-Jews, Toward a (Jewish) Politics of Vicarious Identity," in *Insider/Outsider*, 254.

14. Lynne C. Lancaster and David Stillman, *When Generations Collide: Who They Are. Why They Clash: How to Solve the Generational Puzzle at Work* (New York: HarperCollins, 2002), 25.

15. Michelle Goldberg, "The New Jew Is Who?" *Jewish World Review*, February 28, 2002; online at www.jewishworldreview.com/0202/new_jew.asp.

16. Steven M. Cohen and Arnold M. Eisen, "The Sovereign Self: Jewish Identity in Post-Modern America." *Jerusalem Letter/Viewpoints*, May 1, 2001; online at www.jcpa.org/jl/vp453.htm. See also their *The Jew Within: Self, Family, and Community in America* (Bloomington, IN: Indiana University Press, 2000).

17. See www.rebooters.net.

18. Matthew Baigell, *American Artists, Jewish Images* (Syracuse, NY: Syracuse University Press, 2006).

19. Hollinger, "Jewish Identity," 52.

20. Biale, "Melting Pot," 30.

21. Vincent J. Cheng, *Inauthentic: The Anxiety over Culture and Identity* (New Brunswick, NJ: Rutgers University Press, 2004), 86.

22. Quoted in James E. Young's "After-images of the Holocaust in Contemporary Art," in *After Images* (Frankfurt: Neues Museum Weserburg Bremen & Revolver, 2004), 20.

23. Leon Wieseltier, *New Republic*, May 27, 2002, 22.

24. Schorr, in "German Brutality and Roman Sensuality: Pictures of Soldiers in the Landscape," *Art:21*, season 2, episode 6 (PBS); online at www.pbs.org/art21/artists/schorr/clip1.html.

25. Schorr, in Edith Newhall, "Out of the Past," *New York Magazine*, December 3, 2001, 87.

26. Haendel, artist statement, "Thoughts on Being an Artist Now," February 2004.

27. Haendel, in *Anna Helwing Gallery Conversations: Karl Haendel and Mario Ybarra, Jr.* (Los Angeles: Anna Helwing Gallery, 2006), 44.

28. See Caryn Aviv and David Shneer, *New Jews: The End of the Jewish Diaspora* (New York: New York University Press, 2005).

29. Krieger, e-mail correspondence with the author, April 25, 2006.

30. Zackin, artist statement, 2006.

31. Tauber, artist statement, 2001.

32. Ibid.

33. Biale, "Melting Pot," 32.

34. Meyerson, e-mail to Galerie Emmanuel Perrotin, Paris, 2004.

35. Kina, e-mail correspondence with the author, February 14, 2007.

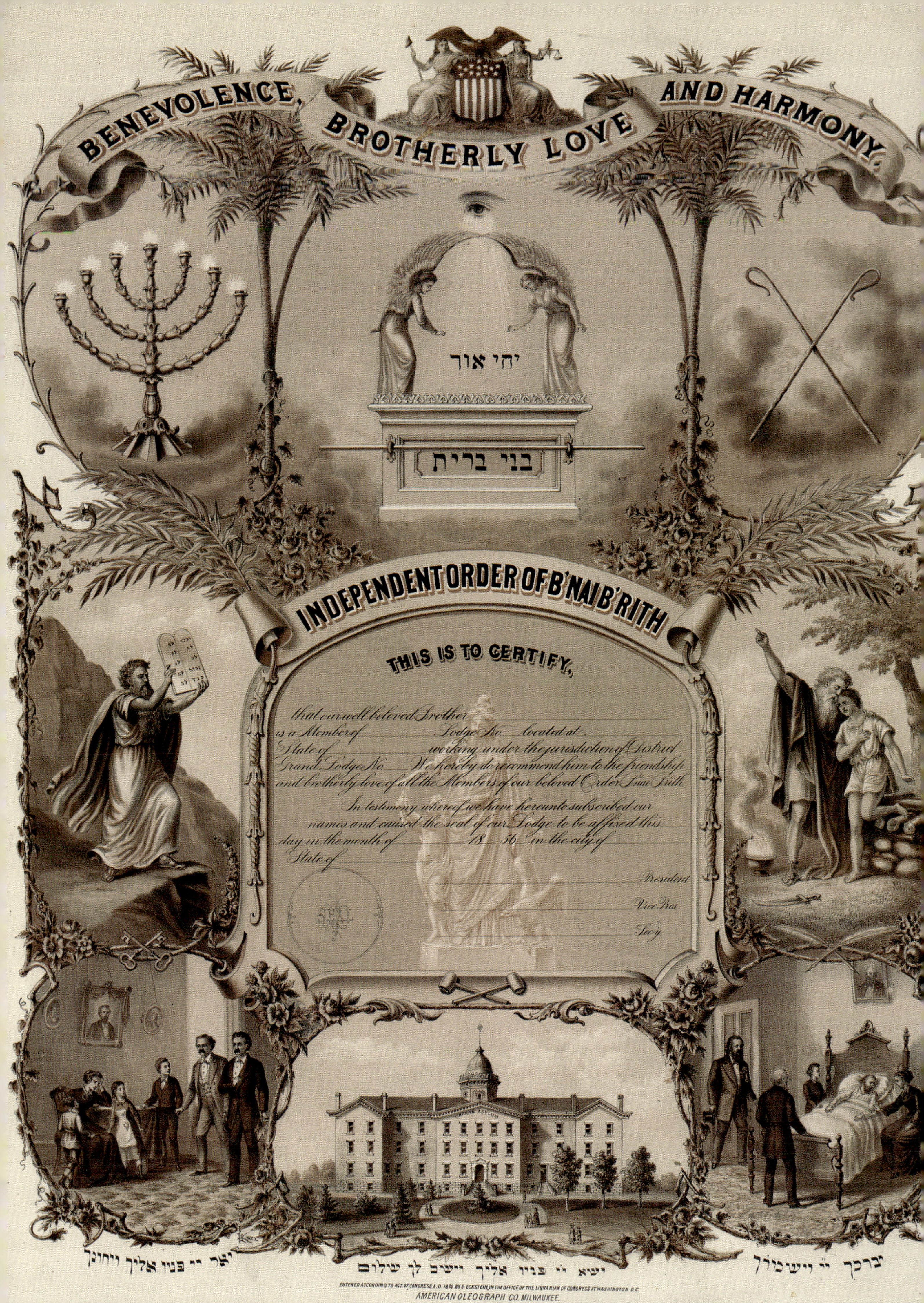

BENEVOLENCE, BROTHERLY LOVE AND HARMONY.
יחי אור
בני ברית
INDEPENDENT ORDER OF B'NAI B'RITH
THIS IS TO CERTIFY,
that our well beloved Brother
is a Member of   Lodge No   located at
State of   working under the jurisdiction of District
Grand Lodge No   We hereby do recommend him to the friendship
and brotherly love of all the Members of our beloved Order B'nai B'rith.
In testimony whereof we have hereunto subscribed our
names and caused the seal of our Lodge to be affixed this
day in the month of   18 6   in the city of
State of
President
Vice Pres.
Secy.
SEAL
יֹצֵר יְיָ בָּנָיו אֵלָיו יֵחוֹנֵן
יִשָּׂא יְיָ פָּנָיו אֵלֶיךָ וְיָשֵׂם לְךָ שָׁלוֹם
בְּרֶכְךָ יְיָ וְיִשְׁמְרֶךָ
ENTERED ACCORDING TO ACT OF CONGRESS A.D. 1876 BY S. ECKSTEIN, IN THE OFFICE OF THE LIBRARIAN OF CONGRESS AT WASHINGTON D.C.
AMERICAN OLEOGRAPH CO. MILWAUKEE.

Between Memory and Messianism: A Brief History of American Jewish Identity

by Stephen J. Whitfield

FOR MOST OF THE FULL SPAN OF JEWISH HISTORY, WHICH IS MEASURED IN MILLENNIA,
Jewish identity has been indistinguishable from Judaism. Until the seventeenth century, when the excommunicated Dutch philosopher Baruch Spinoza (1632–1677) opted to forego the formalities of creed or ritual yet still call himself a Jew, religion is what separated Jews from everyone else. Since Spinoza's choice, Jewish secularism has gathered momentum. In the United States in particular, Jewish identity has often been severed from both worship and belief and expressed instead within the larger template of culture (both high and popular). Here, Jewishness has characteristically been defined as ethnicity or as a sense of people-hood—at its fullest as communal participation and at its thinnest as shared culinary memories. Jewishness can even be so elusive as to defy any precise markings at all. What this essay is intended to suggest is that a Jewishness that is unattached to Judaism also has a history, and has circulated, however ambiguously, within American culture for at least a century and a half. This history has been expressed in film, theater, and literature, as well as in visual art. The past is therefore a prelude to the emergence of the "New Authentics," who are helping to shape the consciousness of our postmodern era.

When does the expansive sense of an American Jewish identity begin? I move the nomination of 1843, when a fraternal and service organization, the B'nai B'rith, was formed. Its membership requirements were strikingly liberal: anyone agreeing to subscribe to the Jewish religion *or* to associate with the Jewish people could join (see fig. 19). This definition of a Jew was not ecclesiastical, not ancestral, not legal. It was subjective—if you call yourself a Jew, you're a Jew. Even the religious criteria that the organization sanctioned were imprecise rather than *halakhic*; Judaic law was inapplicable. As historian Cornelia Wilhelm has noted, the B'nai B'rith "offered Jewish solidarity and identity conceived in broad terms: candidates from mixed marriages who professed Judaism as their faith and those with a Christian mother could, in

Fig. 19 **B'nai B'rith membership certificate**, designed by Louis Kurz, published by Milwaukee American Oleograph Company (1876). Library of Congress, Prints & Photographs Division.

principle, join the lodge; the prerequisite was their simple affirmation that they were Jews by religion."[1]

No wonder then that by the mid-nineteenth century, the Bohemian-born Rabbi Isaac Mayer Wise (1819–1900) had noticed something peculiar about the United States: "Here everyone does as he chooses, preaches as he thinks fit, and expounds the Law as he understands it."[2] The German Jewish immigrants who are largely responsible for inventing the religious, social, and political institutions that would ensure continuity down to our own time had become Jeffersonians, holding truths to be self-evident rather than inherited from political or religious authorities on high. The rationalism, liberalism, and nationalism that had been stirring in the Germanies were already corroding the verities of Judaism, and made the immigrants and their progeny in the United States already receptive to self-definition. Further, a republic that was so enlightened as to lack an established church and a society teeming with a bewildering variety of Protestants had taught the Jewish minority that it was free to do its own thing. This was the groove into which the masses of Eastern European Jews arriving in the final decades of the nineteenth century were learning to fit. So loose was the structure of American Jewry that when Rabbi Hayim Vidrowitz (1836–1911) landed in New York from Tsarist Russia in 1893, he hung out a sign that proclaimed him to be the "Chief Rabbi of America." But when asked who had bestowed so exalted a rank, Vidrowitz was compelled to reply: "The sign painter."[3]

Such newcomers, who were fleeing Tsarist persecution and poverty a century ago, arrived as anti-immigrant sentiments were becoming rampant. These heightened anxieties coagulated into nativism, which posed some urgent questions: Could the nation absorb so many diverse and exotic peoples streaming across the Atlantic and the Pacific? Could Asians, Italians, Greeks, or Slavs ever be "Americanized"? Could those whom even the poet Emma Lazarus (1849–1887), channeling the voice of Lady Liberty, portrayed as "wretched refuse" join a line stretching back to Pilgrims and patriots? The American-born descendants of those whom Lazarus had described as "homeless" and "tempest-tost" knew that the doubts of the nativists proved unwarranted, and their fears gave way to an affirmative pride in the sheer cussed plebeian variety of the populace. In the 1981 comedy *Stripes* (scripted by Len Blum, Harold Ramis, and Dan Goldberg), the military misfit played by Bill Murray exhorts his comrades: "We're not Spartans—we're Americans!" At his fellow soldiers, he shouts: "That means that our forefathers were kicked out of every decent country in the world. We are the wretched refuse. We're the underdog. We're mutts. Here's proof." Murray touches a soldier's face. "His nose is cold."[4]

Struggling to find secure footing in the New World, Russian Jews and their children sought to placate hostility by honoring the dominant ideals of homogeneity and unity. They invoked the right to be equal, but often at the expense of the right to be different. Many subscribed to more demanding versions of Judaism than had their German counterparts, but few were willing to mount a direct challenge to a public culture that considered diversity to be divisive. The ideal to which Americans were expected to adhere was Anglo-Saxon. But Jews generally did not settle in privileged Protestant neighborhoods where direct encounters with those of English ancestry were likely. Instead they encountered the Irish. Their toughness could be physically threatening and violent; their Roman Catholicism could be downright forbidding.

But as native speakers of English, the Irish struck many Jews as a model minority, proof of the process of Americanization. Though they could boast of reaching the New World earlier than did Eastern European Jewry, the Irish bristled with historic resentments and grievances, and in the New World faced accusations of promoting the conspiratorial infiltration of the Vatican. The Irish were therefore outsiders as well as insiders. The power of the Anglo-Saxon ideal had the effect of discouraging ethnic pride and self-respect among the Jews, even if Protestants themselves were rarely their neighbors. Hence "it was the Irish and the Irish alone we Jews admired," according to essayist Harry Golden (1902–1981), who grew up on the Lower East Side. Indeed the highest praise that a Jewish infant could earn from its parents or grandparents, Golden recalled, was the exclamation that the baby looked Irish.[5]

Luckless babies might at least grow up to marry Irish. The Jazz Age marked the blazing popularity of interfaith romantic comedies like Anne Nichols's *Abie's Irish Rose* (1922) on Broadway (see fig. 20), as well as a film scripted by Alfred A. Cohn, *The Cohens and the*

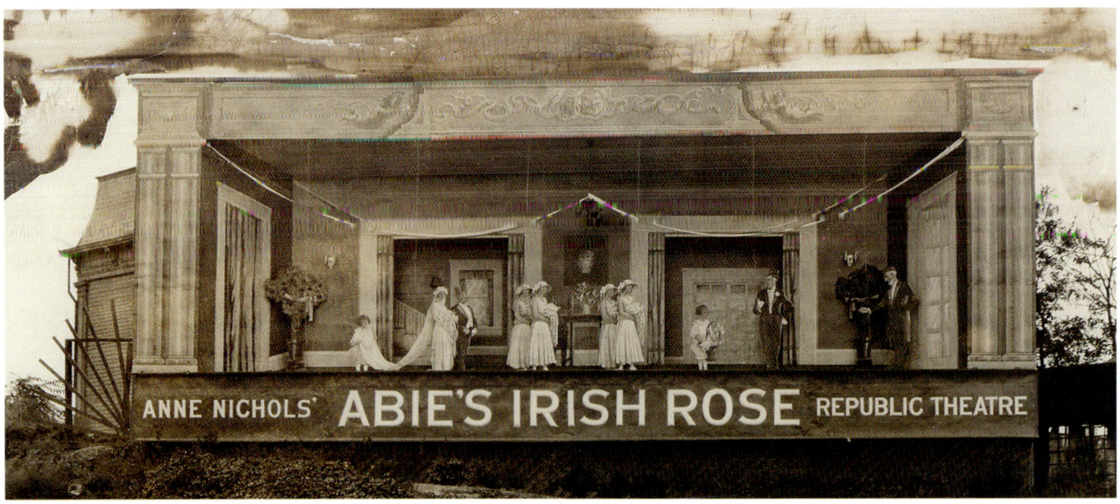

Kellys (1926), that generated six cinematic sequels over the next several years.[6] (When Spencer Tracy got to Hollywood, he discovered a distinctive sort of interaction, noting that out there "the Kellys are working for the Cohens."[7]) The tradition of interfaith comedies waned but did not entirely disappear. As late as 1989, the television sitcom *Chicken Soup* entangled the last authentic legatee of Borscht-Belt humor, Jackie Mason, with Lynn Redgrave, playing an Irish Catholic. Despite respectable reviews and ratings, the show was cancelled, partly due to Jewish complaints that the prospect of intermarriage was cast in too favorable a light.[8]

To be faux Irish was another option. The Chicago-based oral historian Louis Terkel (1912–) called himself "Studs" in honor of James T. Farrell's most famous fictional protagonist, Studs Lonigan of the city's South Side. The Bronx-born Sidney Aaron Chayefsky (1923–1981) maximized his promising career as a playwright in 1943, when he named himself "Paddy."[9] The boxing maven Abbott Joseph Liebling (1904–1963) grew up in Far Rockaway, New York. Pudgy, bespectacled, puny, uncoordinated, and bookish, he scarcely resembled the domineering working-class Irish kids in his neighborhood. But Liebling's "enthusiasm for Catholic toughs," his biographer has conjectured, stemmed from a desire "to cut himself off from the emasculating Jewish tradition."[10] And finally, in Norman Mailer's tale of high-stakes sex in Greenwich Village in the 1950s, "The Time of Her Time," the lover whom Denise Gondelman taunts is not exactly ethnically indistinct. His name is Sergius O'Shaughnessy, an alter ego of the novelist himself.[11]

In the leftward tilt of their politics, the Jews differed sharply, however, from the Irish—and indeed from most other Americans as well. Messianism had of course begun as an ancient Jewish idea, and for many secular Jews in particular the world into which they were born was badly in need of redemption—so much so that only radical mobilization would suffice. Against the injustices associated with capitalism, only a radiant ideology like socialism would presumably

Fig. 20 Outdoor diorama advertising Anne Nichols's **Abie's Irish Rose** at the Republic Theatre in the Bronx, 1922.
Billy Rose Theatre Division, The New York Public Library for the Performing Arts, Astor, Lenox and Tilden Foundations.

be effective. In the Jewish messianic interpretation, the redemptive event will occur publicly, not merely privately (as in Christianity). That anticipation suggested the enlistment of the wretched of the earth rather than the salvation of individual souls.[12] Tolstoy encapsulated the message of the Savior as "resist not evil." But the ethics of Judaism mandated the opposite: resist evil. The implication was evident: politics is necessary to move history forward in a progressive direction and to hasten redemption. Jewish modernists and secularists easily adapted messianism to suggest that collective action might achieve a much better world, arising from the remains of this one. Simultaneously, radical dissatisfaction with the status quo and fervor for justice intensified by the political and religious oppression experienced in the Old World pushed Jews disproportionately to the left. Even in America, Jews continued to bear scars from the wounds that Tsarism had inflicted. Such scars bred activism: not only was the Yiddish *Forverts* the most widely read foreign language daily newspaper in the nation, its editor, Abraham Cahan, who had translated Upton Sinclair's socialist novel *The Jungle* (1906) into Yiddish, sought to make the newspaper into a "workingmen's organ" to achieve "the liberation of mankind— justice, humanity, fraternity."[13] For the Jews, politics was about ideals rather than interests.

For the masses packed into the tenements of the Lower East Side, the Yiddish theater offered a tantalizing refuge from the grinding toil of the sweatshops. But the stage provided more than escapism. *Tsaytbilder* were plays devoted to contemporary political events and especially to Jewish causes. The *tsaytbilder* (or "timely presentations") were topical in an era when entertainment was something to do downtown rather than to be downloaded. For example, in 1911 Mendel Beilis was arrested in the Ukraine, accused of "ritual murder." But so blatant was the frame-up that—even in Tsarist Russia—the defendant was acquitted, in late October, 1913. By early November, plays recounting the fate of Mendel Beilis opened at the city's smaller Yiddish theaters. By Thanksgiving weekend, New York's Yiddish-speaking theater-lovers had the choice of seeing their three favorite actors in the leading role of the following big-budget productions: at the Dewey Theater, Jacob Adler was playing in *Mendel Beilis*; at the National Theater, Boris Thomashefsky was playing in *Mendel Beilis*; and at the Second Avenue Theater, David Kessler was playing in *Mendel Beilis*.[14]

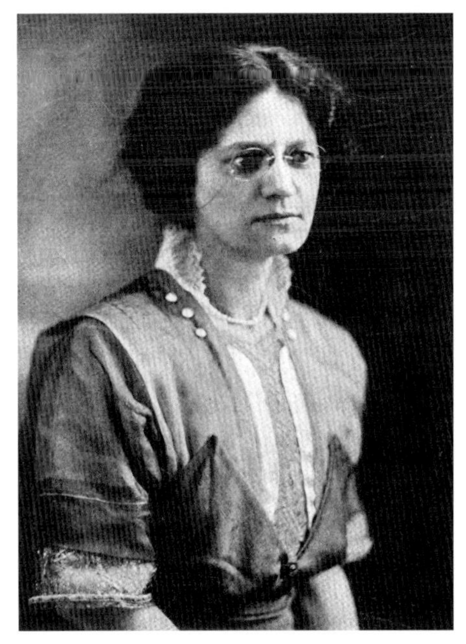

A decade later, however, such lifelines to the old country went slack. In 1924 the United States Congress devised and legalized a quota system, the National Origins Act, which drastically limited immigration for Eastern European Jews and several other unwelcome groups. For the first time the United States became a gated community. Though civic and economic opportunity remained far more advantageous than in Eastern Europe, prejudice and discrimination could not be detached from the experience of American Jews, which helps to explain the empathy that many conveyed toward a far more despised and degraded minority. The American equivalent of a Russian pogrom was a lynching, a mostly Southern horror that inspired only two significant protest songs: "Supper Time" (1933) and "Strange Fruit" (1939). Both were written by Jews: the first, quite surprisingly, by a Republican, Irving Berlin; the second, more predictably, by a Communist, Lewis Allan (né Abel Meeropol). Each song became indelibly associated with a black female vocalist: "Supper Time" with Ethel Waters (who said the song summarized the race problem) and "Strange Fruit" with Billie Holiday (who tried to claim writing credit for so poignant a song).

In the first third of the twentieth century, Berlin and especially George Gershwin became famous for capturing the Negro musical idiom. They did so with such uncanny adroitness that the leading white gentile patron of the Harlem Renaissance, Carl Van Vechten of Cedar Rapids, Iowa, reported from Vienna in 1932: "They don't play Johann [Strauss] here anymore; it's all Gershwin and Berlin."[15] An understanding of the composers' efforts at imitation, which made their identity seem all the more Jewish by painting it black, should not be reduced to exploitation or condescension. There was empathy too, and blacks reciprocated the sentiment. Consider James Weldon Johnson, the general secretary of the National Association for the Advancement of Colored People (NAACP), and also a gifted lyricist who wrote the Negro National Anthem. He exemplified black pride and creativity. Yet in Johnson's autobiography, when he imagines a genie asking him what he would like to be if he were not black, the answer is unequivocal: "Make me a Jew."[16]

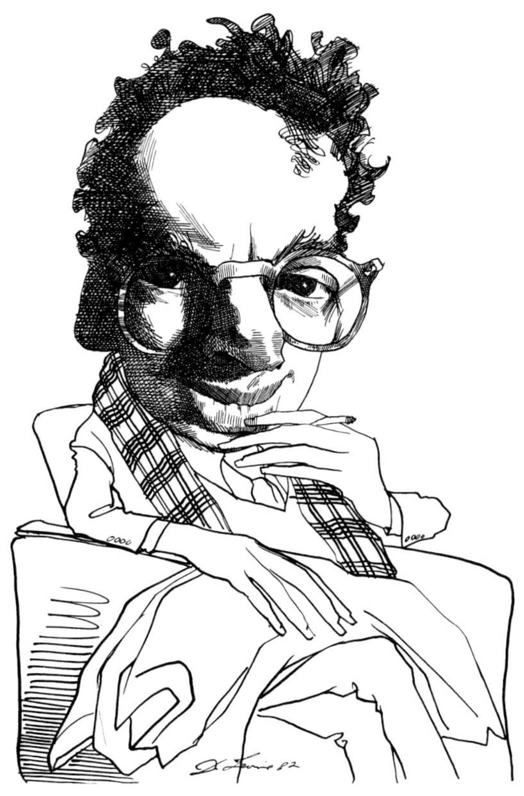

Fig. 22 **Clifford Odets**, illustration by David Levine, 1982.
© David Levine.

This monosyllabic request would not have been imitated by many Jews themselves, had a genie offered them an alternative. For much of the last century, citizenship was more exulted in than ethnicity. A case in point is *The Promised Land*, the autobiography of an immigrant from the Russian Pale of Settlement, and the biggest non-fiction best-seller of 1912. The favorite trope of its author, Mary Antin (1881–1949; fig. 21), was the repudiation of the past and its pain, to be replaced by the fresh start that Lazarus's Mother of Exiles offered. Constructing a new identity, Antin presented herself as an American Eve; her American Adam was the Lutheran minister's son whom she married.[17] Jesse Lasky, the Hollywood movie mogul, would have understood. In 1958, when he collapsed and was rushed to the hospital, an attendant asked him his religion. "American" was his reply, and was also his last word on earth.[18] (Cut, and print!)

Or take Clifford Odets (1906–1963; fig. 22). No playwright of the 1930s managed to capture with greater fidelity the ordeal of the lower middle-class Jewish family. Odets had started his career as the dramatics counselor at Jewish summer camps; he ended up as a Hollywood scenarist. After writing his theatrical masterpiece, *Awake and Sing!* (1935), Odets was troubled that whatever he pecked at on the typewriter somehow came out ethnic. He once told a friend: "I have a serious artistic problem. I don't feel I write completely American characters; they always come out a little Jewish."[19] Bewitched by the ideal of assimilation, Odets had not realized that "a little Jewish" was not a badge of shame, nor a limitation upon his art, but instead the natural expression of his imaginative energy. This desire to escape from the "ghetto" rather than to affirm its spirit was echoed by another playwright on the left, Arthur Miller (1915–2005), whose autobiography expresses a commonplace yearning to forsake a "parochial narrowness of mind, prejudices, racism, and the irrational," and "to identify myself with mankind rather than one small tribal fraction of it."[20]

Had such universalist proclivities persisted, without provoking any sort of particularist counterforce, American Jewry would have disappeared. Indeed, in 1964 *Look* magazine published an article ominously titled "The Vanishing American Jew." The vital signs of the community were seeming to dim. Nevertheless the American Jew did not vanish (though *Look* itself did). Why? Perhaps the conventional quest for inclusion at the cost of particularity had produced its own form of resistance; the drive for utter assimilation may have instigated its own antithesis. This effort to legitimate Jewish difference, which could be detected even as expiration seemed imminent, has continued to flourish right down to the twenty-first century—the era of the "New Authentics" in Jewish art.

When did this counter-trend begin? I move the nomination of 1960, at the dawn of the decade when several of the "New Authentics" were born. In 1960, for the first time in American history, a candidate who was not a Protestant was elected President, making the Electoral College a little safer for diversity. In Buenos Aires in 1960, Israeli agents captured a former Obersturmbann-führer of the SS, Adolf Eichmann, who would be put on trial in Jerusalem and rivet attention on the Holocaust. (That word was not yet commonly used to describe the extinction of European Jewry.) And also in 1960, a best-selling novel published two years earlier, Leon Uris's *Exodus*, was adapted to the screen. *Exodus* had been published when the philanthropic and political interest of American Jewry in Israel was subdued, and when tourism and communal program-ming were—by later standards—low.[21] Since then, over nearly half a century, the book has never gone out of print. No one could have predicted the impact that a pro-Zionist epic would have on countless Jewish readers, for whom the path toward unmodulated Americanization seemed utterly unobstructed.

As influential as Uris's novel was, Otto Preminger's film version was probably even more im-portant in marking a new direction in American Jewish identity (see fig. 23). The movie foregrounds the romance between a native-born Israeli, Ari Ben Canaan (Paul Newman), and a gentile nurse, Kitty Fremont (Eva Marie Saint). In depicting how inter-ethnic or inter-religious love might sur-mount primordial hatred, the love story seemed to perpetuate the staples of earlier popular films. Overlooking the Jezreel Valley, Kitty proclaims that "all these differences between people are made up. People are the same, no matter what they're called." But Ari disagrees: "Don't

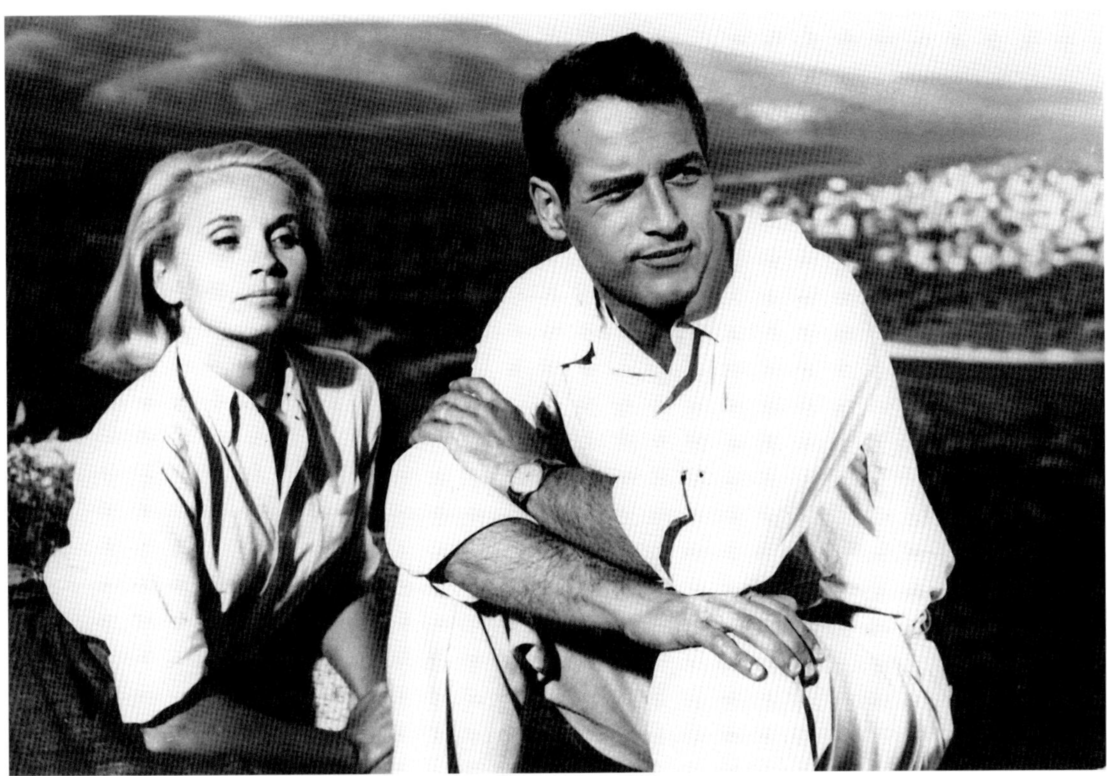

ever believe it. People are different. They have a *right* to be different. They *like* to be different. It's no good pretending differences don't exist. They do. They have to be recognized and respected." Still, Kitty nourishes the hope that if Ari can briefly forget that he is a Jew, she will no longer feel so much a Presbyterian from Indiana. "There *are* no differences," she whispers as they kiss.

But this is not a happy ending, sealed with a kiss, as Ari gets the final word: "We *are* different. . . . I'm a Jew," he tells Kitty. And finally she realizes that he is right, and thus is not Mr. Right.[22] Despite its deal-breaking consequence, however, the meaning of Ari's Jewish identity is never elucidated. He comes across as entirely secular, as though he were a Canaanite, a man of the land, rather than a believer in Judaism. Yet while *Exodus* leaves unsolved the enduring mystery of Jewish identity, its ending contradicts the authority of the American majority culture when its incarnation, Kitty, decides to join the Israeli independence fighters. A tectonic shift had thus occurred: Jewish nationalism is no longer to be dismissed as a parochial embarrassment, a residue of the tribal past, but instead as a living proposition (one worth dying for, even for a gentile). In the United States, the contours of Jewishness were widening as never before, even as advancing multiculturalism was building a big tent for all varieties of identity, with every minority enriching the mosaic.

At first the efflorescence of an overt American Jewish identity was almost too subtle to notice. One night in 1963, for example, the audience numbered only six at San Francisco's hungry i nightclub for a program that paired two Brooklynites. The stand-up comedian was Woody Allen. The singer was Barbra Streisand.[23] Each would become an icon of a performative Jewishness, of an ethnic distinctiveness that could neither be concealed nor suppressed. Allen and Streisand offered proof in their own ways of the hospitality and elasticity of American popular culture. By the time Mandy Patinkin sang Irving Berlin's "White Christmas" in Yiddish on his 1998 album *Mamaloshen*, Jewish identity had become a spur to pride, an almost "natural" fact to be invoked—so much so that when Monica Lewinsky wanted President Bill Clinton to understand her through her heritage, she presented him with a copy of a book called *Oy Vey! The Things They Say: A Guide to Jewish Wit.*[24] And by 2004 so transformed was Hollywood that it released a film with a soundtrack mostly in Aramaic. From the perspective of Jewish continuity, that's the good news. (The bad news was that the movie was Mel Gibson's *The Passion of the Christ.*)

None of Christ's followers played a more decisive role in the founding of what became the United States than did the Episcopalians. But their political influence is fading. In the current Congress, Jews outnumber them (43 to 37). The head of the Episcopal Church, Katharine Jefferts Schori, is no embattled sectarian, however, mourning a lost hegemony. She is open to eclectic influences, having told an interviewer: "I like the word 'shalom.' I use it in my correspondence. I use it in my sermons, and that's how I sign my e-mails—'shalom.' To me it is a concrete reminder of what it is we're all supposed to be about. It means far more than peace," she added. "I think it's a vision of human community. Those great visions of Isaiah— every person fed, no more strife, the ill are healed, prisoners are released."[25] Her invocation of a Hebrew prophet in describing the contemporary condition is a confirmation of the promise of America, and also implies an enduring conundrum. Even within a postmodern culture, even when the comforts of prosperity might have erased all traces of peculiarity and divergence, Jewish identity is suspended between memory and messianism.

1. Cornelia Wilhelm, "Community in Modernity—Finding Jewish Solidarity within the Independent Order of B'nai B'rith," in *Simon Dubnow Institute Yearbook*, I (Stuttgart: Deutsche Verlags-Anstalt, 2002), 299, 303, 305–6, 313.

2. Quoted in Marc Lee Raphael, *Judaism in America* (New York: Columbia University Press, 2003), 49.

3. Quoted in Irving Howe, with Kenneth Libo, *World of Our Fathers* (New York: Harcourt Brace Jovanovich, 1976), 195.

4. Quoted in Tad Friend, "Comedy First," *New Yorker*, April 19 & 26, 2004, 164.

5. Harry Golden, Preface to *Hutchins Hapgood, The Spirit of the Ghetto* (New York: Schocken, 1966), ix.

6. Ted Merwin, *In Their Own Image: New York Jews in Jazz Age Popular Culture* (New Brunswick, NJ: Rutgers University Press, 2006), 126–27, 135, 146.

7. Quoted in Larry Swindell, *Spencer Tracy* (New York: World, 1969), 139.

8. Vincent Brook, "'Ya'll Killed Him, We Didn't': Jewish Self-Hatred and The Larry Sanders Show," in *You Should See Yourself: Jewish Identity in Postmodern American Culture*, ed. Vincent Brook (New Brunswick, NJ: Rutgers University Press, 2006), 301.

9. Judith E. Smith, *Visions of Belonging: Family Stories, Popular Culture, and Postwar Democracy, 1940–1960* (New York: Columbia University Press, 2004), 260, 387n.

10. Raymond Sokolov, *Wayward Reporter: The Life of A. J. Liebling* (New York: Harper & Row, 1980), 24–25, 28, 30, 40, 42.

11. Norman Mailer, *Advertisements for Myself* (New York: G. P. Putnam's Sons, 1959), 478 503.

12. See Gershom Sholem, *The Messianic Idea in Judaism and Other Essays on Jewish Spirituality* (New York: Schocken, 1971), 1–36.

13. Quoted in Moses Rischin, *The Promised City: New York's Jews, 1870–1914* (Cambridge, MA: Harvard University Press, 1962), 160.

14. Joel Berkowitz, "The Mendel Beilis Epidemic on the Yiddish Stage," *Jewish Social Studies* 8 (New Series) (Fall 2001), 199.

15. Quoted in Charles C. Alexander, *Here the Country Lies: Nationalism and the Arts in Twentieth-Century America* (Bloomington: Indiana University Press, 1980), 174.

16. James Weldon Johnson, *Along This Way* (New York: Viking Press, 1933), 136.

17. See Alice Payne Hackett and James Henry Burke, *80 Years of Best Sellers, 1895–1975* (New York: R. R. Bowker, 1977), 76, 78; and Joyce Antler, *The Journey Home: Jewish Women and the American Century* (New York: Free Press, 1997), 18–26.

18. Neal Gabler, *An Empire of Their Own: How the Jews Invented Hollywood* (New York: Crown, 1988), 420.

19. Quoted in Margaret Brenman-Gibson, *Clifford Odets: American Playwright, 1906–1940* (New York: Atheneum, 1981), 411.

20. Arthur Miller, *Timebends: A Life* (New York: Grove Press, 1987), 70.

21. David Biale, *Power and Powerlessness in Jewish History* (New York: Schocken, 1986), 184.

22. Deborah Dash Moore, "*Exodus*: Real to Reel to Real," in *Entertaining America: Jews, Movies, and Broadcasting*, eds. J. Hoberman and Jeffrey Shandler (Princeton, NJ: Princeton University Press, 2003), 207–219.

23. See Jesse Kornbluth, "Play It Alone, Brickman," *New York Times Magazine*, February 24, 1980, 29.

24. Jeffrey Toobin, *A Vast Conspiracy: The Real Story of the Sex Scandal That Nearly Brought Down a President* (New York: Random House, 1999), 163.

25. Deborah Solomon and Katharine Jefferts Schori, "State of the Church," *New York Times Magazine*, November 19, 2006, 21.

The History of Love

by Nicole Krauss

4. I SEARCHED OUT OTHER FORMS OF LIFE

"Where's Brighton Beach?" I asked. "In England," my mother said, searching the kitchen cabinets for something she'd misplaced. "I mean the one in New York." "Near Coney Island, I think." "How far is Coney Island?" "Maybe half an hour." "Driving or walking?" "You can take the subway." "How many stops?" "I don't know. Why are you so interested in Brighton Beach?" "I have a friend there. His name is Misha and he's Russian," I said with admiration. "Just Russian?" my mother asked from inside the cabinet under the kitchen sink. "What do you mean, *just* Russian?" She stood up and turned to me. "Nothing," she said, looking at me with the expression she sometimes gets when she's just thought of something amazingly fascinating. "It's just that you, for example, are one-quarter Russian, one-quarter Hungarian, one-quarter Polish, and one-quarter German." I didn't say anything. She opened a drawer, then closed it. "Actually," she said, "you could say you're three-quarters Polish and one-quarter Hungarian, since Bubbe's parents were from Poland before they moved to Nuremberg, and Grandma Sasha's town was originally in Belarus, or White Russia, before it became part of Poland." She opened another cabinet stuffed with plastic bags and started rooting around in it. I turned to go. "Now that I'm thinking about it," she said, "I suppose you could also say you're three-quarters Polish and one-quarter Czech, because the town Zeyde came from was in Hungary before 1918, and in Czechoslavakia after, although the Hungarians continued to consider themselves Hungarian, and briefly even became Hungarian again during the Second World War. Of course, you could always just say you're half Polish, one-quarter Hungarian, and one-quarter English, since Grandpa Simon left Poland and moved to London when he was nine." She grabbed a piece of paper from the pad by the telephone and started to write vigorously. A minute passed while she scratched away at the page. "Look!" she said, pushing the paper over so I could see it. "You can actually make *sixteen different* pie charts, each of them accurate!" I looked at the paper. It said:

Russian	Polish		Polish	Polish		Polish	Polish		Russian	Polish
German	Hungarian		German	Hungarian		Polish	Hungarian		Polish	Hungarian

Russian	Polish		Polish	Polish		Polish	Polish		Russian	Polish
Polish	Czech		Polish	Czech		German	Czech		German	Czech

Russian	English		Russian	English		Russian	English		Russian	English
German	Czech		Polish	Czech		Polish	Hungarian		German	Hungarian

Polish	English		Polish	English		Polish	English		Polish	English
German	Czech		German	Hungarian		Polish	Hungarian		Polish	Czech

"Then again, you could always just stick with half English and half Israeli, since—" "I'M AMERICAN!" I shouted. My mother blinked. "Suit yourself," she said, and went to put the kettle on to boil. From the corner of the room where he was looking at the pictures in a magazine, Bird muttered: "No, you're not. You're Jewish."

David Altmejd

Cheselyn Amato

Johanna Bresnick

Shoshana Dentz

Lilah Freedland

Matthew Girson

Karl Haendel

Laura Kina

Fawn Krieger

Jin Meyerson

Collier Schorr

Mindy Rose Schwartz

Ludwig Schwarz

Joel Tauber

Shoshanna Weinberger

Jennifer Zackin

Artist essays by Sarah Giller Nelson and Lori Waxman

David Altmejd

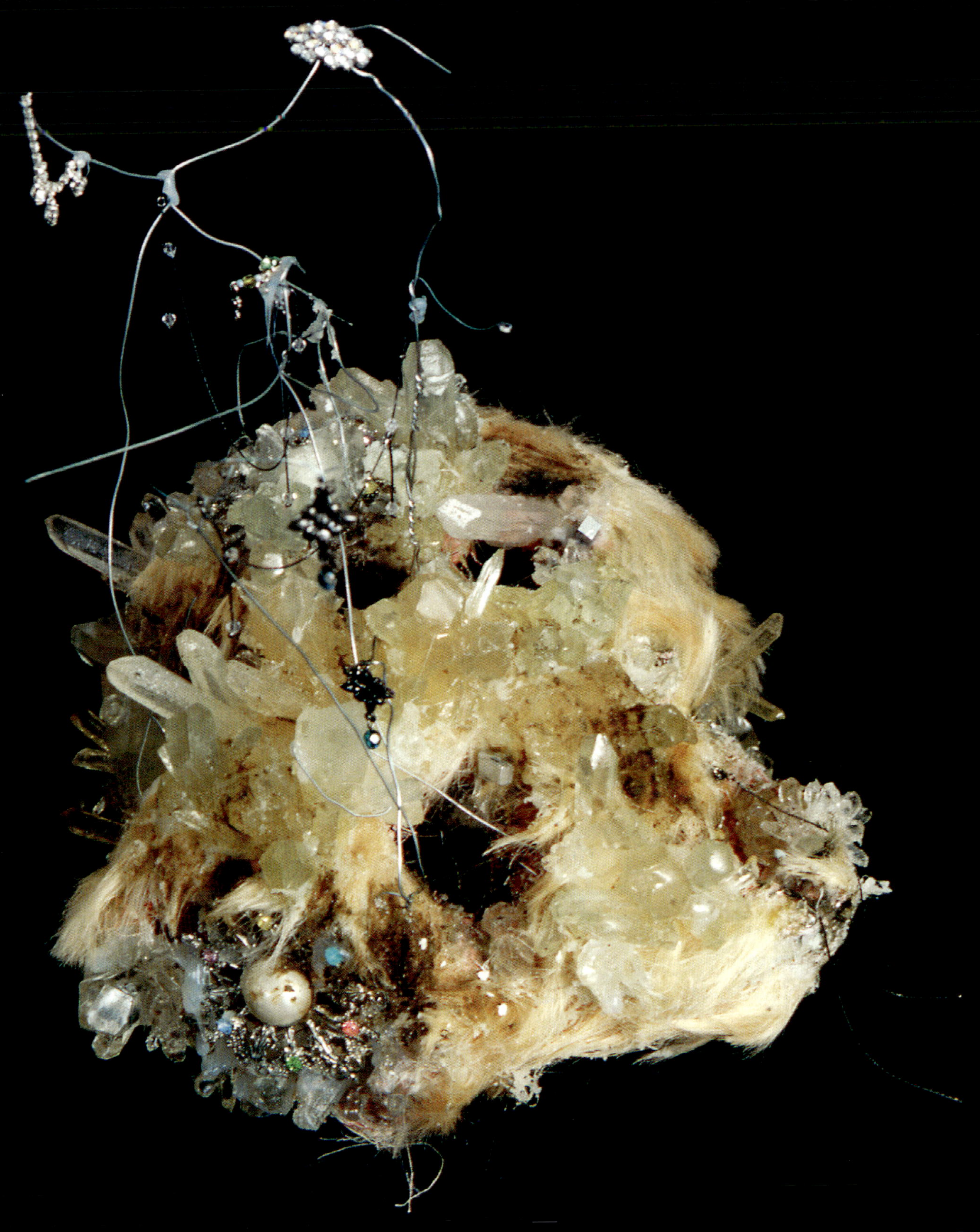

SCULPTOR DAVID ALTMEJD INVENTS PERSONAL SYSTEMS FOR CREATING COLLECTIVE MEANING.
His idiosyncratic visual lexicon includes everything from werewolves, crystals, and thin gold chains to Stars of David, glitter, taxidermied squirrels, and chalky white bones. He sets these chosen motifs, which brim with what the artist calls "symbolic potential,"[1] atop platforms that play off modernist architecture and design. It's a paradigm shared by such artists as Louise Bourgeois, Matthew Barney, and Matthew Ritchie, all of whom deploy their respective eccentric vocabularies within distinctive "sites," both literal and conceptual. Bourgeois places hers in her cage-like *Cells*, Barney in his *Cremaster* films, Ritchie in his invented cosmology. There, as on Altmejd's sculptural bases, strange and often pungent elements take on rich, unpredictable lives of their own.

The temptation when faced with potent objects arrayed in unexpected juxtaposition can be to treat them like a new language, to expect that, given the right key, everything will fit together into a lucid narrative. The title of *Clear Structures for a New Generation*, 2002 (figs. 24 and 25), also the title of the artist's first solo exhibition in New York, seems to suggest as much. But how do we read this combination of bewigged crystallized heads, abstract chain structures, and mirrored cubic geometries? The title misleads if "clear" is understood as "clarity" rather than "transparency," which is the very surface quality that generates a prismatic labyrinth from a jumble of structures—Jorge Luis Borges meets Mies van der Rohe. In any case, Altmejd refuses the linguistic metaphor. "Rather than a language," he explains, "I am more interested in how the elements create energy. . . . The energy of these living abstract organisms depends on the meanings of the work being unresolved, uncontrolled."[2]

Energy in this context is a slippery concept. One way to understand it, however, is in the literal sense of the power that is lost or gained when a substance changes form, as when water

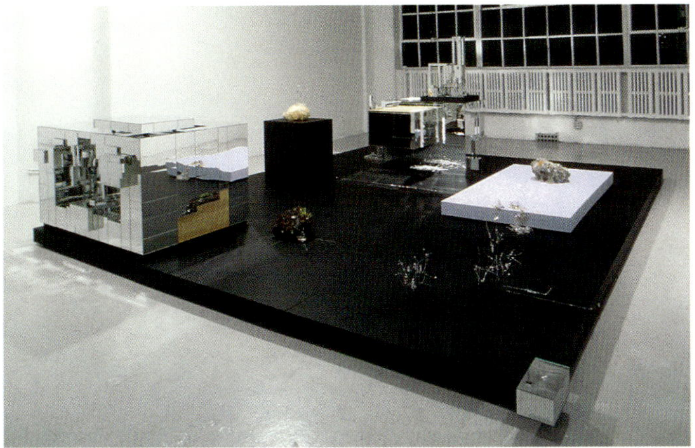

Fig. 25 **Clear Structures for a New Generation**, 2002, wood, paint, mirror, resin, plaster, polymer clay, synthetic hair, jewelry, wire, chain, beads, and glitter, 60 x 180 x 192".

Fig. 24 **Clear Structures for a New Generation** (detail), 2002.

Fig. 26 **The Old Sculptor**, 2003, wood, paint, mirror, cement, resin, synthetic hair, synthetic flowers, foam, polymer clay, wire, chain, paper, jewelry, beads, and glitter, 48 x 126 x 84".

Fig. 27 **Delicate Men in Positions of Power** (detail), 2003, wood, paint, Plexiglas, mirror, lighting system, plaster, resin, foam, synthetic flowers, fabric, synthetic hair, paper, jewelry, wire, chain, beads, and glitter, 96 x 192 x 180".

evaporates into gas, liquid solidifies into crystal, or man metamorphoses into werewolf. Both crystals and werewolves figure prominently in Altmejd's constructions, as the end results of transformative processes but also as participants in them. In *The Settler*, 2005 (fig. 11), a beastly, hirsute figure lies prostrate on a mirrored plinth. Though lifeless, the werewolf gives life, as a mountain of glinting stalagmites, cubes, and crystals grows from

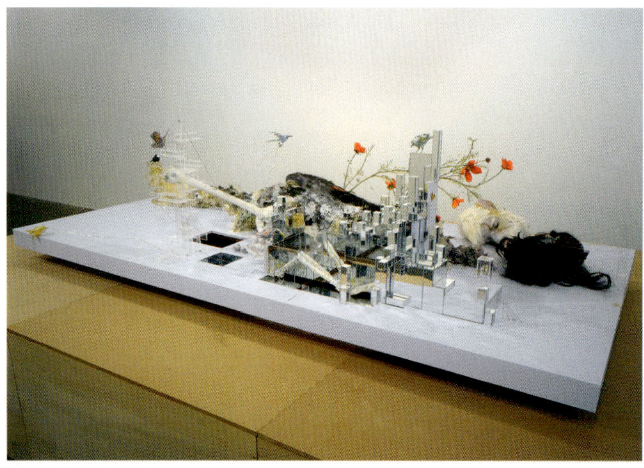

its body. Small trees made of twisted wire and beads sprout nearby—as synthetic flowers do in *The Old Sculptor*, 2003 (fig. 26)—like plants drawing nutrients from the land around graves. Mirrors act as further channels for energy, endlessly multiplying and distorting light, color, hair, and fragmented body parts. In other sculptures fine gold chains do this work, conducting glittery energy between disparate objects.

The potency of Altmejd's constructions emerges from these unexpected and energized intersections of materials and forms, but also from the chosen elements themselves. Various subtexts emanate out of powerful, recognizable symbols like the Star of David, scrawled in a childish hand across a leg bone here or a finger bone there (see fig. 27). An early work, *Anne Frank 2*, 1999 (fig. 28), traces the heroine's name across a wall in spidery, barely legible clusters of beaded filaments. So loaded are these symbols it is impossible not to ask if the artist is Jewish—and he is, in part, the son of a Jewish father who emigrated to Canada in the late 1960s, a biographical fact that adds to *The Settler*'s orbit of meaning.

More pervasive are allusions to gay culture, traceable in lavender platforms, the kitschy glamour of mirrors and glitter, the camp of plastic flowers, titles like *Delicate Men in Positions of Power*, stained Calvin Klein men's underwear, *The Settler*'s pierced nipple, and the repeated use of wigs—though wigs, of course, have a Jewish connotation, too, as head coverings for observant women. These two subtexts come together explicitly when Altmejd graffities the phrase "DISSENT QUEER BUILD CLEAR," with a Jewish star at either end, onto the side of *Clear Structures*. If taking these various sexually and religiously charged markers out of their individual sculptural contexts, as I am here, lends them the clarity of isolation and the force of a critical mass, note that they often lie partially concealed, lost amid the perverse proliferation of parts that compose each large-scale construction,

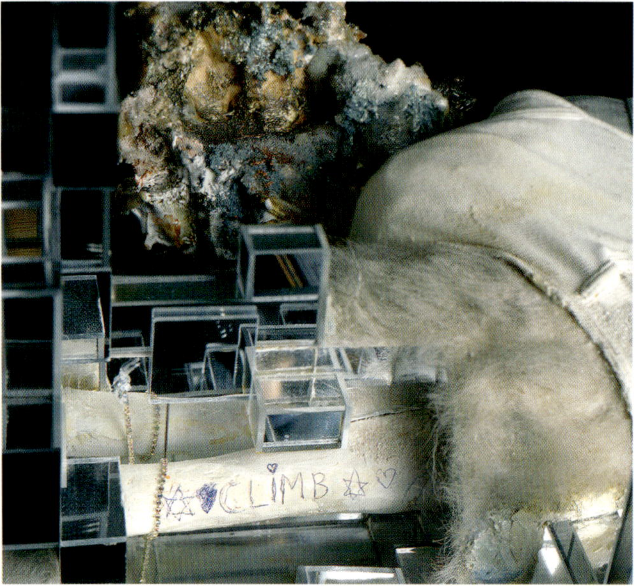

Fig. 28 **Anne Frank 2**, 1999, wood, wire, glass beads, paint, and pencil, 72 x 120".

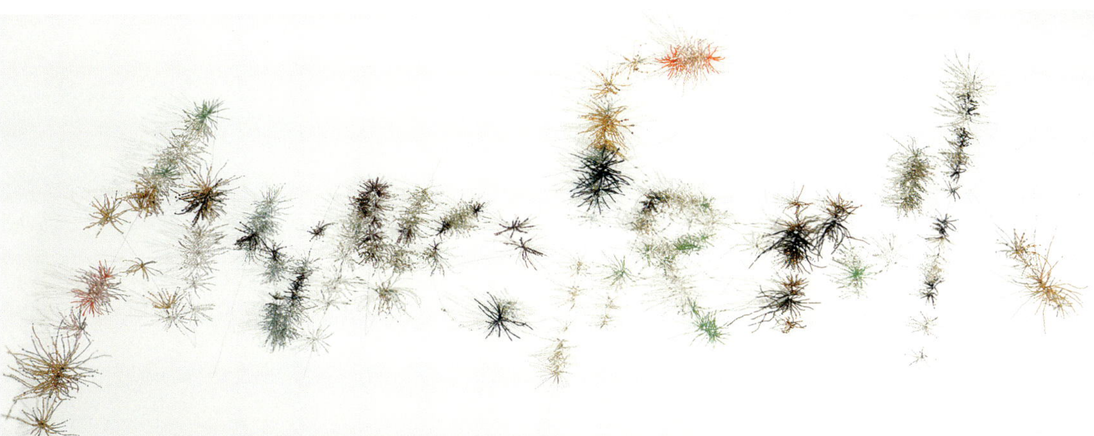

lost also amid the promiscuity of possible meanings. Undeniably and indelibly there but also hidden, they are closeted personalities, double identities waiting to be found.

The structures on and in which Altmejd arrays these charged materials seem relatively reserved. But if his multi-tiered platforms are modern and minimalist, they bare the repressed excesses of their lineage through labyrinthine irregularity, hidden cavities, and the endless, distorting refractions of mirrored surfaces. Deliberately shoddy construction—paint drips, exposed plywood supports, misaligned joints— further weakens any sense of purity. Modern architecture espoused control and truth; Altmejd tests these promises when he perches pretty little birds atop Bauhaus-style structures and hairy, decaying body parts within, investing modernist geometries with the unpredictable and the transient. The possibilities for generating meaning from these weird juxtapositions arc almost endless, a proposition made explicit in *The University 1*, 2004 (fig. 29), a mirrored open-work cube sculpture that recalls the modular structures of Sol LeWitt but upends their reliance on a rational, closed system through reflection and irregularity.

Filled with gory details, Altmejd's work has been positioned within a "Modern Gothic" trend that includes artists such as Sue de Beer and Banks Violette.[3] But where their works wallow in teen angst and irony, Altmejd's Gothic vein runs through a nineteenth-century Romantic vision, an optimistic one that sees vulnerable beauty in the monstrous, that finds organic potential in corpses. "The basis is disaster," he explains, "but then it's about how things grow on top of that."[4] Paradoxically hopeful, his strange conjunctions of the grotesque and the minimalist, the fantastical and geometric,

continuously circulate meaning. If in dead bodies the blood no longer flows, here its coagulation is fabulously crystalline and endlessly generative.

—LORI WAXMAN

1. Altmejd, in Randy Gladman, "David Altmejd: 21st Century Werewolf Aesthetics," *C International Contemporary Art* (Summer 2004); online at www.akrylic.com/contemporary_art_article40.htm.

2. Ibid.

3. Jerry Saltz, "Modern Gothic," *Village Voice*, February 4–10, 2004; online at www.artnet.com/Magazine/features/Jsaltz/saltz2-4-04.asp.

4. Altmejd, in Robert Enright, "Learning from Objects: An Interview with David Altmejd," *Border Crossings* (November 2004), 69.

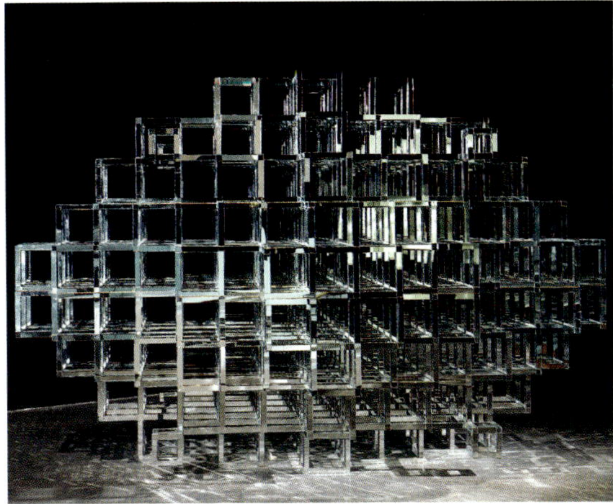

Fig. 29 **The University 1**, 2004, mirror and wood, 66 x 71 x 106".

Cheselyn Amato

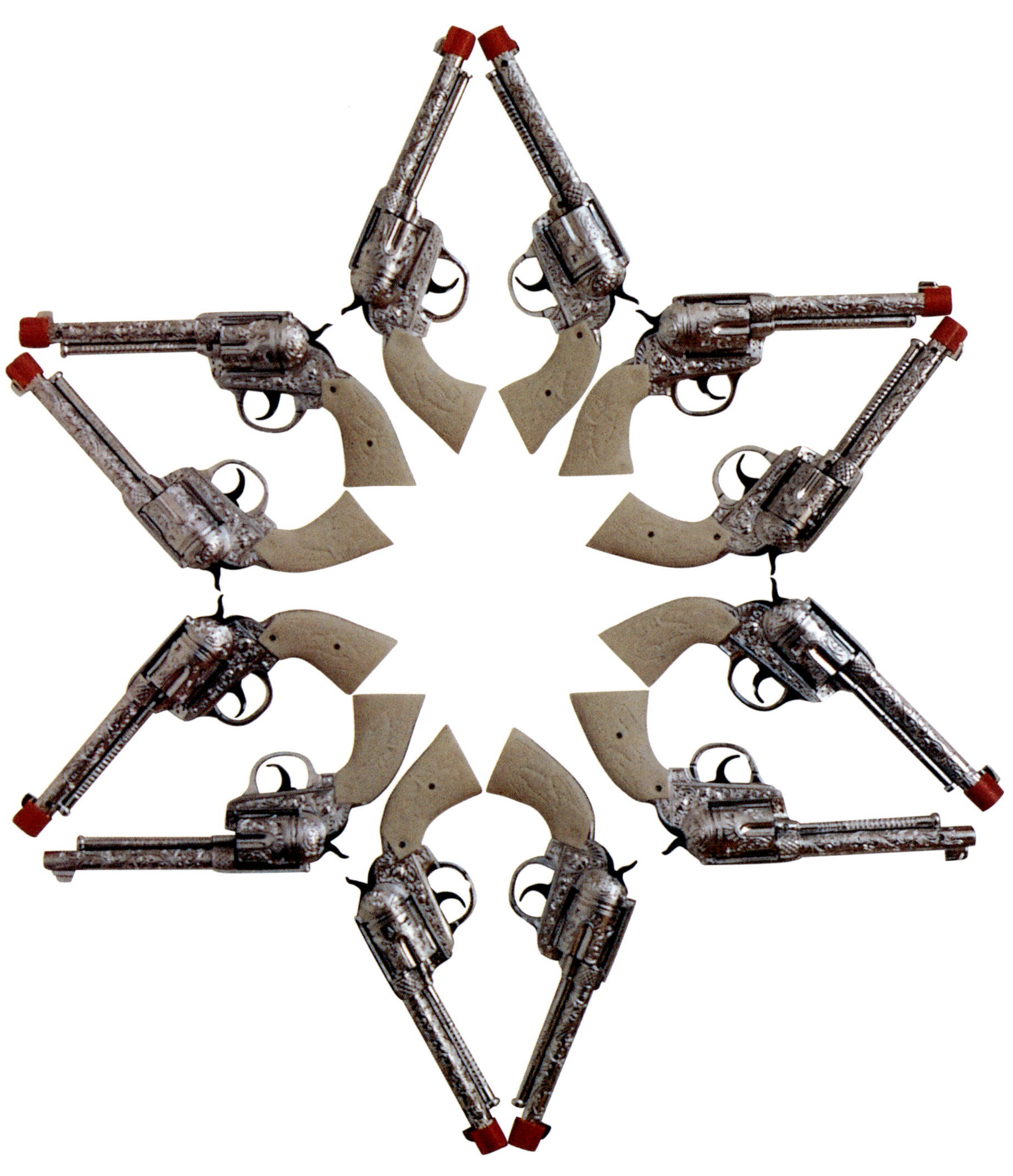

WE LIVE OUR LIVES SURROUNDED BY AN EVER-INCREASING AMOUNT OF STUFF.

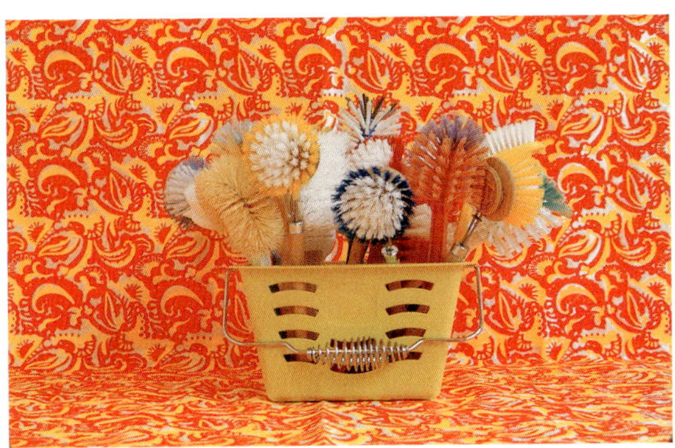

Fig. 31 **Flower Arrangement (#1)**, 2003, inkjet print, 23 x 32".

◀ Fig. 30 **Six-Pointed Star in Silver with Orange Tips**, 2006, plastic toy guns, 24 x 24 x 4".

Fig. 32 **Effluxes** (detail), 2004, radiant film with wood, wire, and light, dimensions variable.

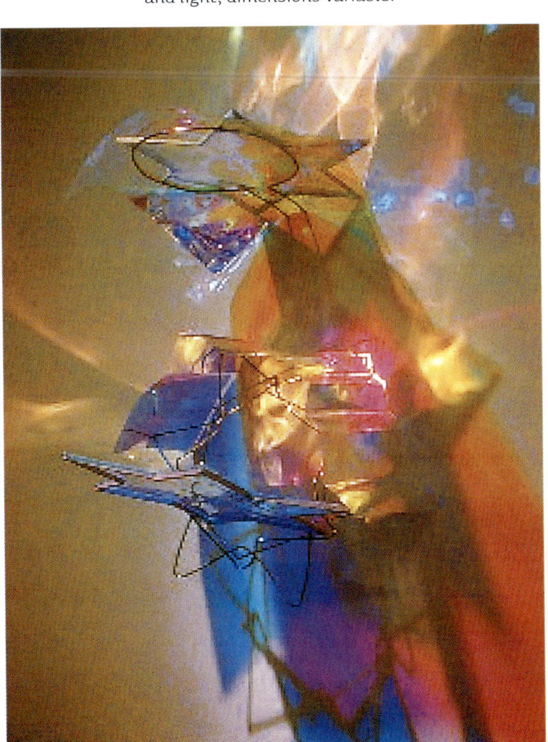

Stuff we find, stuff we're sent, stuff we eat, stuff we store, stuff we wear, stuff we buy, stuff we throw away. These everyday objects have an intended purpose, be it to feed, clothe, inform, or otherwise occupy us. But objects can also be used against their intentions, as demonstrated when Marcel Duchamp made a sculpture from a urinal, Meret Oppenheim from a teacup covered in fur, and Robert Rauschenberg from a stuffed angora goat. Such metamorphic tactics lie at the core of Cheselyn Amato's inventive body of mixed-media works.

How else to explain the transformation of a bucket full of scrub brushes into a work aptly described by the title *Flower Arrangement (#1)*, 2003 (fig. 31)? The witty repositioning of quotidian things evident in this and Amato's other "bouquets" provides a fresh look at common objects rarely beheld for more than their cleaning power. The work's charm rests in the incongruity of finding prettiness in something banal, of the goods simultaneously existing as sweet flowers and crappy cleaning implements. A strikingly different effect ensues when Amato uses similar means but dissimilar materials, arranging twelve plastic guns on a wall in the form of a Star of David. Here too a magical kind of transformation occurs, of cheap toys morphed into a symbol central to both Judaism and Islam. Unlike the more innocuous floral apparition, *Six-Pointed Star in Silver with Orange Tips*, 2006 (fig. 30), blatantly mixes the sacred and the profane, questioning the intermingling of religion and violence, as well as one of the ways in which the latter becomes part of daily life, namely through children's play.

This transformation of ordinary material into something stranger and more meaningful can occur at various stages in an artwork's life, from studio process through viewer reception. In the installation *Effluxes*, 2004 (fig. 32), Amato makes this metamorphic moment visible within the exhibition space itself. Sheets of radiant film,

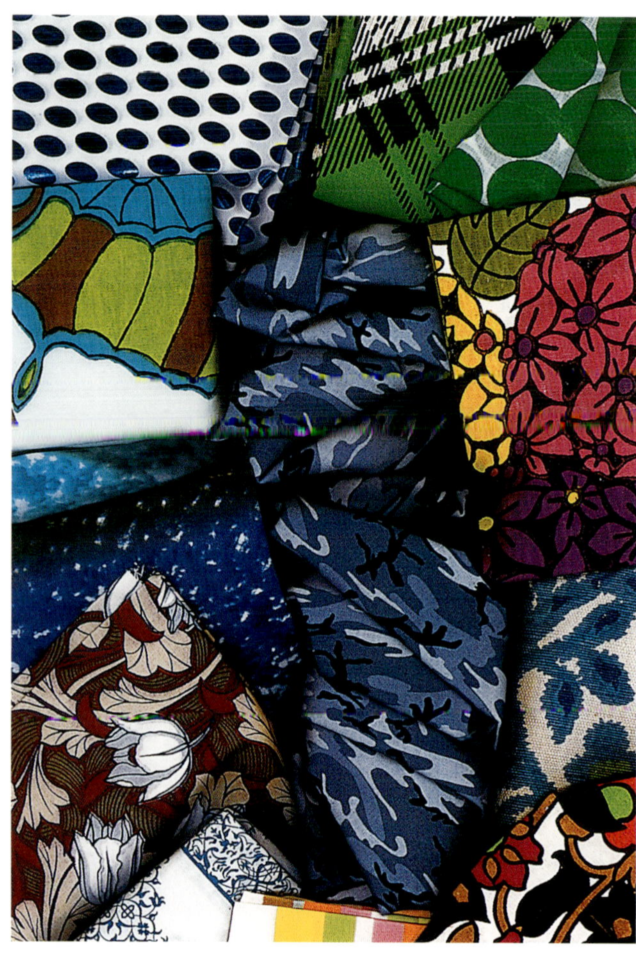

the mix, as in *Fabric Collage (Placemats, Napkins, & Deathcamps)*, 2004 (see fig. 5). Here, dully pleasant geometric patterns layer beside the deep maroon of a Nazi concentration camp plan, whose identification—encouraged by an explicit title—abruptly interrupts the expected aesthetic pleasure of viewing.

That promise of visual pleasure suggested by Amato's rich swaths of color and pattern is also complicated by the underlying organizational concern of the series "Dot Collages/Tree of Life Chronicles," 2000–2006 (see fig. 35). Here composition is predetermined in both form and meaning: it is based on the Tree of Life, a central symbolic icon of kabbalistic teaching that vertically diagrams the ten Sephiroth, which are commonly understood as the ways in which God is made visible in the world.[3] In Amato's many versions of this Jewish mandala, the Sephiroth materialize as small circles of paper cut from a variety of found printed matter, including packaging, children's drawings, and advertising. These rest atop equally unconventional grounds, from wallpaper to sewing patterns, whose linear designs serve to connect the dots. Links between individual Sephiroth are also drawn in traditional Tree of Life schema, but here they are made playfully and aesthetically, the happy accident of overlapping stripes, dots, and curlicues. The double title of the series seems to suggest that a purely formal reading can be as valid as a spiritual one.

Amato's use of base materials to fashion sacred symbols found a new challenge in *Tablets*, 2005 (fig. 36), for which she turned to that most ubiquitous of common goods, commercial product packaging, to create the image of biblical tablets and the tabernacle. By opening flaps and flattening boxes, and then laying the results one atop the other—complete with glue spots and torn paper—she created assemblages that elevate the ugly everyday not just to the level of aesthetic worth but even further, to that of religious icon.

suspended between a series of lightweight wood and wire frames, colorfully refract the light of a nearby projector, throwing dazzling effects onto the wall. The artist describes these works as "visual events,"[1] highlighting their ephemeral and spectacular nature, but also pointing to the importance of the act of creating, an act that occurs literally and repeatedly as the viewer witnesses *Effluxes'* spectral shift.

The transformative power of the artistic process alights at a different but equally transitory moment in a series of fabric collages that Amato has been making since 2000. Rather than glue her material elements together, the artist reinvents the collage process by arranging her swatches directly on a digital scanning bed and printing the results, a method that allows her to reuse materials and even compositions from one work to the next. Amato includes textiles ranging from camouflage to a MacDonald tartan to psychedelic flowers and polka dots; by simply adding or subtracting, she can shift a work's formal and thematic pattern (see fig. 33). Achieving a visual balance between these cacophonous juxtapositions is a primary goal of the work, and is helped by the seamlessness of the scanning technique.[2] Nevertheless it's a precarious equilibrium, growing even headier when historical imagery enters

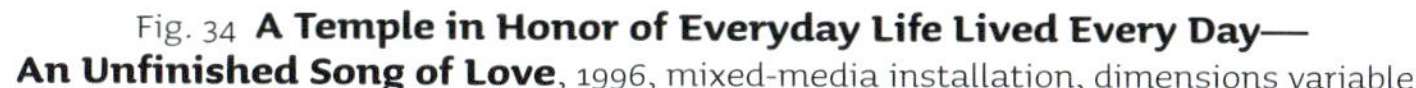

Fig. 34 **A Temple in Honor of Everyday Life Lived Every Day— An Unfinished Song of Love**, 1996, mixed-media installation, dimensions variable.

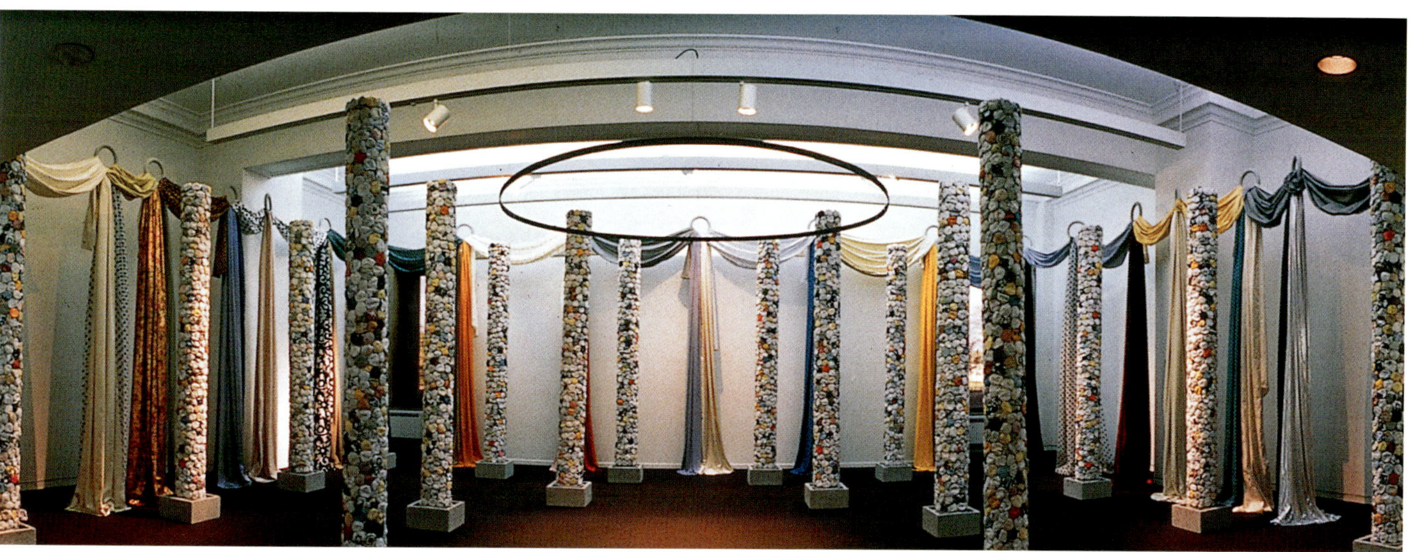

This work harks back to *A Temple in Honor of Everyday Life Lived Every Day—An Unfinished Song of Love*, 1996 (fig. 34), an early room-size installation for which Amato covered eighteen columns in twenty-five thousand paper balls made from twelve years of personal notes, junk mail, photographs, and so on, to create a kind of secular sacred space that symbolically aired the artist's personal life and freed her from it, or at least from the materiality of it.

Each of these acts is simultaneously iconoclastic and spiritual, recognizing potential in the lowliest materials and contriving to redeem them through imaginative and unexpected reuse. Like so much of Amato's work, the stuff-of-life columns and the box-top tabernacles evidence a Midas-like vision—she is able to turn everything from junk mail to cereal boxes to cheap toys into gold. It's a powerfully useful vision in the everyday world of direct-mail campaigns, supermarkets, and dollar stores in which we live.

—LORI WAXMAN

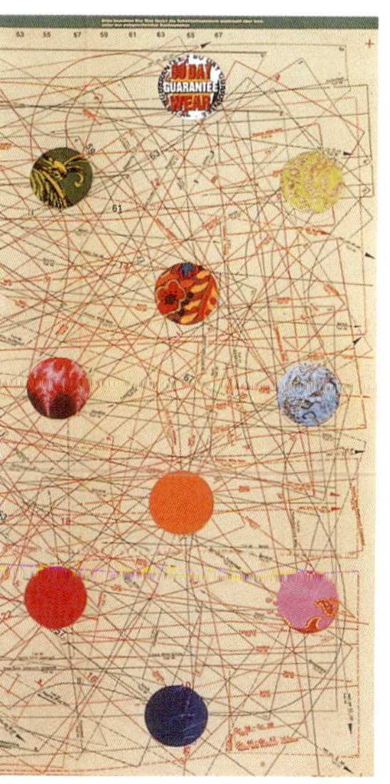

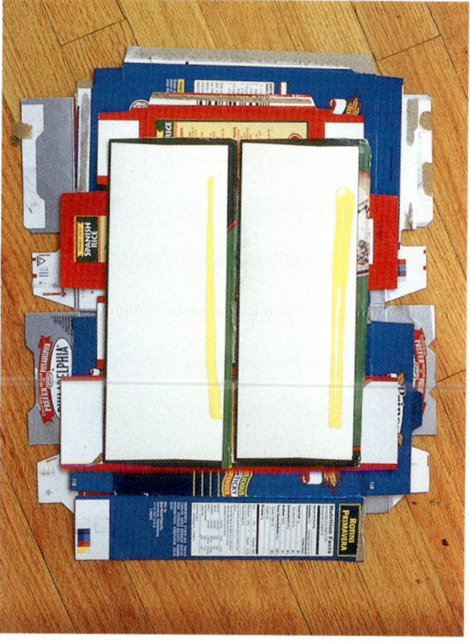

Fig. 35 **Dot Collages/Tree of Life Chronicles (German apparel paper)**, 2000, paper collage, 21 1/2 x 10 3/4".

Fig. 36 **Tablets**, 2005, cardboard and plastic packaging materials, 24 x 18".

1. Amato, artist statement, "Effluxes, Effluence, Effulgency & Effluviums," 2006.

2. Amato, artist statement, "The Fabric and Textile Collages," undated.

3. See Miriam Seidel, *The Hidden Garden: Three Artists Explore Kabbalah*, exh. cat. (Philadelphia: Borowsky Gallery, The Gershman Y, 2005).

Johanna Bresnick

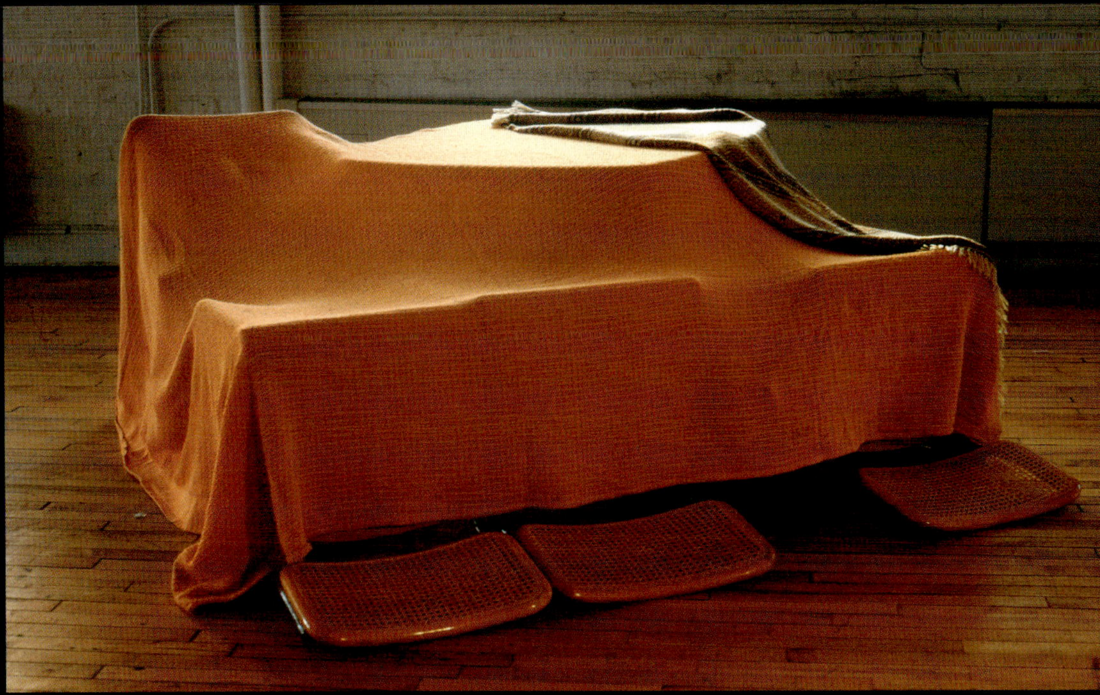

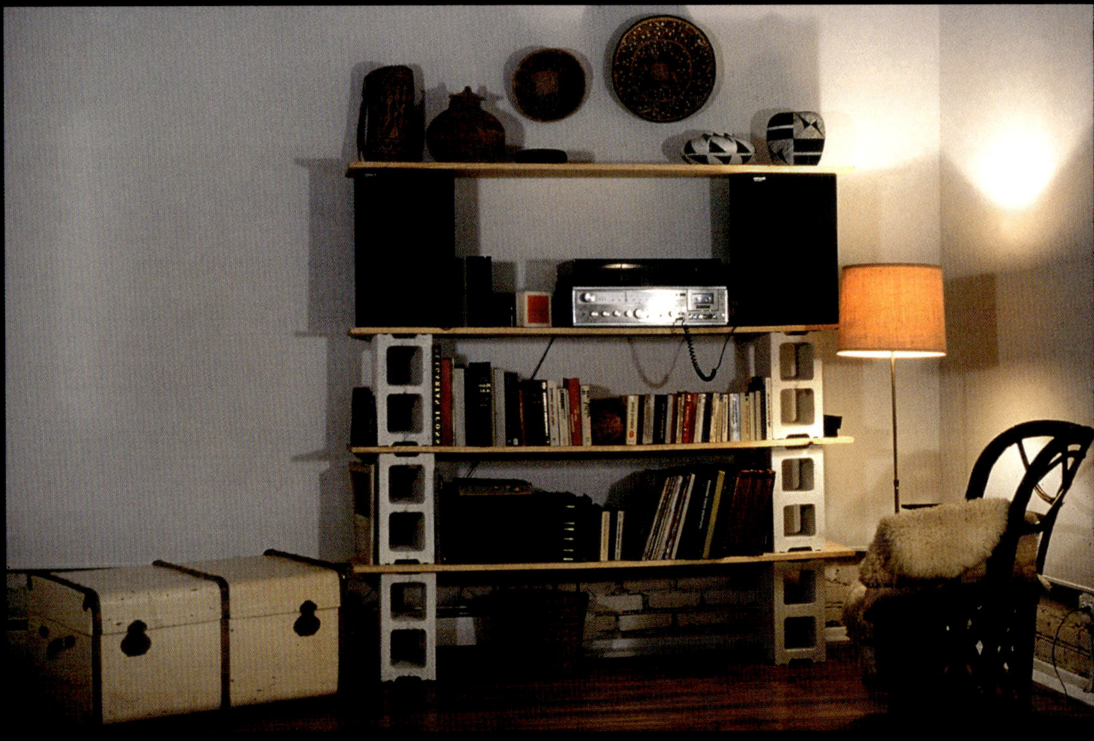

Fig. 37 **Fort Orange**, 2001, blankets, tables, pillows, and chairs, 32 x 70 x 84".

Fig. 38 **The Incubator, Palo Alto, 1973**, 2001, shelving unit, hi-fi, chair, fur throw, baskets, pottery, trunk, sculpture, books, albums, and painted wooden blocks, 90 x 108 x 96".

THE HUMAN NEED FOR SHELTER IS ONE OF OUR MOST BASIC MOTIVATIONS, and is of course intrinsically tied to a more general need for security—the security of family and friends, of personal finances, of geopolitical situations. It's a drive that resides at the core of Johanna Bresnick's multifarious sculptural oeuvre, from her critical explorations of modernist architecture to her cheeky recreations of autobiographical spaces. The latter include *Fort Orange*, 2001 (fig. 37), a sculpture of overturned chairs and draped blankets, a veritable children's fort created with an eye to color coordination and period furniture. When kids build such forts they reveal an understanding of the comfort and importance of physical shelter, as well as a desire to intervene into the adult space around them. Bresnick parses that adult space, and its developmental impact, in *The Incubator, Palo Alto, 1973*, 2001 (fig. 38), an environmental replica of her childhood home that leaves the uncontrollable human element—baby Johanna and parents, soon to be divorced—out of the picture.[1] Instead the architectural and cultural space of nurture is foregrounded, down to the smallest tchotchke, but not out of a nostalgic or idealizing impulse: some of those books, it turns out, are just painted blocks.

If these investigations of familial space soften under their macramé '70s aspect, Bresnick's studies of the modernist built environment are literally hard-edged. Motivated by the visible discrepancies between Chicago's crumbling housing projects and its gleaming International Style office towers, she built "Millennial HUD Projects," 2000–2003, a series of sculptures that critically re-envision Cabrini Green and ABLA Homes as the utopian structures they were meant to be (see fig. 39).[2] Constructed from one-way police glass, the sculptures appear alternately as dazzlingly opaque reflectors, glowing jewel boxes, or grossly transparent panopticons, depending on the light. More recently, the artist has mapped Hurricane Katrina's destruction of the New Orleans Superdome and the man-made

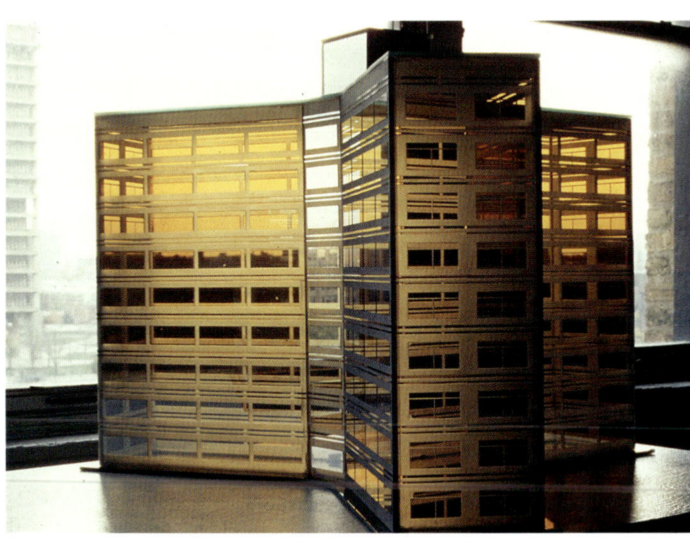

Fig. 39 **ABLA Homes**, 2000, mirrored glass, 20 x 30 x 30".

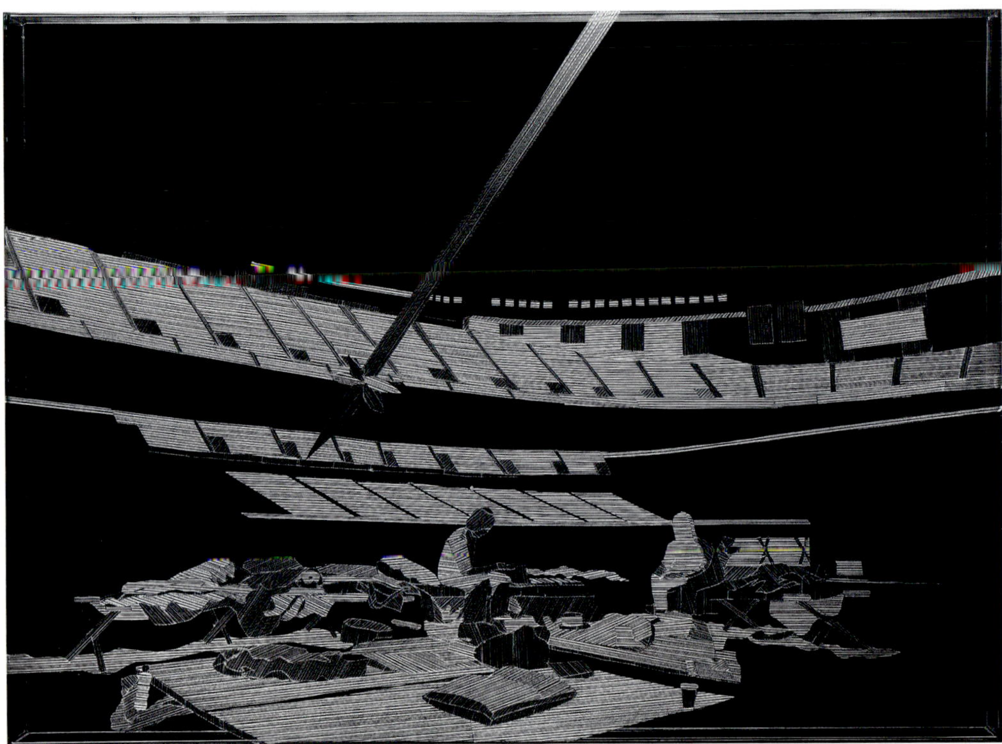

implosion of the New Haven Coliseum using an inventive technique of placing white filament tape on Plexiglas to sketch the crippling consequences of man's architectural hubris (see fig. 40). The resulting images, in their illuminating play of light and shadow, offer an ironically delicate record of ruin.

It's a kind of ruin that stems in great part from what Bresnick identifies as "the intrinsic human need to impose geometry on nature."[3] She takes her exploration of this core desire beyond architecture in "Panama Canal," 2000–2002, a multi-media series that probes the geopolitical arrogance of one of the most difficult engineering projects ever undertaken. In the photograph *Digger's Tattoo*, 2000 (fig. 41), a white woman inks a map of the canal onto the back of a darker-skinned man, in a surprisingly intimate, if consensual and dominating, translation of the canal's reshaping of the land between two oceans. Performed by Bresnick and her Ecuadorian husband, the piece also interrogates the very possibility of knowing a foreign person or place, a line of questioning highlighted in *Self-Deceptive Thought Circuit*, 2001, an imaginary map of the canal's topography as traced by a polygraph test that Bresnick, who has never visited the canal, submitted herself to.

The autobiographical impetus that runs through *Fort Orange*, *The Incubator*, and "Panama Canal" finds another kind of outlet in "Mamzer Loshen," 2005–2006, a collaborative project by Bresnick and artist Michael Cloud that centers around their self-proclaimed identity as "modern Jews of dubious faith."[4] Their series of tongue-in-cheek sculptural installations puns on the burning bush (in their version, a red, wax-dipped branch with wicks), Orthodox sexual myths (a sheet with a hole in it), and the Torah (torn up and stuffed into gel caps for communion-like consumption), and it begins with *The Upsetters (Set It Off)*, 2006 (fig. 42), a piece of drywall that has seen better days. Topped with unraveling razor

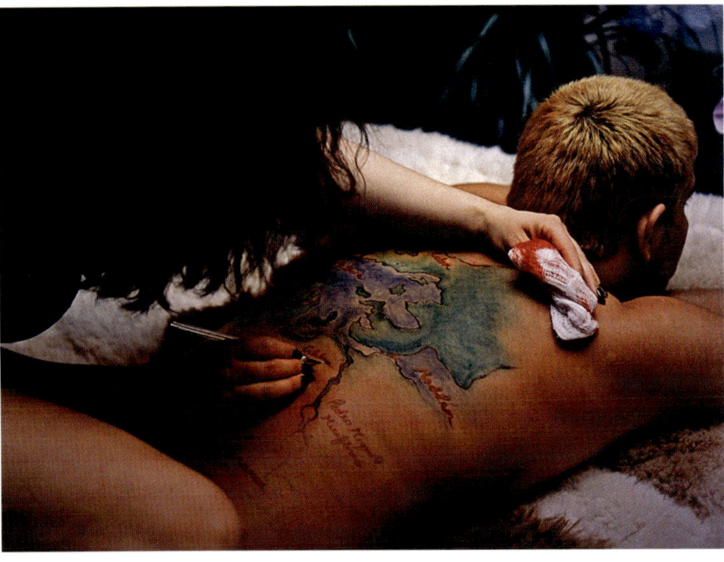

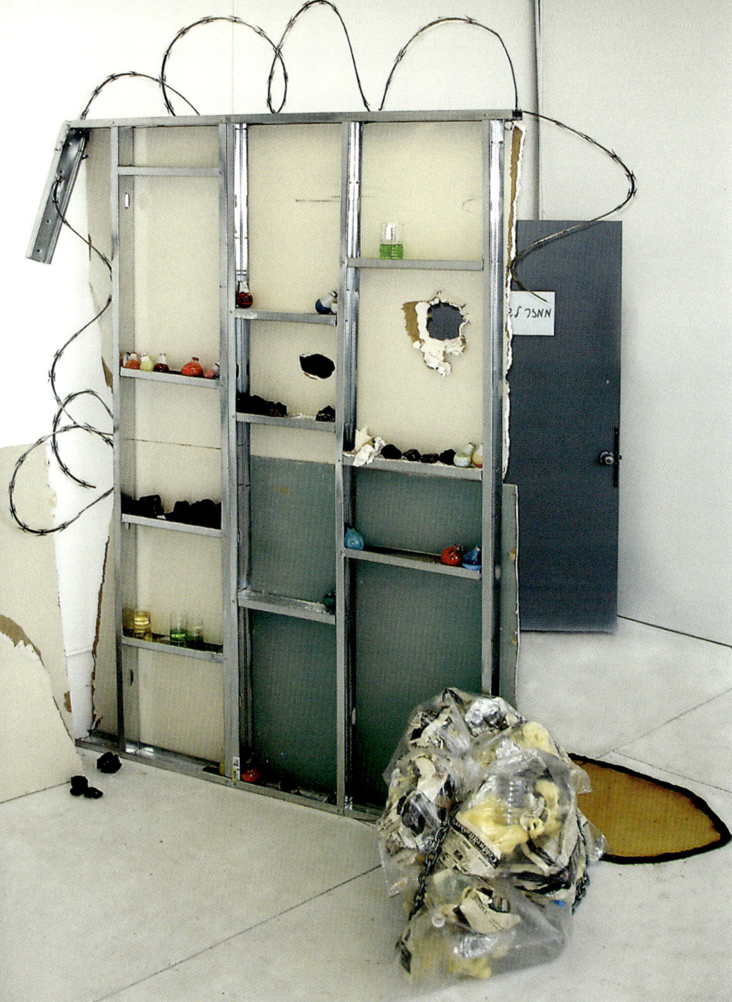

Fig. 42 **The Upsetters (Set It Off)**, 2006, drywall, metal studs, garbage, grease, oil, razor-wire, rocks, spray-foam, light bulbs filled with paint, and cleaning fluids, 120 x 108 x 108". In collaboration with Michael Cloud.

Fig. 43 **Ohne Lebensraum** (detail), 2004, rug, mannequin, wood, foam, and latex paint, 40 x 92 x 140".

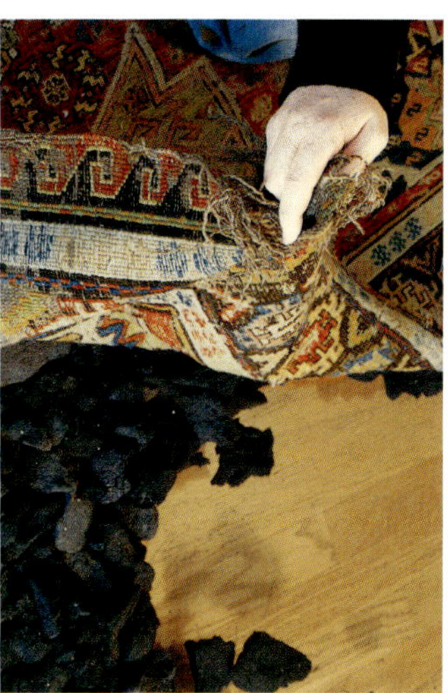

wire, surrounded by a grease spill, and penetrated by fist-size holes, the wall references the Jew-on-Jew unrest then raging in the Gaza Strip, when the Israeli army was charged with evicting settlers, who fought back with irritating but not murderous weapons—paint-filled light bulbs, cleaning agents, and rocks, objects here arranged within the sculpture's metal stud framing. The topical allusion need not be understood in order for *The Upsetters* to have an impact: its material and configuration speak in general of attempts, often frustrated, to achieve security through territorial and architectural aggression.

A far less aggressive but even more frustrated attempt at security lies at the heart of what is perhaps the most autobiographical and allegorical of Bresnick's projects, *Ohne Lebensraum*, 2004 (figs. 2 and 43). The sculpture presents a three-dimensional figure, a self-portrait kneeling on an antique rug acquired by the artist's grandparents during World War II. Unlike the piece of land for which they traded it, the rug was portable, and when they fled Germany for the U.S. it came with them.[5] This story, which speaks of diasporic existence and forced nomadism, is couched in a particular family history but also in the larger one implied by the work's title: an important component of Nazi ideology and its expansionist policies was the idea of *Lebensraum*, or "living space,"

for German population growth. Bresnick flips that concept by adding *Ohne*, meaning "without," but also by suspending the entire assemblage a few inches off the floor, so that it hovers like a flying carpet, afloat as much on the promise of unknown possibilities as it is grounded on a burdensome bed of coal. Lest that coal threaten to drag the whole enterprise down, however, Bresnick has built in an ironic safeguard: as it turns out, it's just painted foam.

—LORI WAXMAN

1. Bresnick, conversation with the author, February 9, 2007.

2. Bresnick, artist statement, undated.

3. Ibid.

4. Ibid.

5. Ibid.

Shoshana Dentz

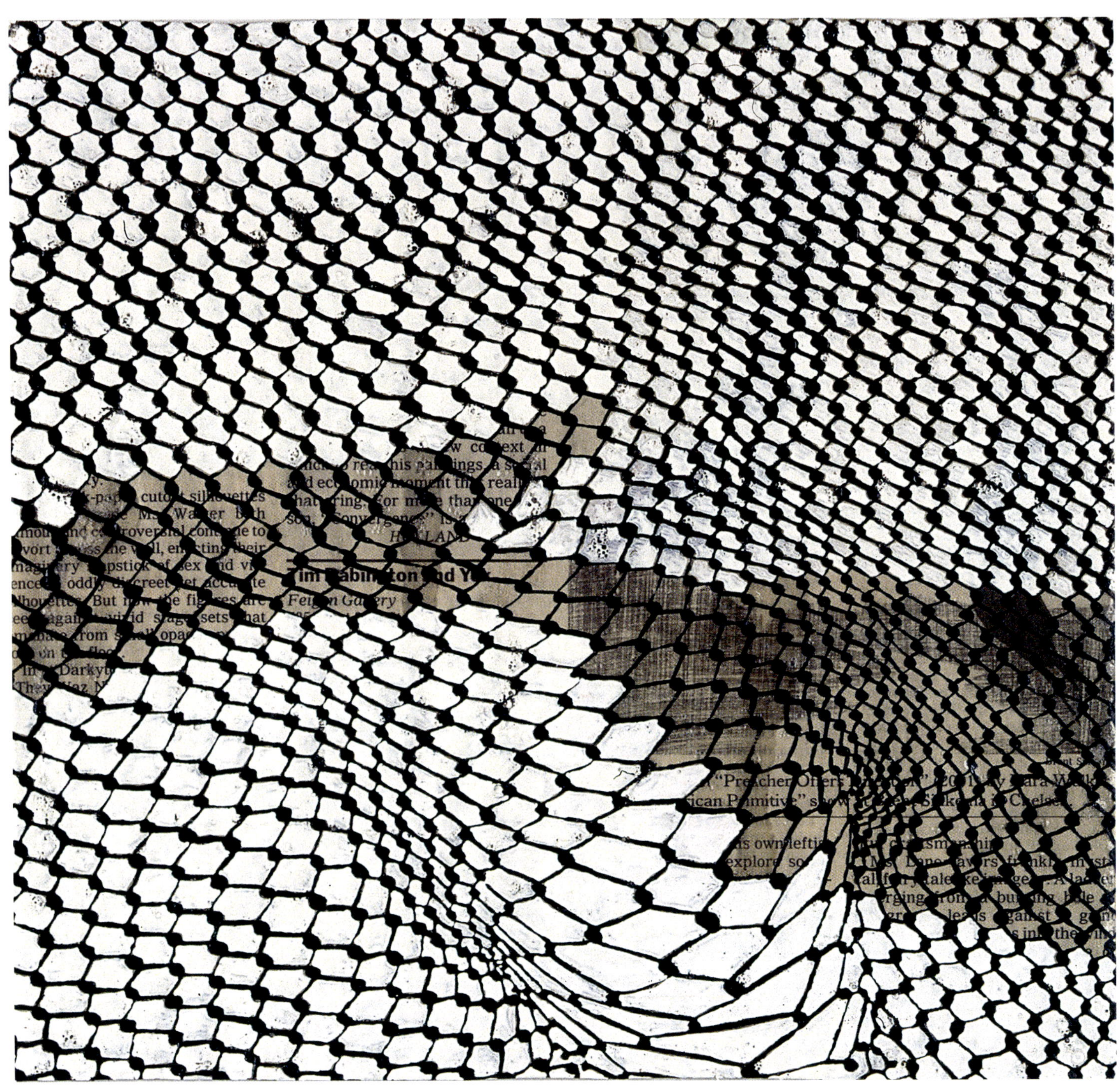

Fig. 44 **no one and everyone #2**, 2002, oil on newspaper, 8 x 8".
Collection of Alanna Heiss and Fred Sherman, New York.

SINCE ITS INCEPTION IN THE EARLY TWENTIETH CENTURY, ABSTRACT ART HAS PROVIDED
a radical means of conveying the human experience. For artists like Mondrian, Malevich, and Kandinsky, abstraction was a vehicle for expressing utopian ideals. In response to the decidedly self-referential work of the New York School and, later, the Minimalists, artists in the 1980s came to believe that abstract painting had to be politicized if it was to have staying power. What followed were works by artists like Ross Bleckner, Donald Moffett, Rosemarie Trockel, and, more recently, Byron Kim, who imbue abstraction with topicality, particularity, and biography. Shoshana Dentz similarly inserts abstraction into the realm of public discourse. Using motifs suggestive of enclosure, Dentz creates abstract paintings that examine the symbolic relationship between physical barriers and the contested places they define.

The artist's inquiry began with the pattern of the keffiyeh, the black-and-white scarf worn as a symbol of Palestinian nationalism. Growing up in an Orthodox Jewish community, she was taught to equate the keffiyeh with the swastika. According to Dentz, her twenty-plus keffiyeh paintings, collectively titled "no one and everyone," 2002–2003 (see fig. 44), chart a determination to relearn the past and to re-see the present by questioning her own indoctrination and response to these symbols.[1] The title of the series, excerpted from Edward Said's remark that "no one and everyone is to blame" in the Israeli-Palestinian conflict, reiterates the artist's ideological challenge. Dentz's repetition of the keffiyeh design across the surface of the small-scale paintings results in an undulating, optical abstract pattern that conjures myriad politically laced references: a shrouded body, a rolling landscape, or a seemingly endless chain link fence, like one that might surround a refugee camp or define a border. By using this explicit symbol in an equivocal manner, the paintings in this body of work offer a

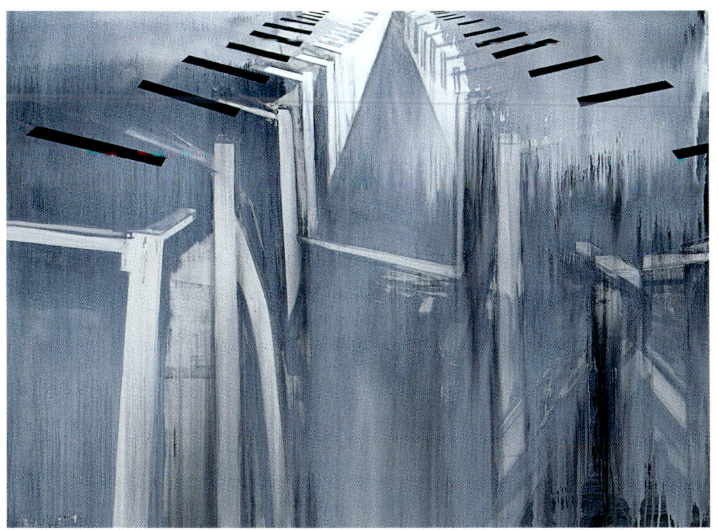

Fig. 45 **Fence I #1**, 2003, oil on canvas, 54 x 70".
Collection of Lewis Pell, New York.

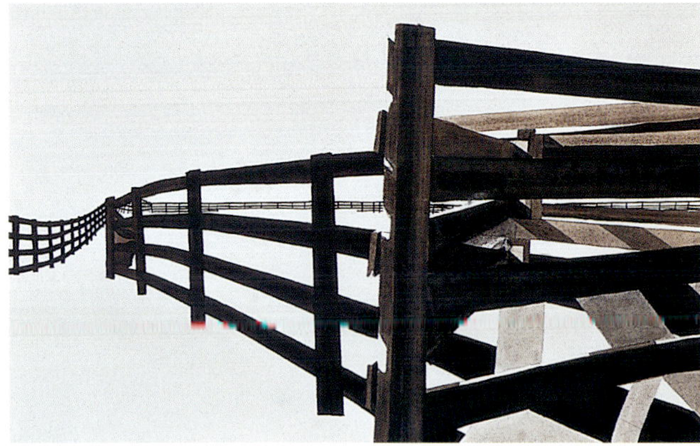

Fig. 46 **Fence II #23**, 2003, gouache on paper, 8 1/4 x 11 3/4".

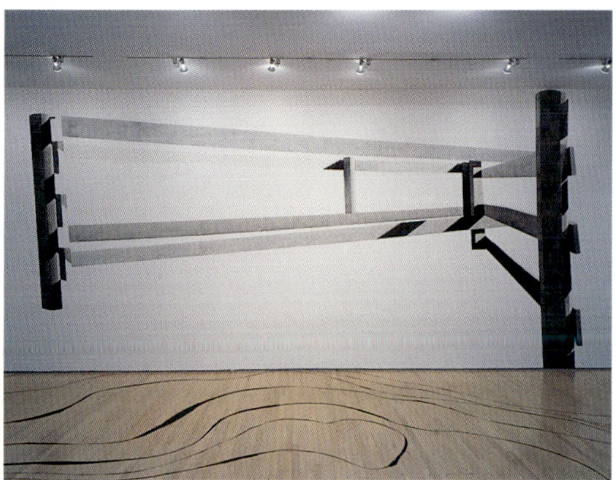

Fig. 47 **Fence II #46**, 2005, gouache on wall, 13 x 25'.
Installation view, The Drawing Center, New York, NY, 2005.

reconsideration of the divisive discourse the keffiyeh engenders.

Dentz's interest in broadening interpretations of charged symbols led her to consider motifs derived from images of concentration camps. *Fence I #1*, 2003 (fig. 45), is based on an archival photograph of a fenced section of the Majdanek camp in Poland. The high horizon line, monochromatic palette, dramatic recession of the central aisle, and ethereality of the posts and landscape endow the work with an eerie sense of confinement. The contrast between the expressionistic brushwork and spatial energy of the "Fence I Series," 2003, and the more neutral treatment of the "Fence II Series," 2003–2005, illustrates one of Dentz's fundamental questions about the inherency of symbolic meaning: the "Fence II" paintings developed as the artist began to consider the kind of content possible were the fence, and the painting itself, not sourced directly from such emotional discourse. The seemingly endless wooden fences featured in works like *Fence II #23*, 2005 (fig. 46), are based on those found at bucolic horse farms in upstate New York. For the artist, the farm suggests "a perfect American ideal, the antithesis of what a Holocaust camp or the security fence in Israel represents."[2] While these paintings are quieter than their predecessors, they also evoke feelings of entrapment, and its corollary, power. Although the deep perspective in *Fence II #46*, 2003 (fig. 47), creates a sense of expanse, no gate—and therefore no escape—is evident.

Dentz further explores the psychological implications of containment in the ongoing series "home lands," begun in 2003 (see figs. 8, 48, 49, and 50). The imagery in these works derives directly from the chain link, razor-wire fences that demark abandoned inner-city areas across the United States. These non-spaces, sites that urban dwellers overlook or even resent, are laden with economic and political implications, especially in rapidly gentrifying areas. The enclosure that inspired one of these works encircles a garbage-strewn waterfront lot near the artist's studio in Williamsburg, Brooklyn, and frames a view of the Manhattan skyline. The multivalent title "home lands" raises more questions than it answers: Who is erecting these fences? Whose "homelands" are they enclosing? Who is being kept out, who is being kept in, and why? Do these fences really solve anything?

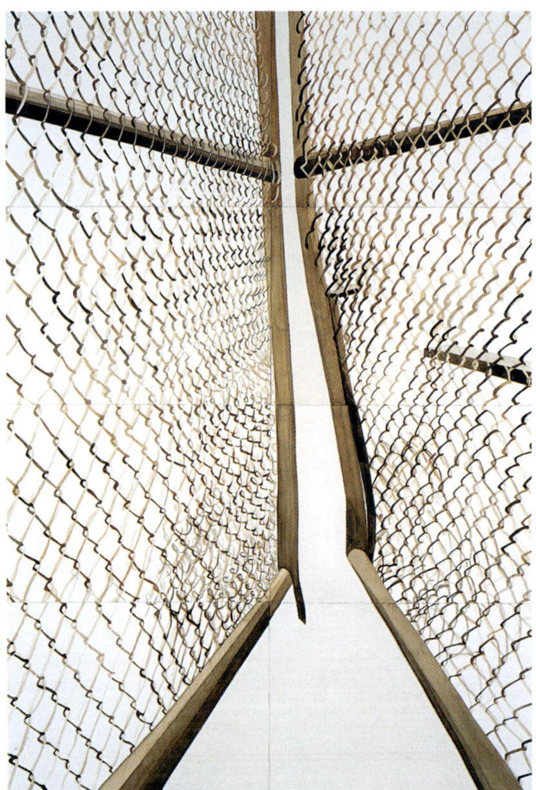

Fig. 48 **home lands #8**, 2004, gouache on paper, eight panels, 88 x 60" overall.

Fig. 49 **home lands #13** (detail), 2004, oil and gouache on canvas, 70 x 140".

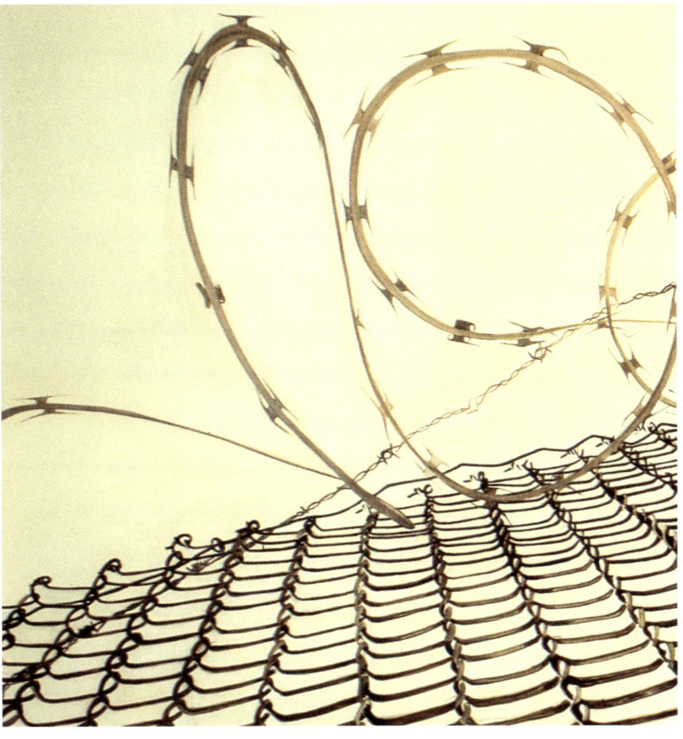

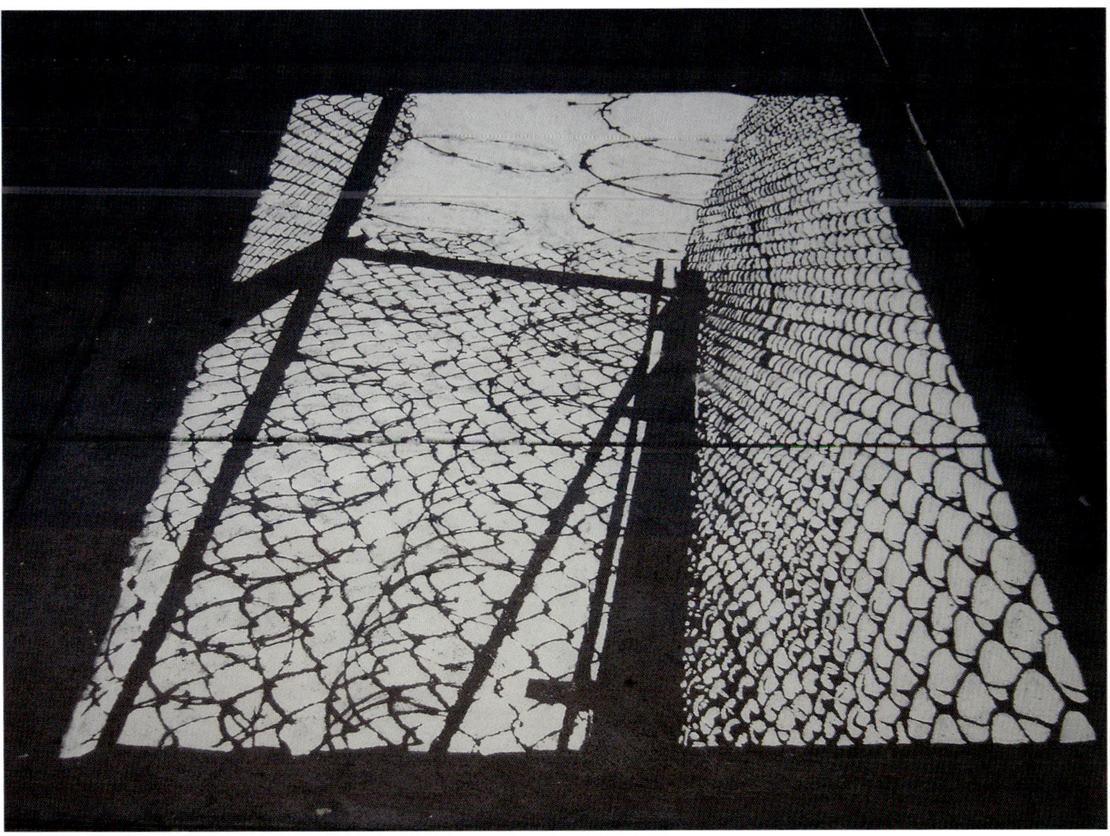

Fig. 50 **home lands on the sidewalk**, 2004, tempera paint on sidewalk, 76 x 48". Installation view, Rubin Museum of Art, New York, NY, 2005.

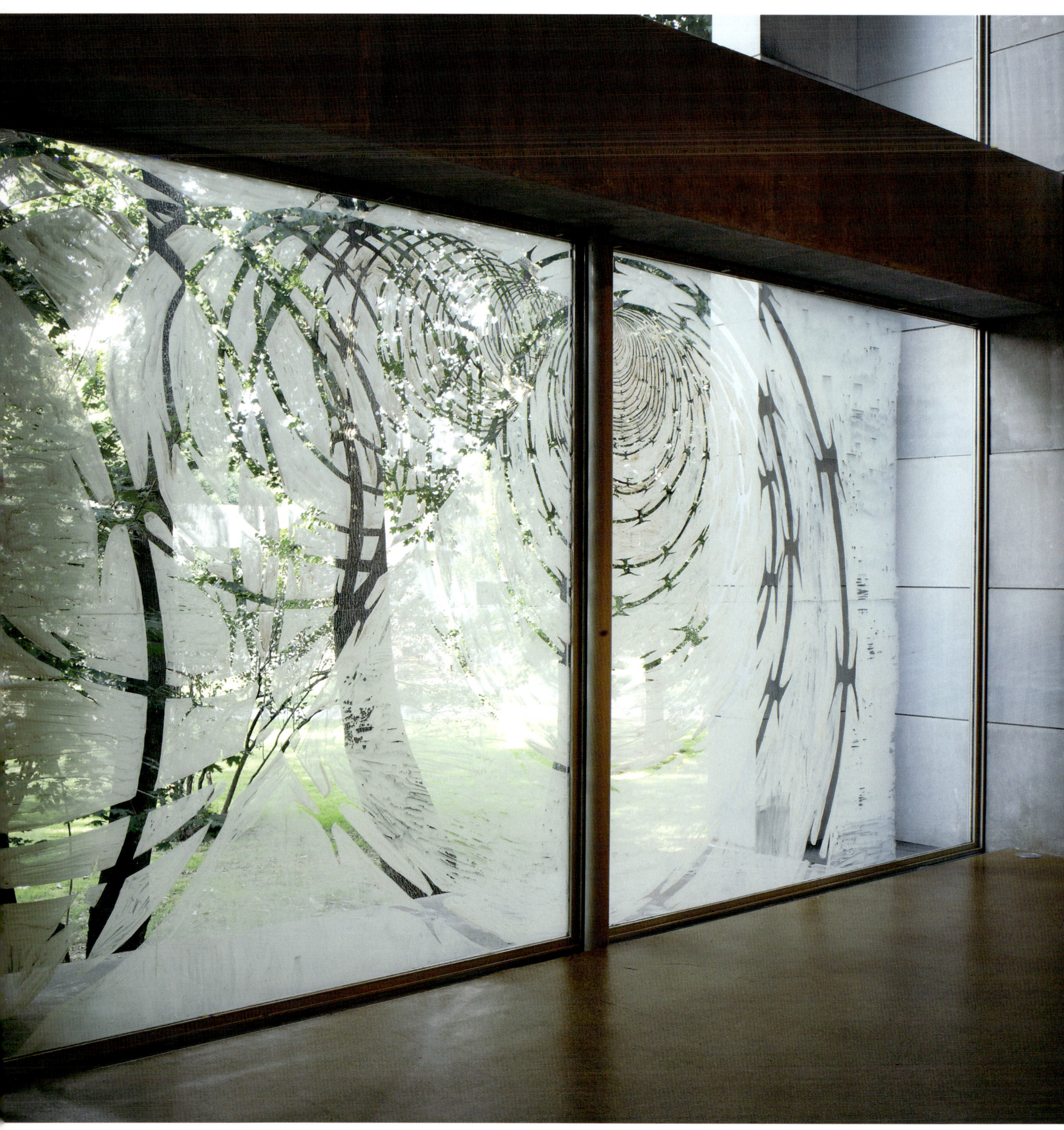

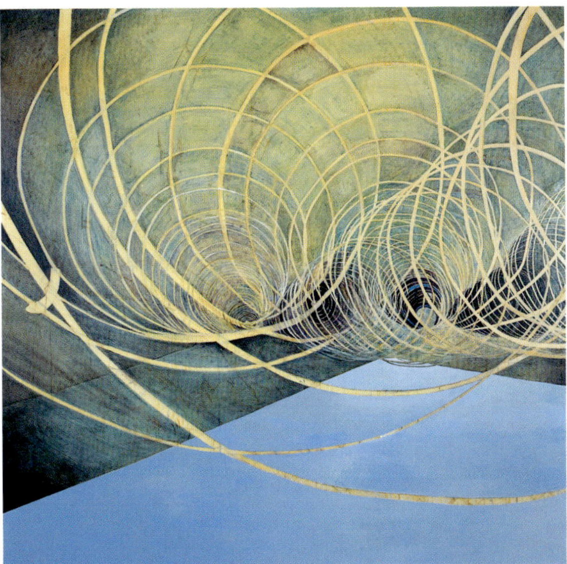

Fig. 52 **Portal #1 (unbarbed)**, 2005, gouache and oil on canvas, 70 x 70".

◄ Fig. 51 **Portal #10**, 2006, gouache on glass window, 10 x 15'.
Installation view, Center for Fine Arts, Wesleyan University,
Middletown, CT, 2006.

The impact of Dentz's images relies as much on formal devices as it does on conceptual queries like these. Using variations in line and color, she plays with positive and negative space, manipulating scale, perspective, and orientation to enclose viewers within the pictorial plane. Dentz's fence imagery is derived from photographs, which she takes and later crops to heightened effect. The dramatic fore-shortening in *home lands #13*, 2004 (fig. 8), for instance, evokes the impending doom of sliding down a sloped chain link floor on the way to being ensnared in a tangle of razor wire. Since the fence is spread, carpet-like, across the entirety of the diptych's two adjoining canvases, there would seem to be no way out. Dentz's lyrical handling of form and delicate variations in color tempers the threat, however, opening up the reading of the painting. The central seam between the two panels further mitigates the illusion of a continuous plane. This seam also features in the public art piece *home lands on the sidewalk*, 2004 (fig. 50). Here, the extreme perspective and inversion of negative and positive space teases the viewer into imagining that one can actually see the sky by looking down.

Dentz's most recent series, "Portals," ongoing since 2005 (see figs. 51 and 52), pushes her abstracted fence imagery and its symbolic content to new limits. The spiral imagery that dominates these compositions—renderings of stretched coils of razor wire—resemble long passageways. The vortex-like forms transport rather than ensnare the viewer, suggesting movement and possibility, rather than enclo-sure and tension. Painted on a glass wall, the site-specific *Portal #10*, 2006 (fig. 51), is semi-transparent, enabling the viewer to see through the physical barrier, furthering the sense of potential progress. Although less overt and more optimistic than their predecessors, the "Portals," encircled with stylized barbs, are as fully infused with political content. Dentz manipulates perspective in the formal sense, and thereby prompts shifts in the viewer's perspective of a conceptual sort. In her work, "What side of the fence are you on?" takes on literal, political, and moral dimensions.
—SARAH GILLER NELSON

1. Dentz, e-mail correspondence with the author, December 5, 2006; see also Carlos Motta, "Interview with Shoshana Dentz," www.artwurl.org/issue5/popup7c.html.

2. Dentz, in Motta, "Interview."

Lilah Freedland

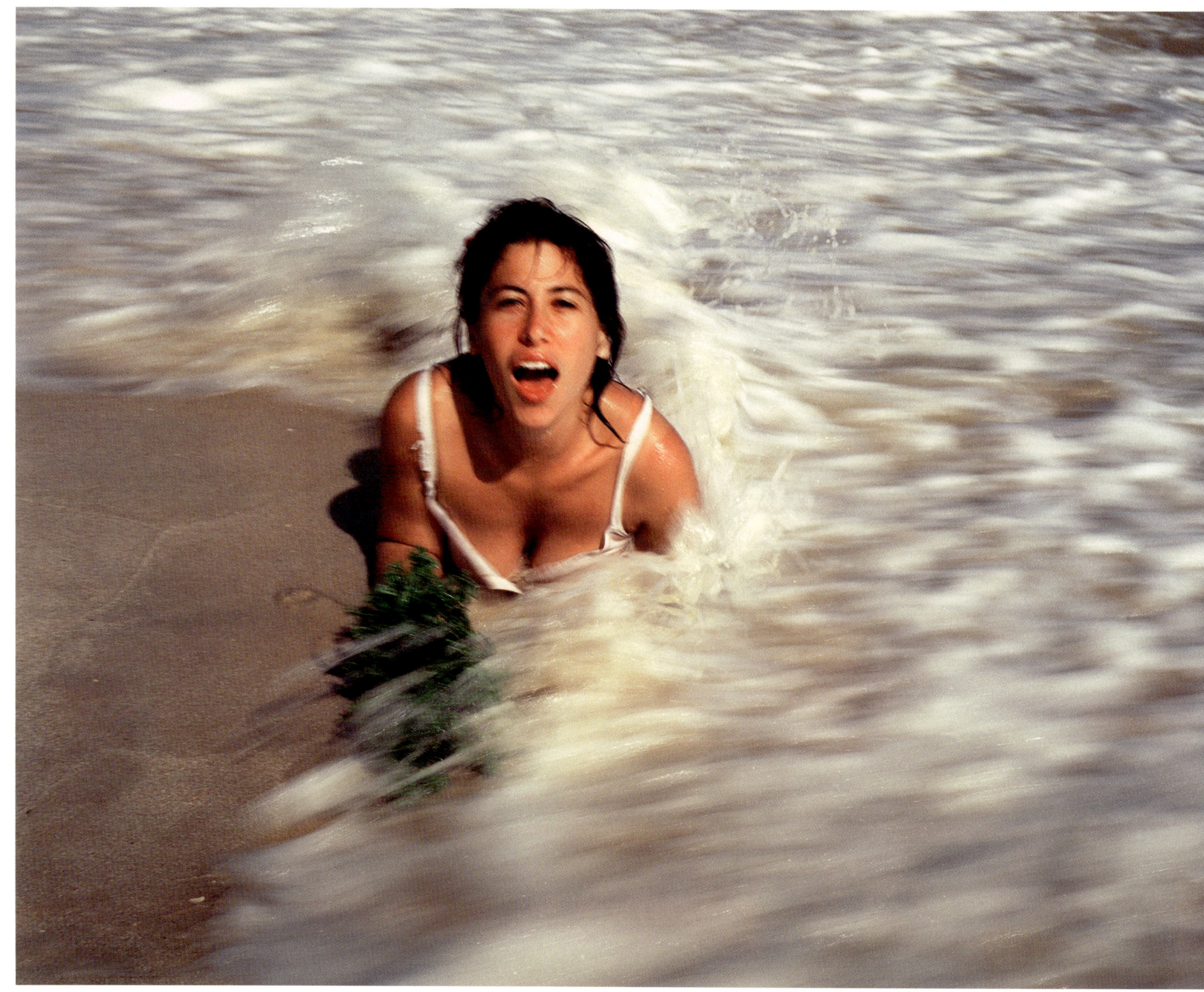

Fig. 53 **dip ya karpas**, 2001, c-print, 20 x 24".

THERE ARE ART FORMS AND THEN THERE ARE ART FORMS. FROM PERFORMANCE TO DOCUMENTARY,

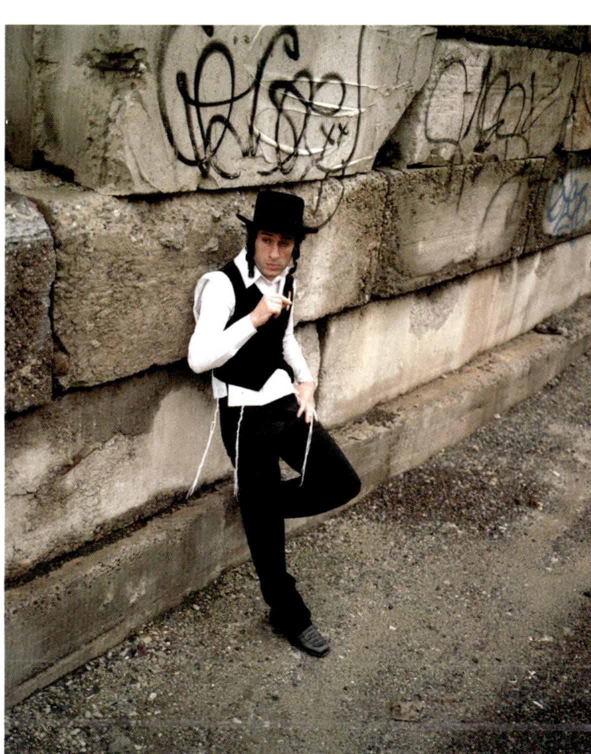

Fig. 54 **dream as though you'll live forever, live as though you'll die today**, 2003, c-print, 24 x 20".

from photography to drawing, from the art of looking sexy to the art of casting spells, Lilah Freedland has dabbled in them all, never to the end of mastering a certain form but rather toward renewing what has grown moribund. Take, for instance, the artist's most striking series, "Hebrew School Pin-Ups," 2001–2005. Mimicking good old American soft porn, these photographs capture Freedland and other women in various clichéd roles: bikini-clad hitchhiker, bathing beauty, girl-next-door. But while the cleavage looks familiar and the set-ups just right, there's always a twist, not unlike that of braided challah. In *dip ya karpas*, 2001 (fig. 53), the lusty model holds a bunch of greenery in her hand as she kneels in the surf: the greens are parsley, the ocean salt-water, the unexpected reference Passover Seder. The hot girl on the side of the road in *next year in the holy land*, 2002 (fig. 14), isn't thumbing it to the beach; her cardboard sign reads "Israel or Bust," and her pouty red lips say she means it. Religion and sexuality clash uproariously in these pictures, but their combination of the sacred and the profane seriously tests certain limits, prompting such questions as: Can there be such a thing as religious pornog-raphy? Is sexiness neutralized by religious content? Or is the taboo mix itself a turn-on?

Freedland pushes these and other limits when she shifts subjects from cheesecake to heartthrob, posing a guy in Hasidic dress as if he were James Dean. Titled after a quote attributed to the actor, *dream as though you'll live forever, live as though you'll die today*, 2003 (fig. 54), anticipates the current hip factor of all things Jewish, but more than that it fetishizes the young men of a certain religious sect, turning forelocks and fringes into something tall, dark, and handsome. Freedland, who at the time she made this image was living in the Williamsburg neighborhood of Brooklyn amid

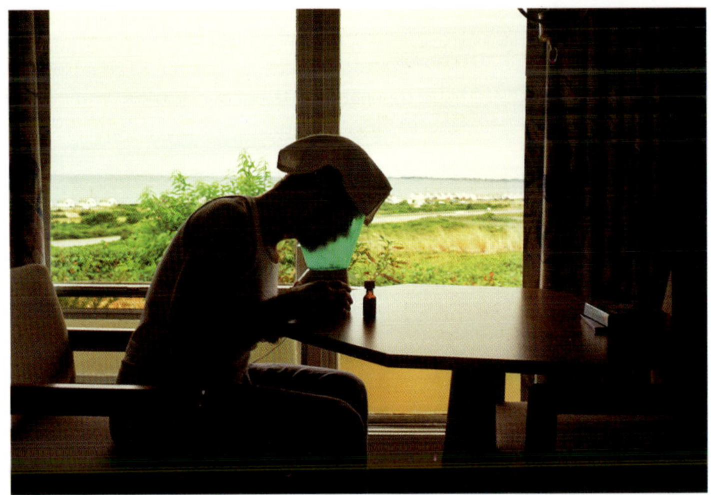

Fig. 55 **todd**, 2003,
c-print, 20 x 24".

a population of artists and Hasidim, explains
that her fascination with the Hasidic community stemmed from their extreme self-denial.[1]
Cigarette in hand, the cool Hasid exhibits just
the opposite behavior, self-indulging as if he
believed the hard-living Dean's words. A rabbi
might chastise him, but the guy in the photo
looks so damn good he should be given a
smoking dispensation—no matter if he ends up
dead at the age of twenty-four.

An equally irreverent and transgressive
approach to Jewish representational forms is
found in Freedland's series "the messiah arrives
and is no longer necessary," ongoing since 2003
(see fig. 55). In this group of photographs,
Freedland presents snapshots of her friends
that reveal moments of super highs and
miserable lows, often prompted by substance
abuse of some kind. The series sets up a sort of
Catch-22. The dark joke is that at either extreme
the messiah isn't going to make a difference:
if you're high as a kite, you don't need
the messiah; if you're grossly hung-over, the
messiah isn't going to be of much help.
Rather than connoting godlessness, however,
the series in the end betrays a belief in the
messiah, even if not in his effectiveness.

For all of their defiant cheek, each of the
above photographic works is explicitly Jewish in
content. It's not Jewish subjects Freedland
seeks to abandon; it's as if she sets out to
reinvent the *form* of typical Jewish art, and no
wonder. As she once said, "Jewish art is so ugly,
you know? All those tchotckes and things."[2]
Nevertheless, in a drawing from 2002 she takes
on Jewish kitsch on its own formal terms, using
ink on paper and a style that in fact wouldn't
look out of place on the wall of my grandparents' den, next to the woodcut rabbi. That is,
if the foreground figure in *god bless video*, 2002
(fig. 56), weren't brandishing a video camera
instead of a siddur. By accessorizing him thus,
Freedland brings the representation of the
faithful into the twenty-first century. Granted,
holding the camera with an arm wrapped
in tefillin isn't exactly kosher, but how better to
record a holy experience in the digital age?
At least the fellow's having a holy experience.

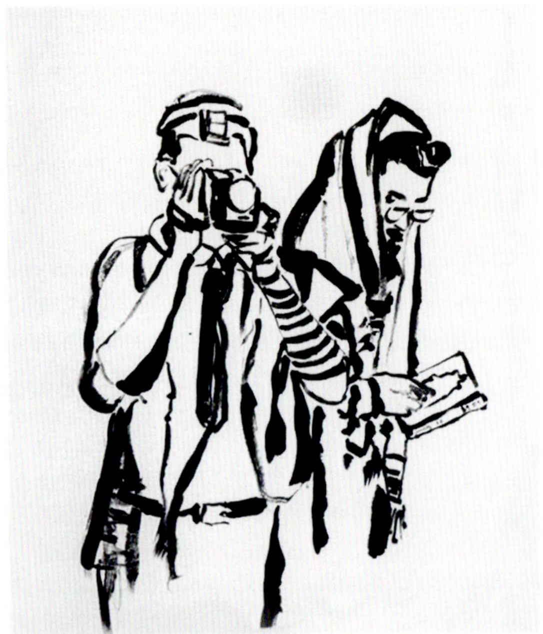

Fig. 56 **god bless video**, 2002, ink and acrylic on paper, 14 x 11".

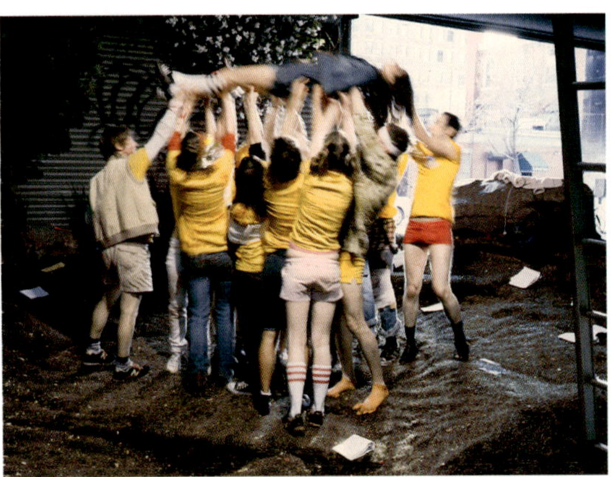

Fig. 57 **light as a feather**, 2006, c-print, 20 x 24".
From the performance *sleepaway*, Scope Art Fair, New York, NY.

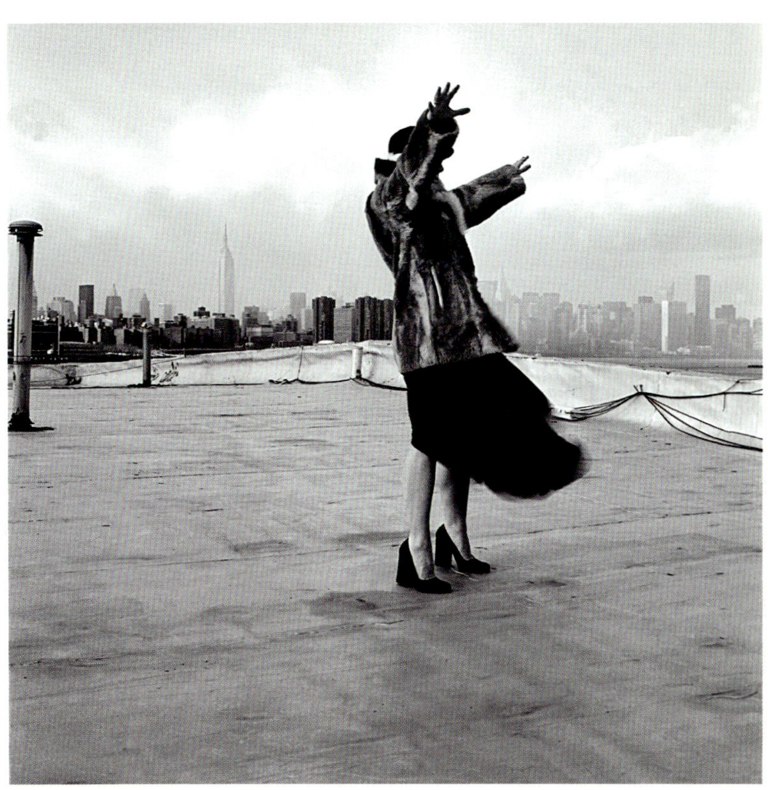

Fig. 58 **spell 02—dome of protection, tri-state**, 2002.
Performance view, Williamsburg, Brooklyn, NY.

Freedland's reinvigoration of waning art forms doesn't stop at Jewish art. Over the past few years, she's tested the mettle of various performance styles—from Duchampian personae to Marina Abramović–style endurance to Sophie Calle–esque voyeurism—as if to see what is still doable as an artist and believable for the audience. Freedland recently orchestrated a genuinely exhausting eight-hour event for a cast of fifteen. Held on an Astroturf knoll at the 2006 Scope Art Fair, *sleepaway* (see fig. 57) aimed to condense an entire summer of experiences into one day. The participants sang songs, went on a panty raid, threw a pie fight, and endured bloody cuts and bruises, intensely combining joy and chaos under the loose direction of Freedland, who played the role of (camp) director.

A series of private performances, ongoing since 2002, has found Freedland casting spells by writing spontaneous texts in the air. Looking like a cross between Rrose Sélavy and Joseph Beuys, which is to say like an elegant shaman, she radiates a dome of protection over the tri-state area from her rooftop, merely through the power of her thoughts and the movement of her body (see fig. 58). Obviously Freedland is no priestess with magical powers, but as it happens, New York is still safe. You can't trust a trickster, but you can certainly be affected by her. And as a 2004 drawing (fig. 59) twistedly notes, you can laugh, you can always laugh.
—LORI WAXMAN

1. Freedland, conversation with the author, March 13, 2007.

2. Freedland, in various authors, "Stars of David," *Time Out New York*, December 4–11, 2003.

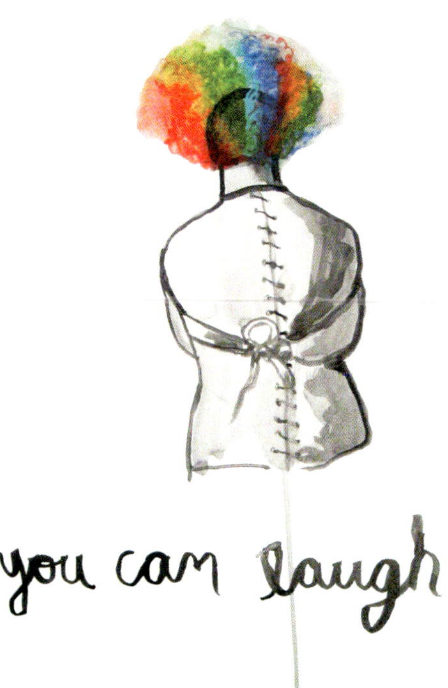

Fig. 59 **you can laugh**, 2004, watercolor and acrylic on paper, 14 x 11".

Matthew Girson

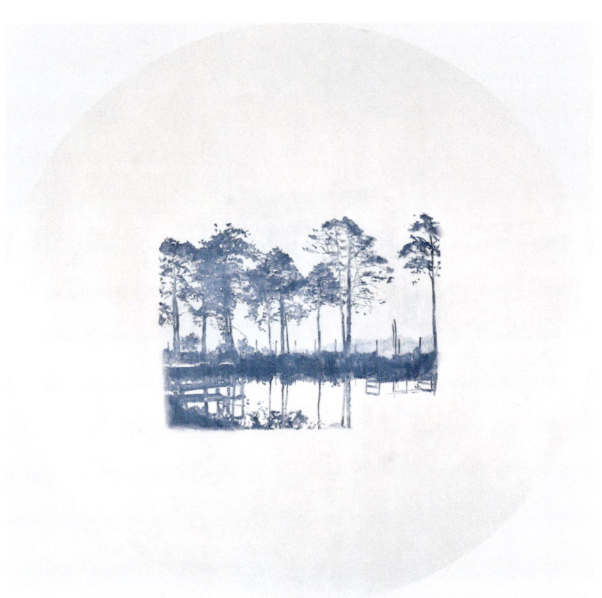

Fig. 60 **Auschwitz**, 1994, oil on canvas, 62 x 62".

Fig. 61 **Untitled (Scotoma)**, 2004, oil on canvas, 62½ x 62½".

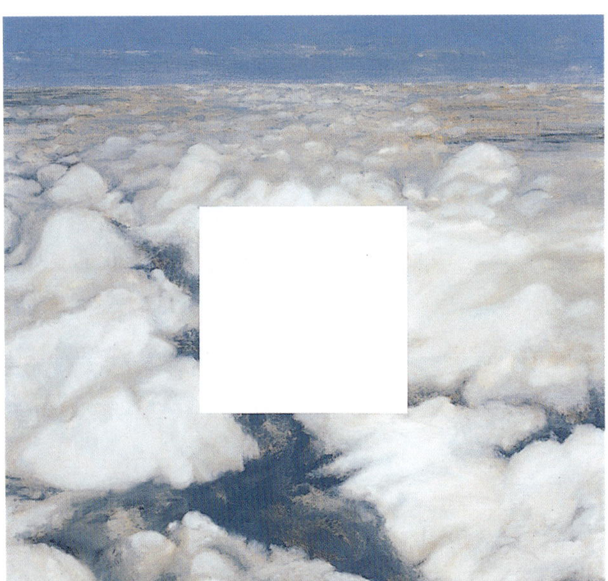

far more nuanced. Kant recognized that in experiencing the sublime—that which exceeds our power of comprehension—terror accompanies our pleasure. Philosopher Edmund Burke made a fine distinction, noting that distance alleviates the former response to sublime events and heightens the latter: "When danger and pain press too nearly, they are incapable of any delight . . . but at certain distances, and with certain modifications, they may be, and they are, delightful."[1] More recently, Jean-François Lyotard extended the notion of the sublime, which previously focused primarily on nature, to all things—experiences, feelings, concepts, and objects—that confound our abilities to synthesize them into knowledge. These three takes on the sublime illuminate the art of Matthew Girson, which represents from afar the pleasure and terror of modern events, phenomena, and objects that exceed the powers of imagination.

Girson's ethical sublime reflects a keen combination of Romanticism and post-Holocaust theory. The sweeping cloudscapes, unpeopled pastoral scenes, and atmospheric drama of his paintings recall the Romantic landscape tradition, specifically that of Caspar David Friedrich, whose paintings helped establish a distinctively German artistic tradition that has been defined by its "aesthetic and emotional engagement with the intangible, the unrepresentable, and the unknowable."[2] While Friedrich attempted to recreate the experience of the sublime on canvas, Girson references the aesthetic tradition of the sublime to explore the challenge that human atrocities force upon artistic and linguistic representation. The Holocaust is Girson's genocidal point of reference, perhaps unsurprising given his own Jewish heritage. The loosely painted images in his "Concentration Camp Series," 1994, for example, seduce viewers with their ethereal allure, only to shock them with the facts of their origin. *Auschwitz*, 1994 (fig. 60), like other works in

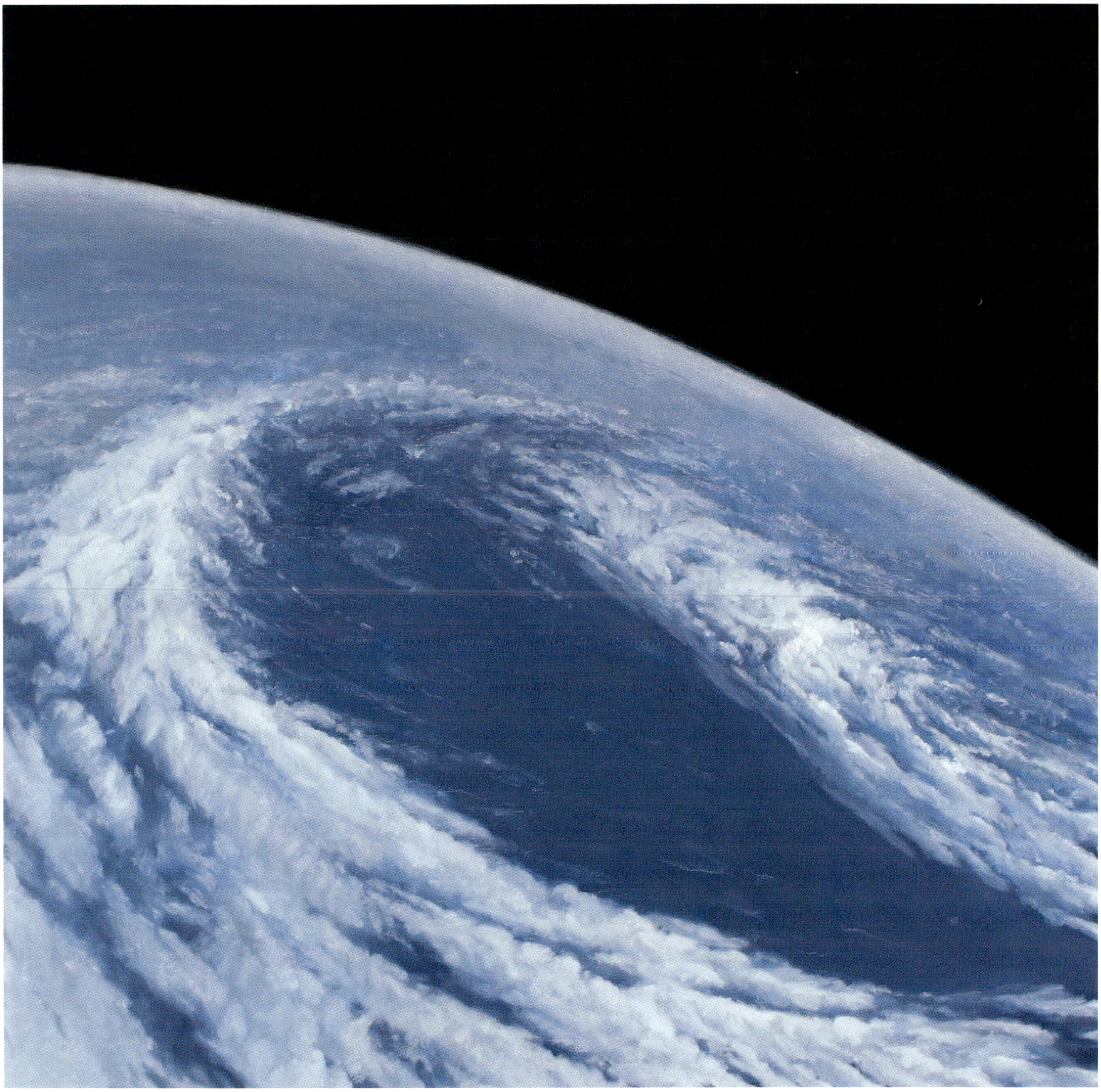

Fig. 62 **Satellite View #3**, 2006, oil on canvas, 63 x 63".

Is my
Vision failing
or is my
failing vision
?

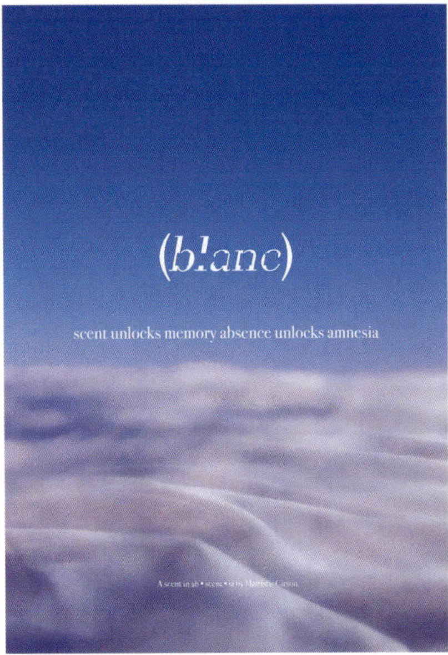

Fig. 63 **Central Scotoma Font Sample**, designed by Matthew Girson and Timothy Straveller, 2001, postcard, 3 x 5".

Fig. 64 Promotional poster for **(blanc) a scent in ab·scent·ia** by Matthew Girson, designed by Matthew Girson and Amit Patel, 2006.

the series, presents a rectangular landscape in the center of a faint white circle that is itself framed by a white five-foot-square canvas. The austere, white-on-white shapes allude to the formal tropes of twentieth-century abstract painters such as Kasimir Malevich, Ad Reinhardt, and Robert Ryman. The delicate stillness of the central scene recalls a contrastingly Romantic Friedrich, and its haziness suggests the passage of time and the loss of memory. As the title of the work indicates, however, there's a sinister history behind this pastoral setting. The image is painted from a photograph of the countryside surrounding Auschwitz. Taken decades after the concentration camp was dismantled, shot from afar, and transposed to a painting, the image is now not so much threatening as it is beautifully terrible and terribly beautiful.

Girson's "Scotoma Series," 1998–2005 (see fig. 61), reverses the compositional scheme of the "Concentration Camp Series." In each of these works, which comprise paintings, drawings, and collages, a large white square occupies the center of the canvas, partially blocking the bird's-eye view of lush landscapes or billowy clouds that activates the periphery. A scotoma is a medical condition in which vision is occluded in a certain area. In Girson's work the "scotoma" functions conceptually, as a metaphor for uncertainty. The artist's blind spot is ambiguous: the square form suggests flatness, absence, and removal, as well as depth, presence, and opportunity. (Blindness is, according to Girson, "a problem as much as a possibility."[3]) It invites the viewer to complete the work, or, alternatively, symbolizes something too profound to be depicted. As Lyotard notes, "We can conceive the infinitely great, the infinitely powerful, but every presentation of an object destined to '*make visible*' this absolute greatness or power appears to us painfully inadequate."[4] (Emphasis mine.) Perhaps Girson's empty square represents this very inadequacy in picturing the infinite power that is the sublime.

Indeed, Girson's scotoma cloudscapes were inspired by a particular image of great, grave power. Adolf Hitler used the imagery of the sublime, particularly Friedrich's, toward his own propagandist purposes: to equate the power of nature with that of the Third Reich. The highly influential Nazi film *The Triumph of the Will* (1935), for instance, opens with a majestic shot of the clouds above Nuremberg as seen from the inside of an airplane—a view most people would have only been able to imagine in 1935, and one Girson has revived in his cloudscapes. By placing a blind spot in the center of *his* images of a sublime sky, the artist infuses it with consciousness of the lapse in humanity and morality that allow genocides to occur.

In 2001 Girson developed a font called Central Scotoma that extends the metaphor of blindness into the linguistic realm. Each letter of the typeface has a blank square in its center that hinders legibility. Girson used it in a series of

Figs. 65, 66, 67 **Dizzy Heights II**, 2005, **Dizzy Heights III**, 2005, **Dizzy Heights IV**, 2005, oil on canvas, 20 x 20" each.

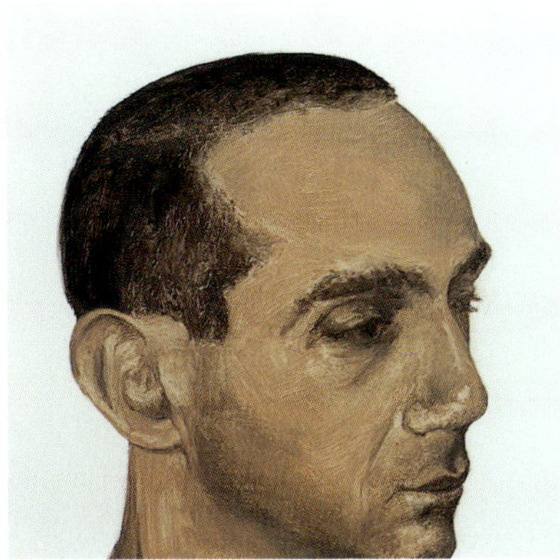
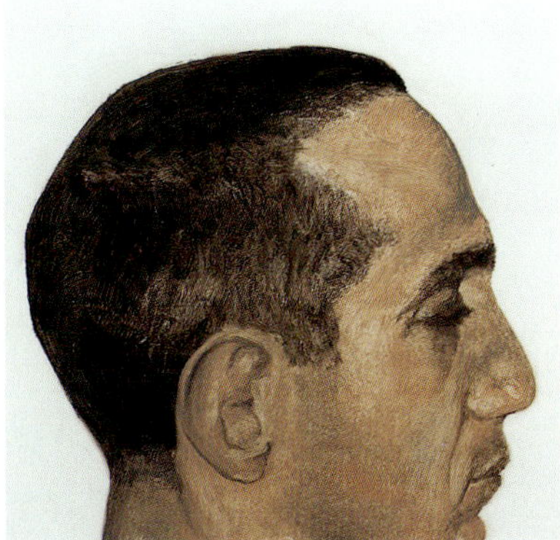
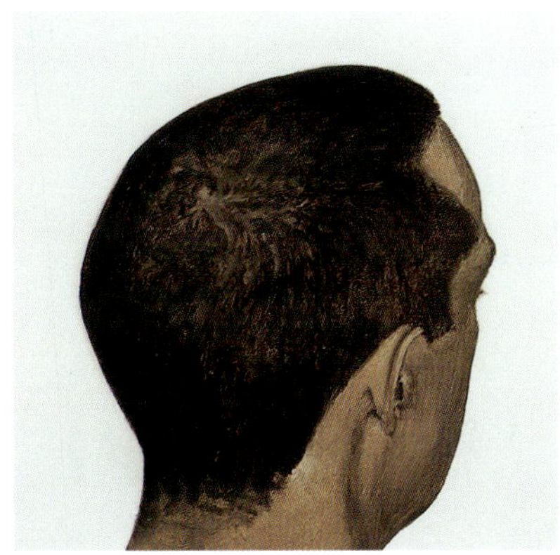

text-based postcards that, like Bruce Nauman's linguistic innovations, toy with language, ontology, and ethics. For instance, one postcard asks: "Is my vision failing or is my failing vision?" (fig. 63). The artist also used the font in the press materials for the launch of an odorless, color-less perfume he satirically calls *(blanc) a scent in ab·scent·ia, 2005 (see fig. 64). (blanc)* is, according to the press release, "extremely subtle and conceptually bold . . . a must for all people strong enough to live in the realm of blank emptiness." While the reference to genocide is less overt here than in Girson's other work, through *(blanc)* the artist reminds us that "scent unlocks memory" and "absence unlocks amnesia."

In his latest body of work, Girson focuses on potential future tragedies rather than those of the past. "Satellite View," 2005–2006 (see figs. 4 and 62), is a series of sensuous, large-scale paintings of hurricanes depicted from the point of view of Earth-orbiting satellites. Peering across the edge of a planet into the expansive emptiness of outer space, the viewer is confronted with Girson's most sublime view of nature to date. At this safe distance, the brewing storm is beautiful rather than fearsome. Girson has exhibited these works alongside a series called "Dizzy Heights," 2005, close-up paintings of the back of his own head (see figs. 3, 65, 66, and 67). These

paintings are the same size as the scotomas in the large cloudscapes and are hung at correspond-ing heights alongside the "Satellite Views," and thus stand in for the blank squares. Likewise, the swirling cowlicks in "Dizzy Heights" provide an unmistakable parallel to the clouds wildly spinning around the eye of the storm in "Satellite Views." As the artist puts it, "Despite how hard I try to build my knowledge, I'm often left feeling dizzy and in the dark."[5] These works, like their predecessors, insist on personal responsibility in facing the sublime terrors of the modern world— no matter how destabilizing and dark it may be.

—SARAH GILLER NELSON

1. Edmund Burke, *A Philosophical Enquiry into the Origin of Our Ideas of the Sublime and the Beautiful*, edited with an introduction and notes by James T. Boulton (Notre Dame, IN: University of Notre Dame Press, 1968), 40.

2. Iain Boyd White, "The Sublime," in *The Romantic Spirit in German Art: 1790–1990*, ed. Keith Hartley (London: Thames & Hudson, 1994), 138.

3. Girson, artist statement, 2006.

4. Jean-François Lyotard, *The Postmodern Condition: A Report on Knowledge*, trans. Geoff Bennington and Brian Massumi (Minneapolis: University of Minnesota Press, 1984), 78.

5. Girson, e-mail correspondence with the author, February 9, 2006.

Karl Haendel

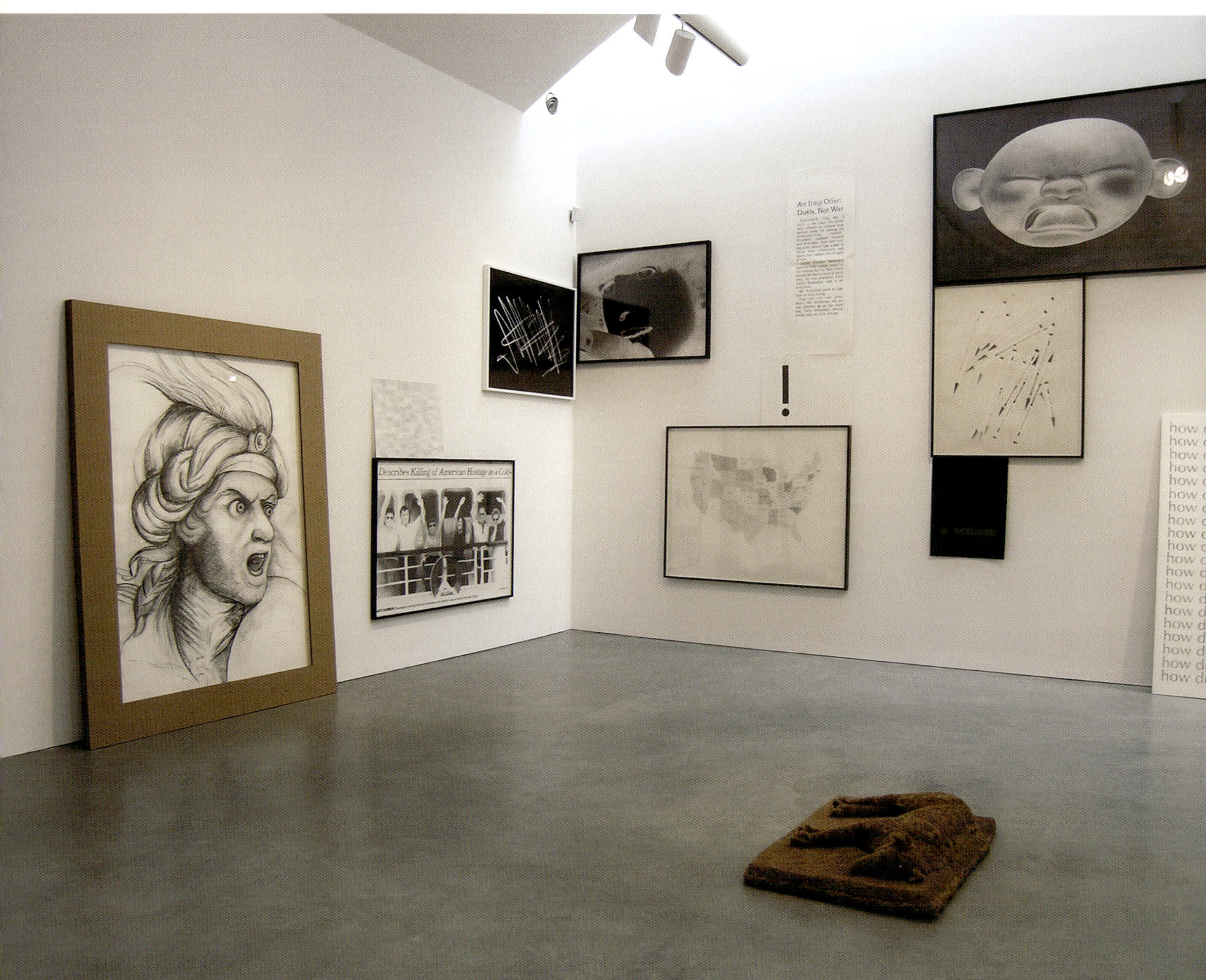

Fig. 68 **Untitled**, 2005. Installation view, *Uncertain States of America: American Artists in the 3rd Millennium*,
Center for Curatorial Studies, Bard College, Annandale-on-Hudson, NY, 2005.

Fig. 69 **Mapplethorpe is dead, Helms is out, Schwarzenegger is Governor**,
2004, pencil on paper, 80 x 45½". Collection of the Orange County Museum of Art, Newport Beach, CA.

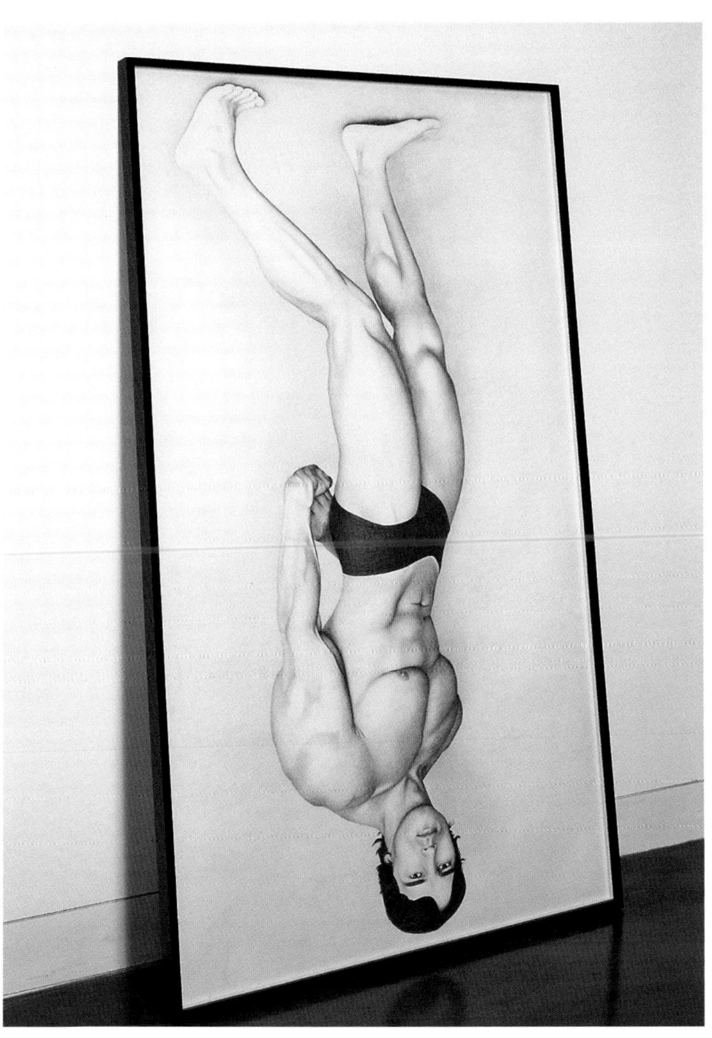

KARL HAENDEL IS AN APPROPRIATION ARTIST AND THEN SOME.
Though known for his meticulous, large-scale pencil reproductions of hard-to-find advertisements, news clippings, abstract scribbles, and high art, which he installs in expansive, salon-style arrangements, Haendel in fact questions the very notion of appropriation art because, as he explains, "as far as I'm concerned, everyone is an appropriation artist at this point."[1] Indeed, there's no avoiding referencing the glut of information that inundates us incessantly, whether through television, the Internet, magazines, bumper stickers, T-shirts, history books, or even museums. Everything we say or do is to some extent a copy, even if it's a rare copy, woven together from what's already out there. What we actually do with this material is another story, or at least that's where the story begins to get interesting.

A typical installation by Haendel, such as the one he arranged for the 2005 group exhibition *Uncertain States of America* (see figs. 7 and 68), finds the following motifs adjacent to one another: a fluffy white terrier, a close-up of one zebra mounting another, the slogan "WE ♥ ABORTION," an exclamation mark, an Associated Press item about an Iraqi vice president proposing to duel Dick Cheney instead of going to war, a scrawl, freed hostages waving from the deck of the Achille Lauro, and a Renaissance sketch. The drawings are framed or not; hung on, propped against, or pinned to the wall; layered atop one another, stacked edge to edge, or displayed independently. They rise to the ceiling, sit on the floor, and lurk in the corner. Their heterogeneous presentation reflects equally diverse sources but masks a consistent process: the artist photographs found materials, projects the resulting transparency onto Arches Hot Press paper, and

Fig. 70 **Let Marys Marry**, 2006, pencil on paper mounted on board, 70 x 44 ½"; **Gay Republicans and Democratic Fetuses**, 2006, pencil on paper mounted on board, 51 x 79"; **We Miss Clinton**, 2006, pencil on paper mounted on board, 74 x 51". From "Protest Group." Installation view, Sorcha Dallas Contemporary Art, Glasgow, Scotland, 2006.

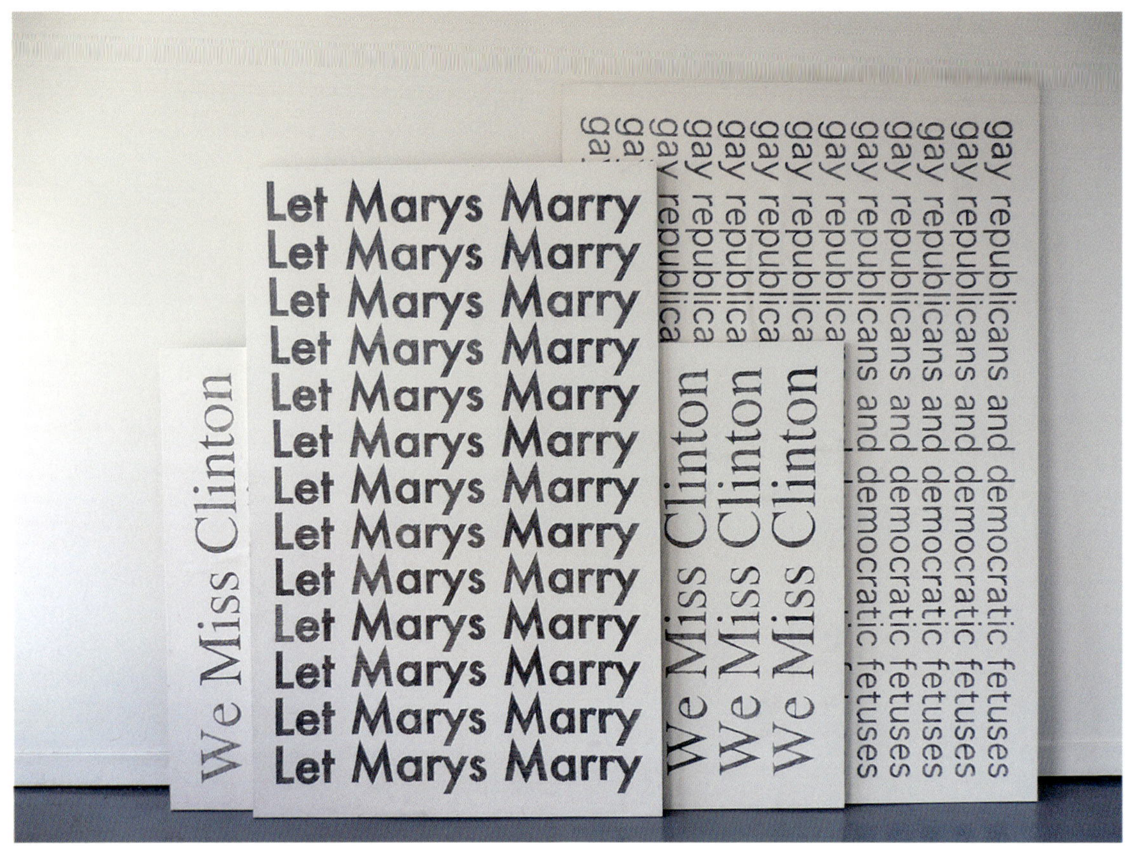

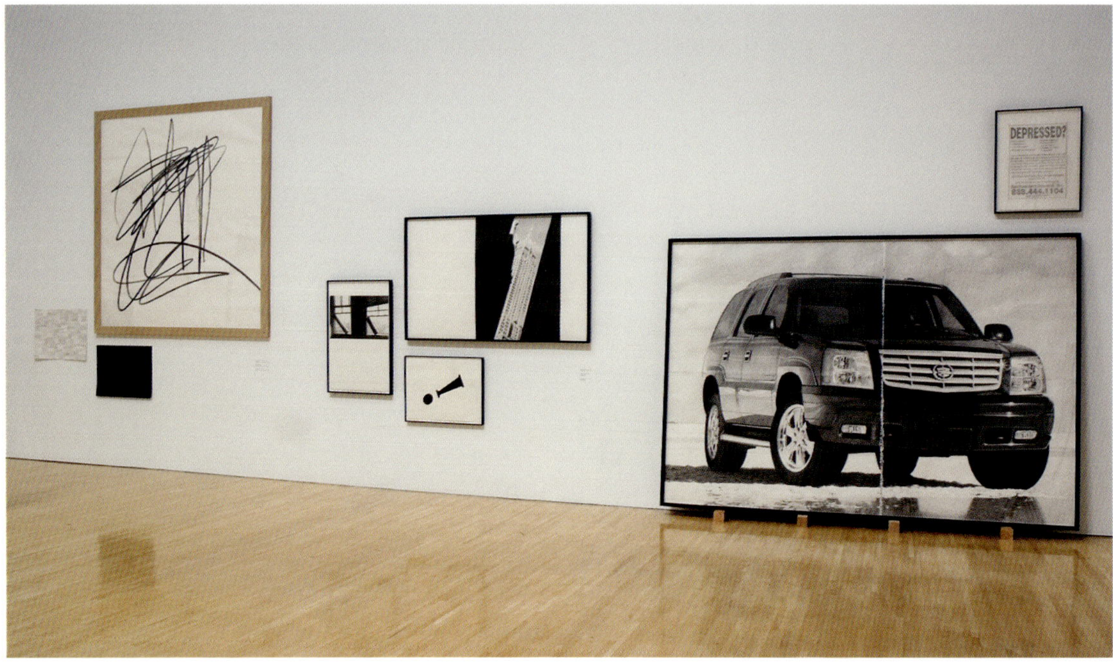

Fig. 71 **MOCA Focus: Karl Haendel**. Installation view, Museum of Contemporary Art, Los Angeles, CA, 2006.

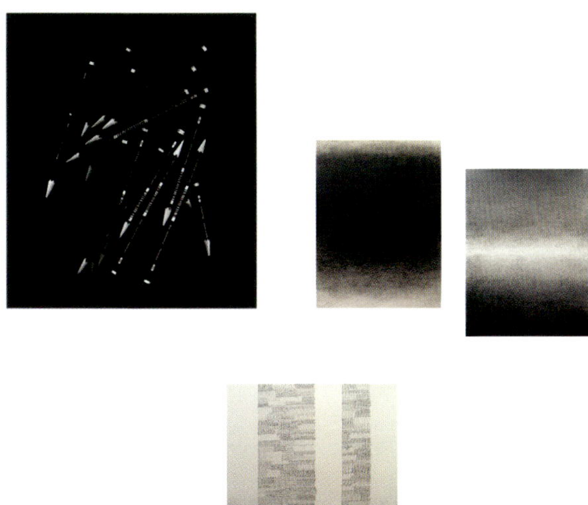
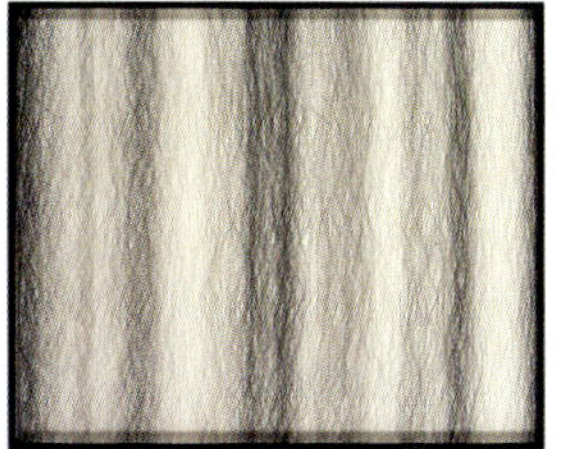
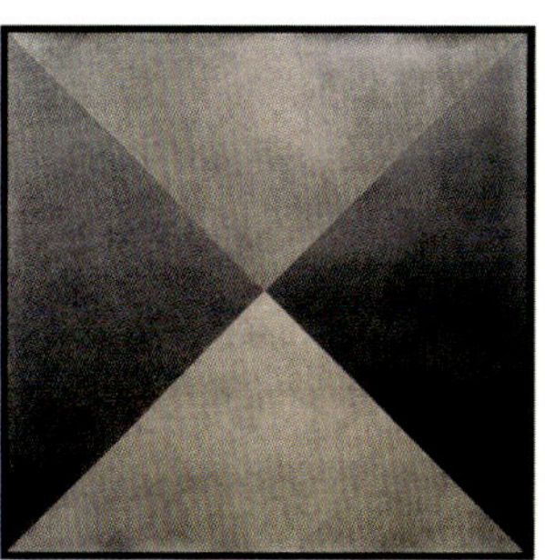

Fig. 72 left to right: **Wasserlack #1 (Ghost Version)**, 2006, unique c-print, 52 x 43"; **Untitled (more me than you)**, 2005, pencil on paper, 22 x 30"; **Abstract Bild 1**, 2006, pencil on paper, 30 x 22"; **Abstract Bild III**, 2006, pencil on paper, 30 x 22"; **Lyndon #4**, 2005, pencil on paper, 41 x 49"; **Abstract Bild II**, 2006, pencil on paper 52 x 52". From "Abstract Group."

carefully traces the cast image, sometimes with the help of studio assistants.[2] (That Haendel occasionally draws the images freehand is merely the exception that proves the rule.)

It's a paradoxical artistic practice: the drawing process is labor intensive and dependent on handwork, while the selection of images and installation are intellectually demanding and fully conceptual. Mechanically reproduced media are transformed into original drawings that bear the artist's touch, but since they are based on projections, these drawings can be and often are traced and retraced, subject to potentially endless reproduction (sometimes they're even photographed and printed as negative "ghost versions" of the "original" drawing). Furthermore, the drawings themselves often undergo the destabilization of accidental staining, peculiar framing, deliberate tearing, and upside-down hanging. It's as if Haendel took the theoretical lessons of Sherrie Levine and Richard Prince, threw in some of the tongue-in-cheek bravado of Julian Schnabel, added the subversive grouping strategies of John Baldessari, and stirred. And those are just the conceptual references. (Formal quotations begin with da Vinci and Rubens, circle around Richter, take a right at Robert Longo, a U-turn at Rodney Graham, and keep on moving.)

Amid all of this simulation, quotation, and re-contextualization arises the matter of

selection. Haendel sees his practice as akin to that of the street photographer, who "observes the world, points, edits, crops, and selects . . . [while] still attempting to get at/to some truth."[3] The motifs of his drawings may appear random, but in fact they evidence careful attention to the stream of stats, slogans, and pictures that unceasingly pass us by. As the artist has noted, his work isn't political in the sense of actively seeking change, but it is in the sense that he acts as a commentator or editorialist.[4] The phrase "Let Marys Marry" repeated thirteen times across a seventy-inch-high board, for instance, or an immaculate (if upside-down) life-size portrait of Arnold Schwarzenegger (figs. 69 and 70)—such oversize, labor-intensive gestures assert importance and demand consideration. What they don't do, however, is state any kind of clear meaning.

Having dealt with the dizzying endgame of how these drawings represent, and the slightly less dizzying one of why they represent, the basic but key question of what they represent remains. It's a slippery one: a sideways exclamation mark doesn't mean much on its own. But when hung near pictures of an SUV, an anti-depression advertisement, two precariously propped-open windows, a giant scribble, and a neck-craning view of a Wall Street skyscraper (see fig. 71), certain

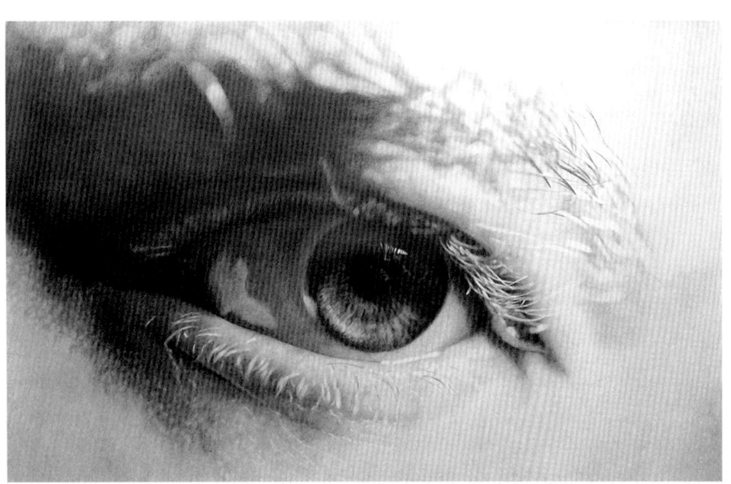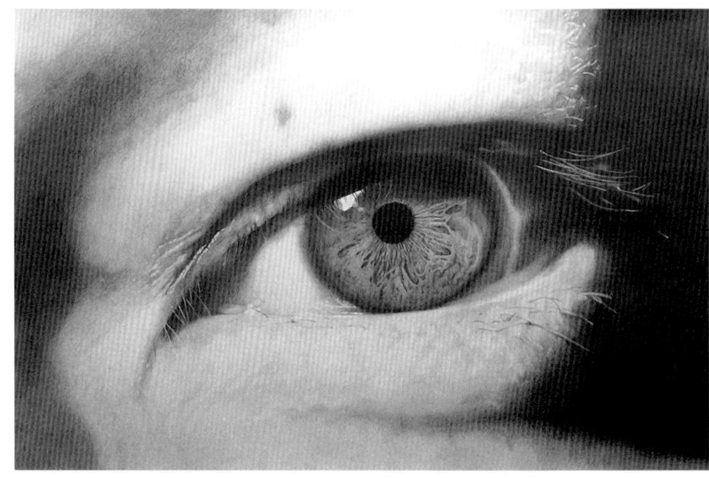

Fig. 73 **Hapa (Karl's Eye)**, 2006, pencil on paper, 52 x 77".
Hapa (Mika's Eye), 2006, pencil on paper, 52 x 75". Hort Family Collection.

associations begin to emerge, for instance about 9/11, speechlessness, and American hubris. Formal connections occur as well, through the play of diagonals and light versus shadow. These and other installations are fluid and open to endless reconfiguration, such that an individual drawing (or one like it) might find itself in an alternate grouping and thereby part of a different orbit of meaning. To wit, *Wasserlack #1 (Ghost Version)*, 2006, displayed beside grayscale abstractions (fig. 72), participates in a discourse about the medium of drawing. But hung amid representations of fighter jets, a screaming child, a joke about the Israeli occupation of Gaza, a Pilates-*cum*-torture device (fig. 76), and two looming, disembodied eyes (fig. 73)—as he has proposed for his *New Authentics* installation—it gets caught up in a frightening and confusing conversation about the powers of the state.

The lesson here is not so much that a picture is worth a thousand words, but that it can tell a number of different stories, depending on how it is deployed. The exception that proves the rule is a rare image that Haendel has chosen to exhibit on its own. Displayed under a spotlight in a darkened room, *Floating Hitler Head*, 2002 (figs. 74 and 75), hangs alone, so over-determined that it is incapable of sharing space with any other image. Instead, Haendel disfigures the oppressive portrait by attaching a clump of his own pubic hair where the Führer's moustache should be. It's a pathetic gesture that insists, even as it performs to the contrary, on the inescapable and consuming power of images.

—LORI WAXMAN

1. Haendel, in Gabriel Ritter, "Interview with Karl Haendel," *MOCA Focus: Karl Haendel* (Los Angeles: The Museum of Contemporary Art, 2006), 68.

2. Gloria Sutton, "Karl Haendel: The things that I am about to tell you are the things that I have come to regard as true," *MOCA Focus*, 11-12.

3. Haendel, artist statement, "Thoughts on Being an Artist Now," February 2004.

4. Haendel, in Ritter, "Interview," 74.

Fig. 74 **Floating Hitler Head**, 2002, pencil, charcoal, and artist's pubic hair on paper, 53 x 45". Collection of the Museum of Modern Art, New York, NY. Installation view, Track 16 Gallery, Santa Monica, CA, 2003.

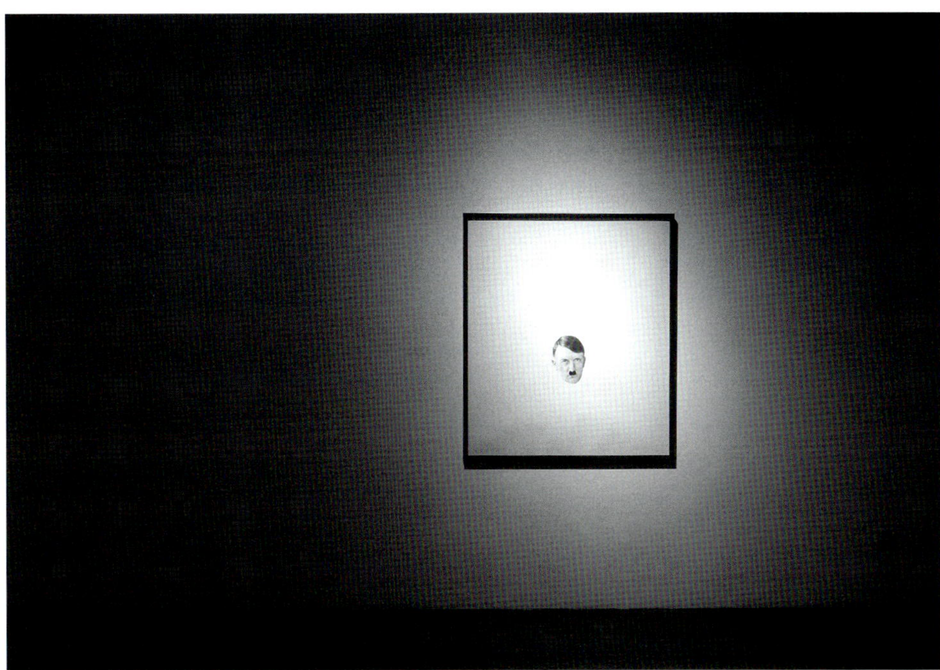

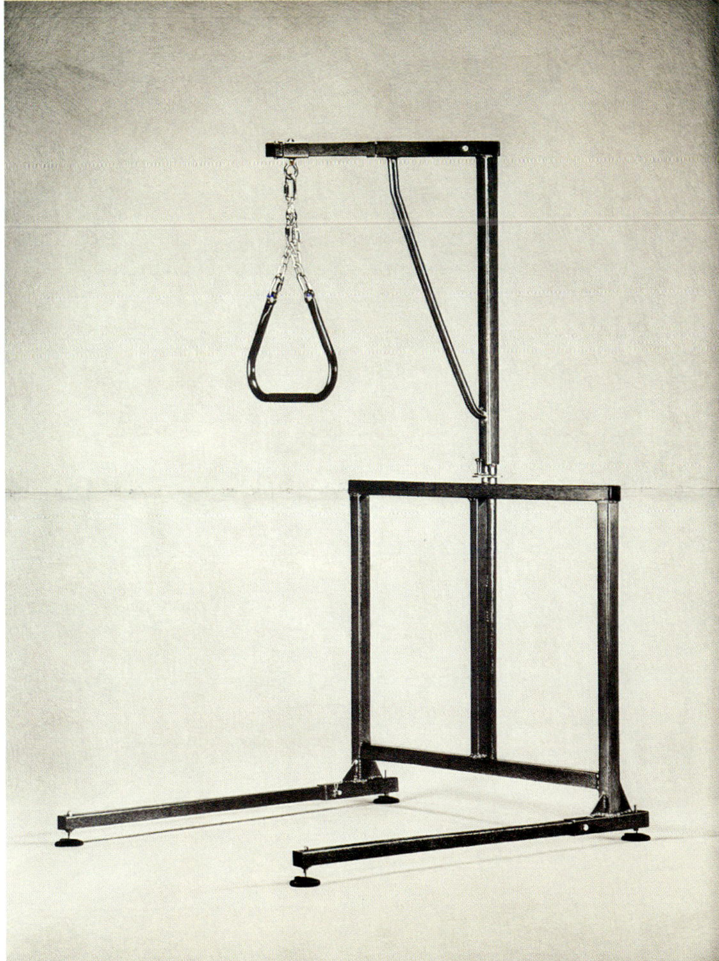

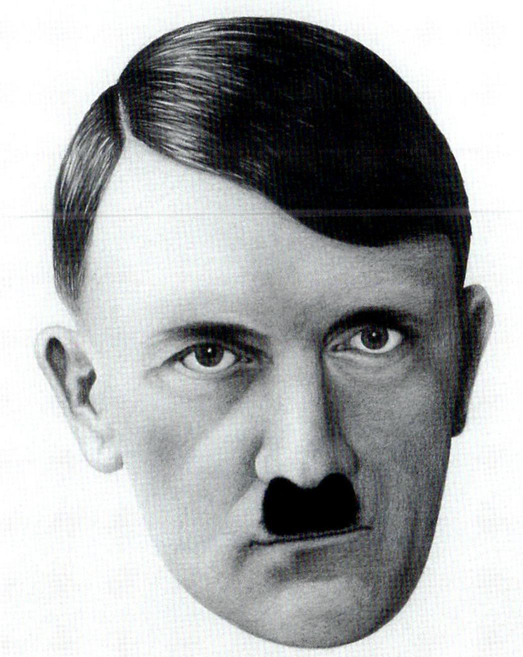

Fig. 75 **Floating Hitler Head** (detail), 2002.

Fig. 76 **Untitled**, 2006, pencil on paper, 90 x 70".
Private Collection.

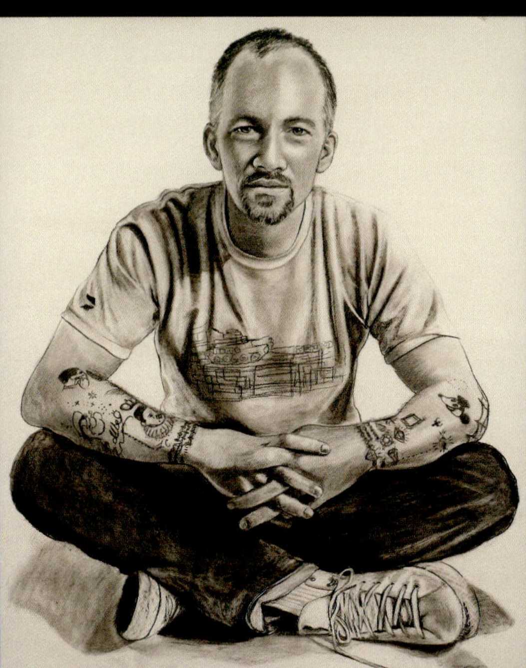

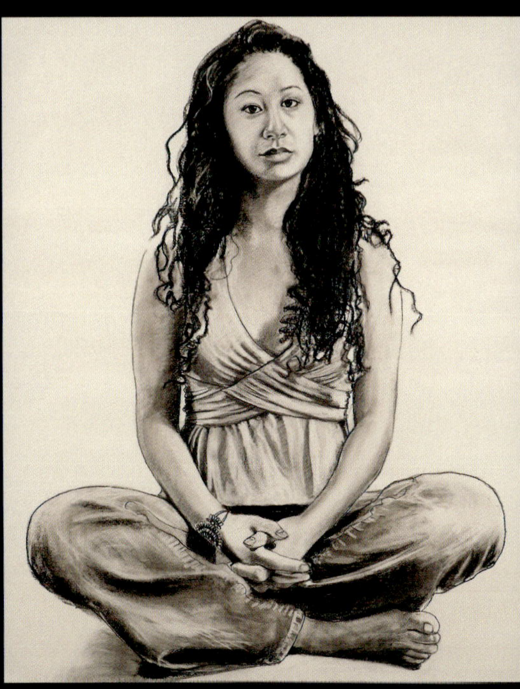

The artist's interest in "the slipperiness of identity" is autobiographical.[1] Raised by a Japanese American father from Hawaii and an Anglo, Spanish American mother from the Pacific Northwest (in a town near Seattle with a strong Norwegian heritage), Kina is now bringing up her own Jewish family in a Chicago neighborhood where the city's Muslim, Hindu, and Jewish communities intersect. In contrast to the often confrontational identity politics that informed much of the activist art of the 1990s, Kina's political images quietly raise the visibility of mixed-race individuals within the art world. Where many of the artist's earlier paintings examined surface appearances, her most recent body of work focuses on the nuances of personality.

"Loving," Kina's 2006 series of life-size photorealistic charcoal drawings of friends and colleagues, captures the inner life of her sitters. The empty backgrounds direct the viewer's attention to the forward-facing figures, who sit cross-legged and tightly contained within the frame. This spatial limitation perhaps mimics the way in which society reductively labels and categorizes the multifaceted personal histories of individuals. At the same time, Kina's monochrome rendering of her mixed-race models obscures the most obvious indicator of their "otherness." Since their identities cannot be assumed based on skin color, the viewer must carefully study body language, attire, and facial expression to interpret the work and gain insight into the figures' subjectivity.

Hunched forward, calmly capturing the viewer's attention with his friendly gaze, the sitter in the eponymous *Scooter LaForge*, 2006 (fig. 77), exudes a confident, approachable demeanor. The images with which he chooses to adorn himself—the aggressive tank on his T-shirt and the sad clown, Popeye, and Mickey

Fig. 77 **Scooter LaForge**, 2006, charcoal on paper, 42 ½ x 34".
Fig. 78 **Elena Rubin**, 2006, charcoal on paper, 42 ½ x 34".

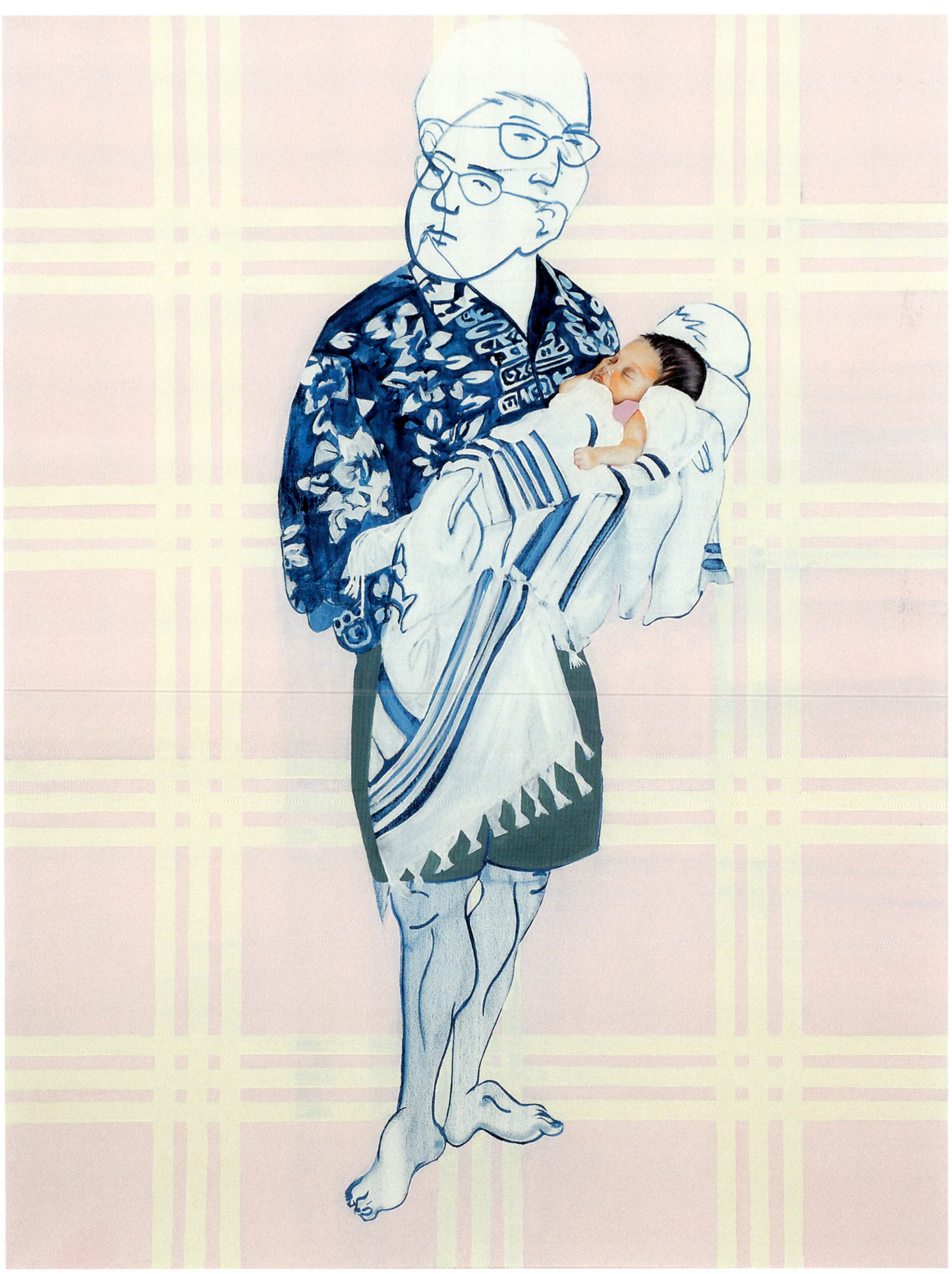

Fig. 79 **Midori's Brit Bat**, 2006, oil on canvas, 48 x 36".

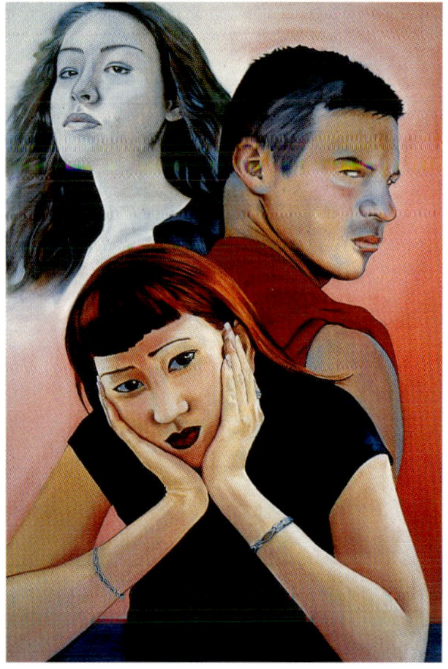

Fig. 80 **Hapa Soap Opera #4 (Ann Marie Lickteig, Justin Frolich, Margaret Erdmann)**, 2004, oil on canvas, 72 x 48".

Mouse tattoos on his arms—suggest a complex individual. For her part, the figure in *Elena Rubin*, 2006 (fig. 78), with her long, flowing hair, slight tilt of the head, and deep, v-neck blouse, conveys a self-assured yet understated sexiness. Kina's sympathy for her subject is evident; it prevents us from possessing her with our gaze and instead makes us aware of her humanity.

Kina's psychologically rich portraits follow earlier "identity studies" that were based almost exclusively on physical attributes. *Midori's Brit Bat*, 2006 (fig. 79), for instance, considers "the changing face of Asian America from a mixed race perspective."[2] The full-length portrait depicts Kina's father holding the artist's newborn daughter, Midori, during her Jewish baby-naming ceremony. Here, style functions as a superficial index of identity, with Kina's father rendered in the flat, abstracted manner of a Japanese Edo-period actor print, and Kina's daughter painted using a more naturalistic Western technique.[3] Perhaps to counteract the cultural reductivism suggested by the artist's use of these emblematic painting traditions (grandfather as "Asian," grand-daughter as "white"), both figures have two heads, one looking back toward the past, and the other looking forward toward the future. Surface details, like the print on the father's Hawaiian shirt and the stripes of the baby's *tallis*, or Jewish prayer shawl, reinforce the multiple cultural and ethnic identities of both sitters. In contrast, the melodramatic "Hapa Soap Operas" series, 2002–2005 (see fig. 80), presents a fantasy of uniform heterogeneity: a world exclusively populated by hapas, people of mixed Asian or Pacific Islander descent.

A series of family portraits from 2001 (figs. 17, 81, and 82) further explores the Jewish side of Kina's hyphenated hapa-Jewish identity. Kina has said that what struck her most during her initial visits to the suburban homes of

her husband's extended Jewish family, namely, the Rosenfelds and the Aronsons, were their high-end refrigerators. Viewing these prized appliances as symbolic expressions of class and identity, the artist created trompe-l'oeil images of refrigerators that imply, rather than present, the bodies and tastes of their owners.[4] In *The Rosenfelds*, a Sub-Zero refrigerator, a domestic status symbol, resides in its custom-made, inlaid-wood cubby. Its sleek facade stands in contrast to the haphazardly adorned face of the generic, middle-class Frigidaire in *The Kina-Aronsons*. In this family self-portrait, a picture of newly married cousins Ayako and Miles is sandwiched between poetry magnets bearing Yiddish words like "kvell" and "yinglish" as well as drawings by Ariel, Kina's Jewish Mexican stepdaughter. Not only do these unframed, life-size paintings metaphorically equate person and possession, they also elide the difference between image and object. Kina's attention to pattern and texture give the realistically rendered cabinetry, grill, and refrigerator doors in *The Rosenfelds* an almost abstract quality. Like a Color Field painter, the artist uses layered washes of color to focus the viewer's attention on the painted surface of the appliance's stainless-steel shell, rather than on the three-dimensional object being represented. While the variety of adornments on the Kina-Aronson fridge indicates a multi-plicity of identities, the interiors of the refrigerators, and, by extension, the inner lives of their owners, remain closed to the viewer.
—SARAH GILLER NELSON

---

1. Kina, artist statement, 2006.

2. Ibid.

3. Kunihiro's wood block print *Gokumon no Shÿebei: Ichikawa Ichizÿ*, 1827, is the source of both the background design and the father's pose.

4. Kina, conversation with the author, August 17, 2006.

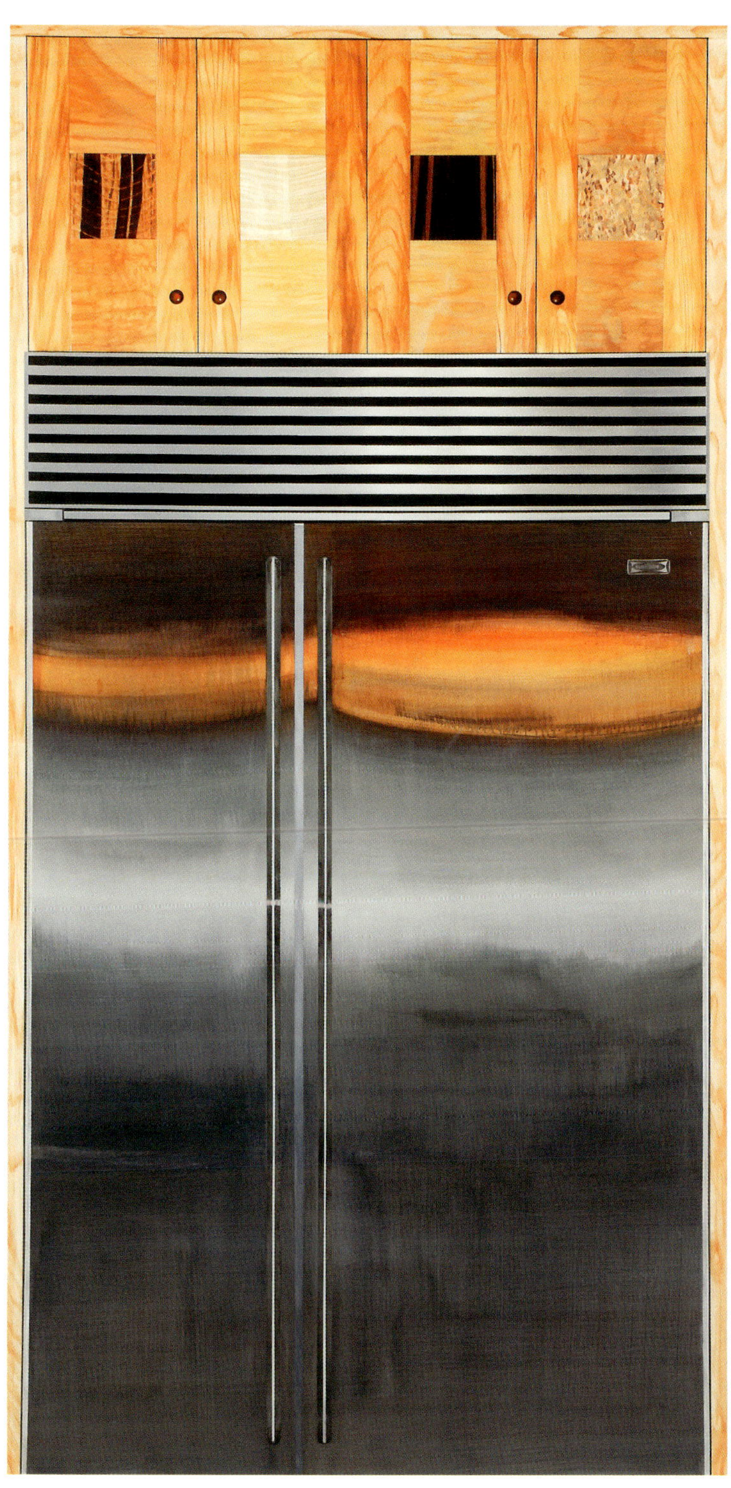

Fig. 81 **The Rosenfelds**, 2001, acrylic on canvas, 103 x 50½".

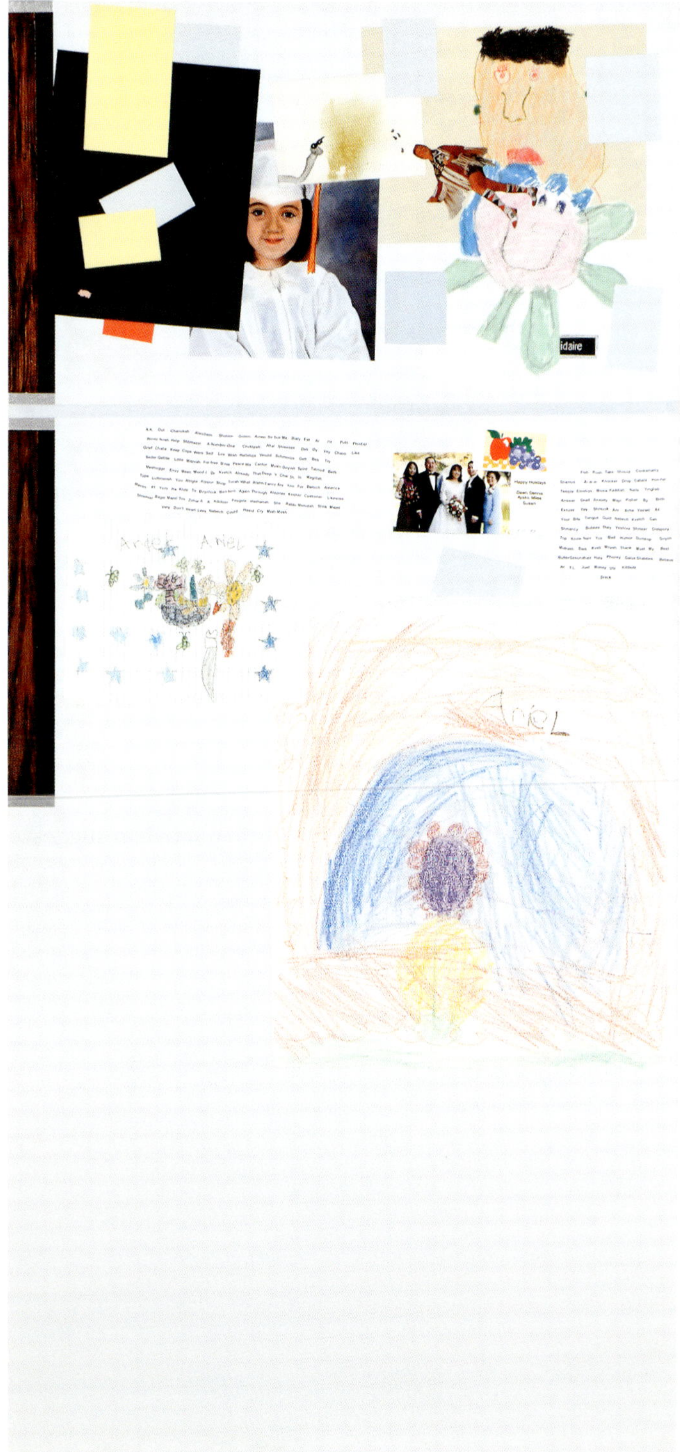

Fig. 82 **The Kina-Aronsons**, 2001,
acrylic, crayon, pen, and collage on canvas, 60 x 30".

Fawn Krieger

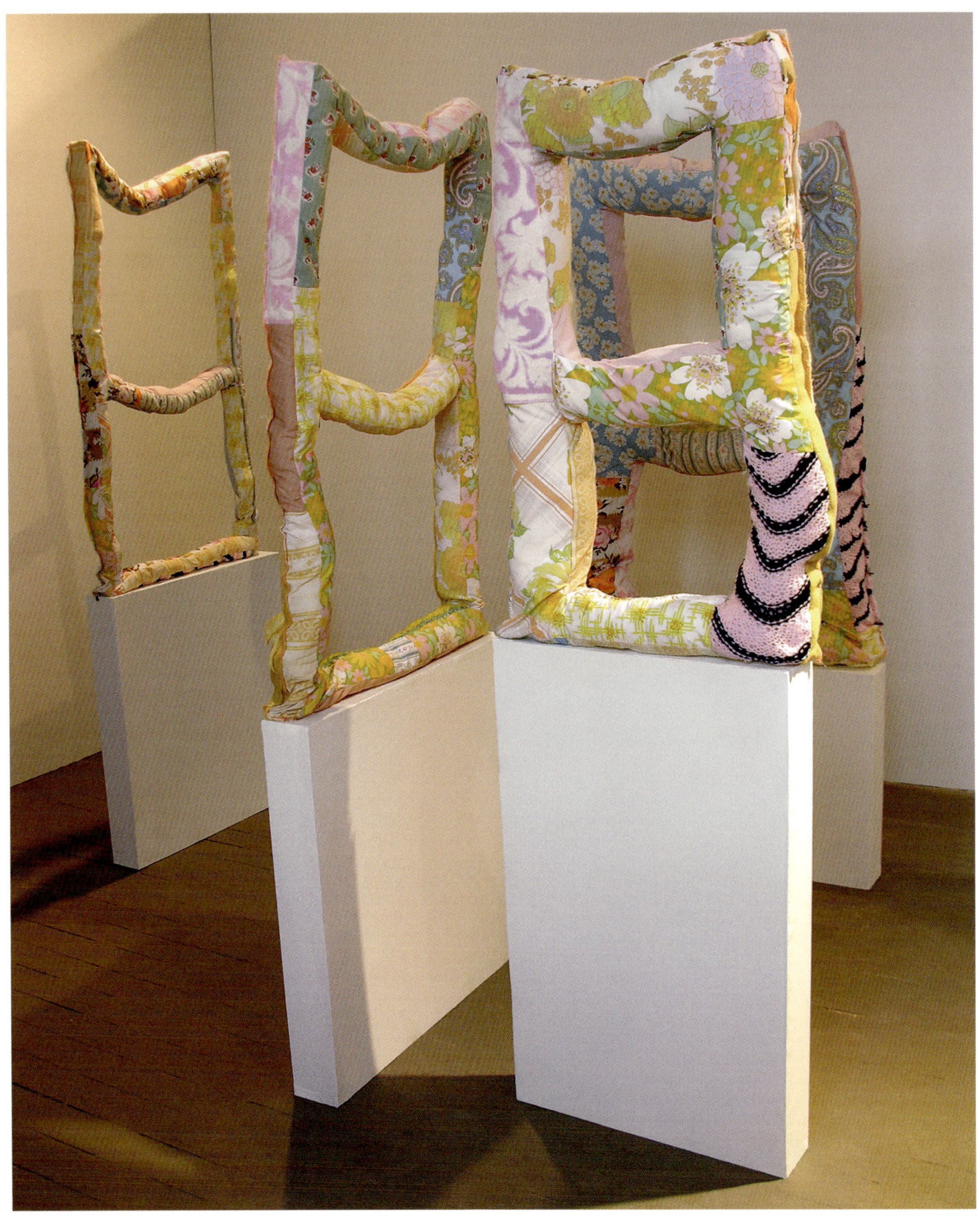

Fig. 83 left to right: **DAWNING 3**, **2**, **4**, and **1**, 2006, fabric, stuffing, and thread with wood bases, 63 ½ to 69 ½" high.

"MY CONCERN IS CENTERED AROUND WHAT IT MEANS TO FEEL HOME, TO BUILD A HOME,

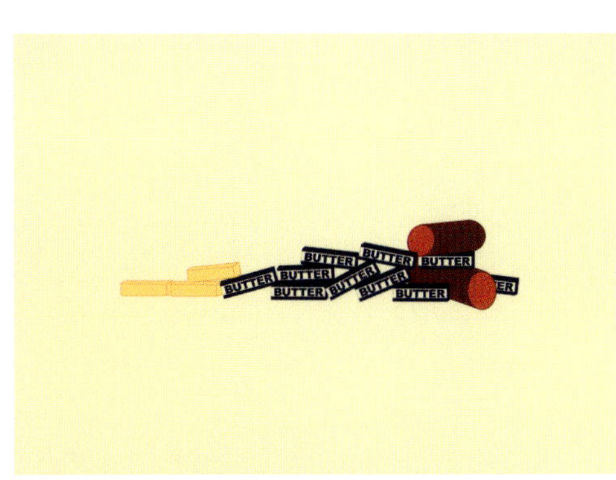

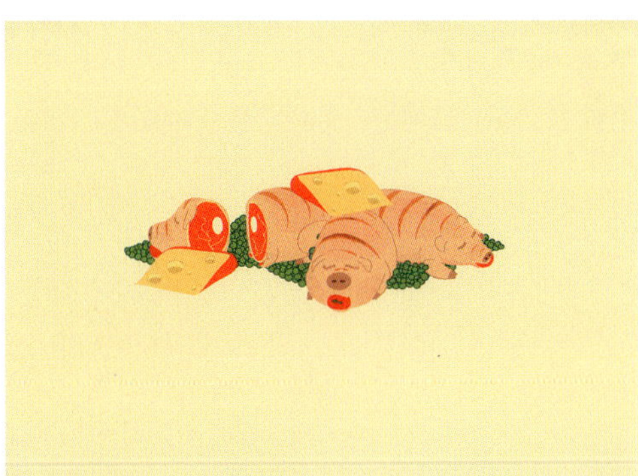

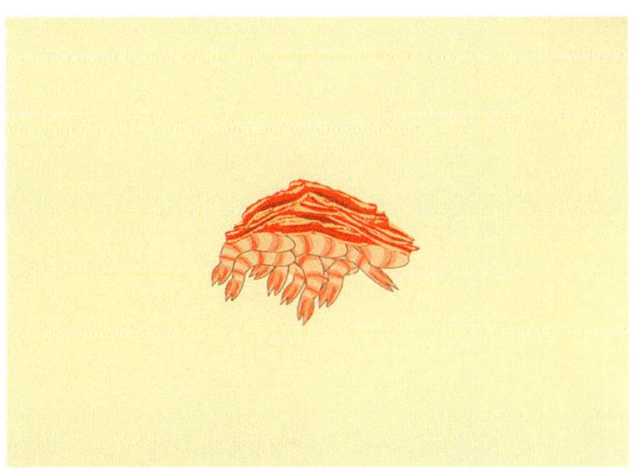

Figs. 84, 85, 86
Meat Composition 7, **17**, and **20**,
2004, inkjet prints on cotton rag paper, 8 1/2 x 11".

to occupy a home, to be protected by a home."[1]
In this statement artist Fawn Krieger not
only identifies home as one of the governing
themes of her work, she also alludes to the wider
definitions that the very concept entails. Home
can be the house in which our parents chose to
raise us, but it can also be any place in which we
find comfort, security, and familiarity. It is the
physical place where one lives, but also the social
and spiritual unit that occupies that place. More
abstractly, home is often a place from which life
originates and happens. As an artist whose
sculptures redefine the spaces they occupy and
whose visionary drawings propose new ways of
inhabiting space, Krieger demonstrates an
activist's understanding of home as a place
that is not given but constantly found, redefined,
and re-imagined.

In "DAWNING," 2006 (see fig. 83), a recent
series of fabric sculptures, Krieger examines the
relationship between the architecture of the home
and those it is intended to protect and care for.
Refashioning old afghans and bed linens from
her grandparents' summer cottage, she sews and
stuffs structures that suggest family members,
while simultaneously acting as freestanding
windows. Experienced in the round, they create a
curiously liminal space, free from notions of inside
or outside, of individual or collective forms. Bereft
of glass panes or any perceivable rigidity (they
rest on wood bases), the windows become upright
comforters that have been ripped, torn, patched
up, and sewn back together. While playful textures
and breezy, worn out pastel textiles define
their forms, the sculptures' central empty spaces
tell their story.

The cartoonish nature of "DAWNING" finds an
edgy parallel in "TREYF," a series of twenty digital
drawings from 2004 that playfully arrange butter
sticks between sausage rolls, cheese wedges
beside suckling pigs, and bacon strips atop shrimp
cocktail (see figs. 84, 85, and 86). The drawings

Fig. 87 **STACKED (study 1)**, 2003,
pen and acrylic on paper, 11 x 8½".

Fig. 88 *****, 2005, wood, fabric, contact paper, marker, hardware,
and paint; table 36 x 96 x 96", chairs 18 x 16 x 16".

Fig. 89 **ROOM 1**, 2005, mixed media, 55 x 30 x 8'. In collaboration
with Wynne Greenwood/Tracy + the Plastics. Installation view,
The Kitchen, New York, NY, 2005.

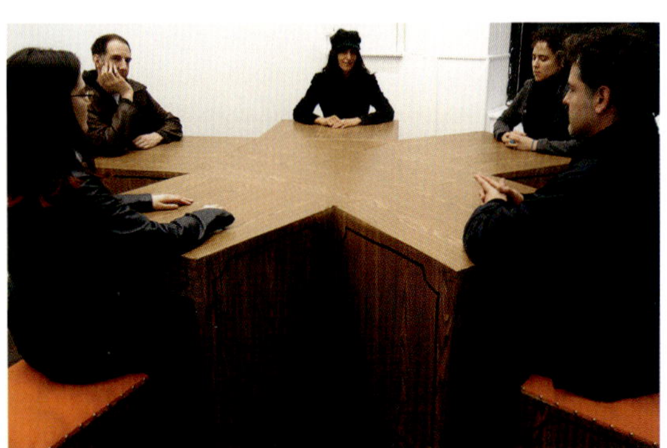

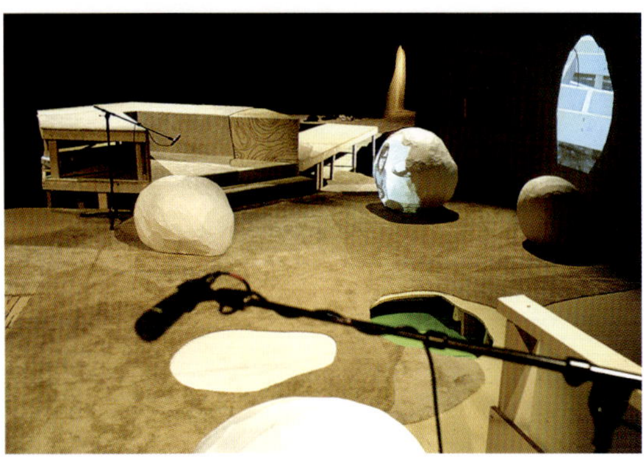

poke fun at Kosher rules, while simultaneously acknowledging them as one way of building a Jewish home. Krieger grew up in a home where pork and cheeseburgers were taboo, but where bacon was sometimes fried up on Sunday mornings, and here she pushes this kind of casual kosher observance as far as it can go.[2] Funny, colorful, and simple, the drawings belie a frisson of illicitness, flaunting the dietary laws of Kashrut as if to test whether something bad might happen in consequence.

An earlier work, *STACKED (study 1)*, 2003 (fig. 87), takes the notion of home building literally, envisioning slabs of bacon as one among many units in a complex imaginary structure. The drawing sketches a weird and impossible proposal out of associatively rich components, and its seemingly haphazard composition evidences an organizational principle central to Krieger's oeuvre. The scattered multiplicity evident in *STACKED (study 1)* abstractly illustrates the artist's investment in "non-hierarchical building," a concept that she explains favors the horizontal over the vertical, dispersion over centralization, exposed structures over those that conceal, and that draws inspiration from the utopian architecture of the 1960s as well as the animal architecture of bees and beavers.[3] The artist has explored this concept in various formats, from visionary drawings like *Capsule 1*, 2003, which diagrams a whimsical landscape of interconnected domes, to sculptural furniture like *, 2005 (fig. 88), which was designed as a conference table for The Generals, a programming committee at Art in General, the nonprofit exhibition space in Lower Manhattan. * radically reinvents the geometry of this office staple such that no one—or everyone—gets to sit at the head of the table, a fitting design for a radical, rotating curatorial panel made up not of curators but of artists.

A collaboration with musician Wynne Greenwood provided an opportunity for Krieger

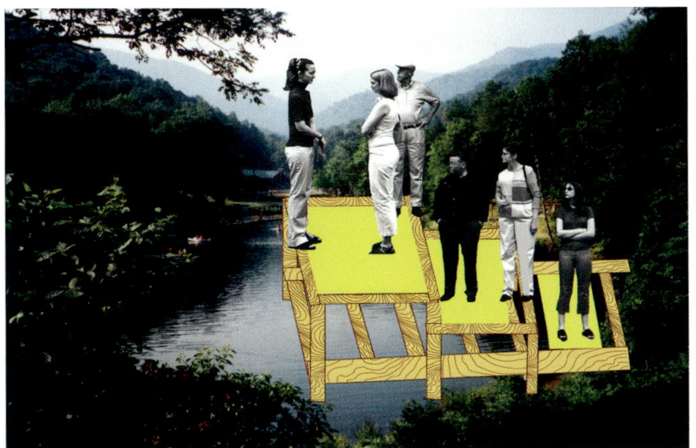

Fig. 90 **HOVER (lake 5)**, 2005, inkjet print mounted on Sintra, 12 x 18".

Fig. 91 **Home for Huck**, 2005, wood, fabric, floatation billets, and hardware, 96 x 120 x 60".

Fig. 92 **PLACE (study 4)**, 2005, acrylic, ink, and pen on paper, 9 x 10".

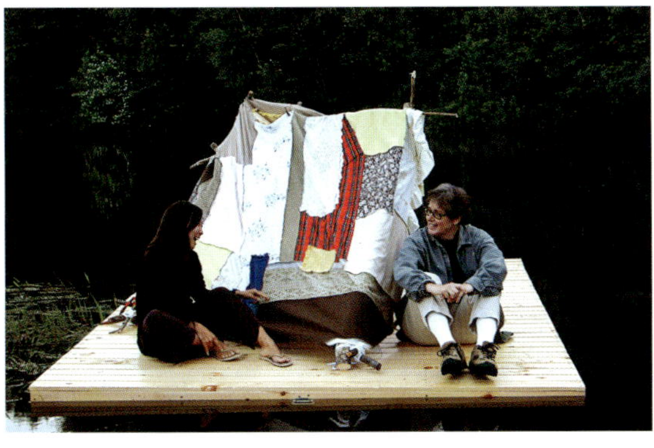

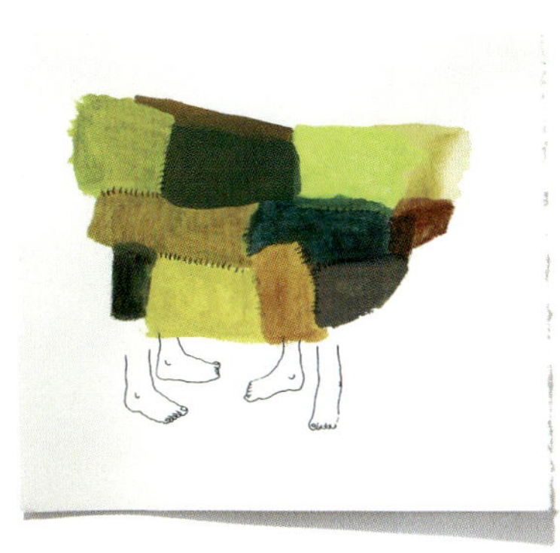

to expand her concept of non-hierarchical building on an environmental scale. Built as the set for Greenwood's art-punk band Tracy + the Plastics, *ROOM 1*, 2005 (fig. 89), was inspired by 1970s feminist consciousness-raising groups.[4] Covered in beige carpeting and filled with throw pillows, stage and seating merged into one continuous, sprawling milieu resembling a suburban living room. Viewers, free to sit anywhere, found themselves in the same space as the show, and therefore as part of a performance that insisted on active participation rather than passive spectatorship. "*ROOM* as a sculpture is not complete without its audience," Krieger has noted, pointing to the social component integral to many of her projects.[5] One doesn't view her art so much as take part in it, and though engagement involves interacting with the built form and the surrounding environment, of primary importance is the collective dialogue that can occur between individuals.

A group of interventions into nature, both visionary and realized, act as catalysts for these kinds of relational encounters. Krieger's series of "HOVER" collages envision spectator platforms afloat amid verdant mountains and lakes, offering a place for viewing beautiful American vistas but more so for encountering other folks (see fig. 90). Ironically, the figures Krieger pictures standing on these sculptural plateaus look disconnected and

touristy, like they're waiting for a bus, eliciting the gap that can exist between the use of a structure and its creator's best intentions. *In Home for Huck*, 2005 (fig. 91), Krieger physically realized one such intervention, installing a raft with a patchwork-and-log tent on a lake in Southern Vermont, where she had a residency. The homey tent, whose fabric was culled from the art center's linen closets, transforms the raft into an intimate space where artist residents can socialize with one another. Set in a scenic environment, the work's focus is less on the surrounding nature than on the social potential of the built structure, an emphasis highlighted in *PLACE (study 4)*, 2005 (fig. 92), a work on paper in which quilted tent and human parts humorously collapse into one hybrid body roughly forming a map of the United States. A home, after all, is only a house until it's inhabited by people.

—LORI WAXMAN

1. Krieger, in Lanka Tattersall, "Interview with Wynne Greenwood (Tracy + the Plastics) & Fawn Krieger," 2005, www.artwurl.org.

2. Krieger, in Mitchell Davis, "Treyf: Drawings by Fawn Krieger," The James Beard Foundation Calendar (November 4, 2004).

3. Krieger, in Tattersall, "Interview."

4. Pamphlet for *ROOM*, by Wynne Greenwood / Tracy + the Plastics & Fawn Krieger, The Kitchen, New York, NY, January 17–February 15, 2005.

5. Krieger, in Tattersall, "Interview."

Jin Meyerson

and, often as not, equally grand scale. Andreas Gursky tackles the globalized present in digitally enhanced, mural-size color photographs of sprawling architectural and commercial sites. Thomas Hirschhorn illustrates our hyper-mediated world through room-size installations containing overwhelming quantities of visual and textual information. Neither of these bodies of work depicts exactly what the world looks like—though sometimes they come uncannily close—rather they achieve a metaphorical embodiment of it, an impression of how we see and feel our greater surroundings. Jin Meyerson's oversize paintings participate in this challenging discourse, achieving through dizzying juxtapositions of abstract and illusionistic imagery a sense of the spectacular, chaotic simultaneity of today.

More references than can be counted pack the canvases in a group of paintings Meyerson created in 2005 and 2006 that weaves in and out of disasters, man-made and natural, at every turn. Buildings collapse, automobiles pile up, trains derail. Sometimes nature wreaks a kind of sci-fi havoc, as when the giant, crippling roots of *Family Tree*, 2006 (fig. 93), overtake a city block like some sort of alien from outer space. The disaster that hits closest to home, however, may be the one most obliquely represented. The title of *Tower*, 2005 (fig. 94), immediately recalls 9/11, but rather than depicting the Twin Towers Meyerson layers Mayan ruins, a banal European streetscape, a postmodern apartment building, stacks of scaffolding, and a bombed-out Gothic cathedral—all of them fallen or threatening to fall. The cross-cultural array of artistic, geographic, and temporal strata continues stylistically as he mimics black-and-white photography, lithography, photorealism, and abstract painting, quoting directly from the work of Mexican muralist Diego Rivera,

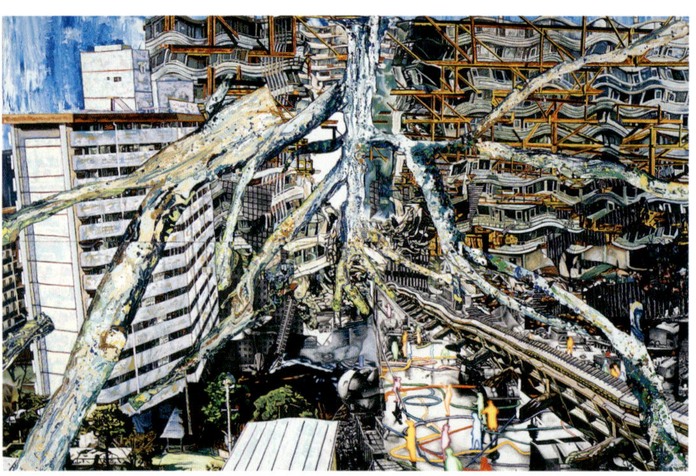

Fig. 93 **Family Tree**, 2006, acrylic and oil on canvas, 135½ x 210".
Vanhaerents Art Collection, Brussels, Belgium.

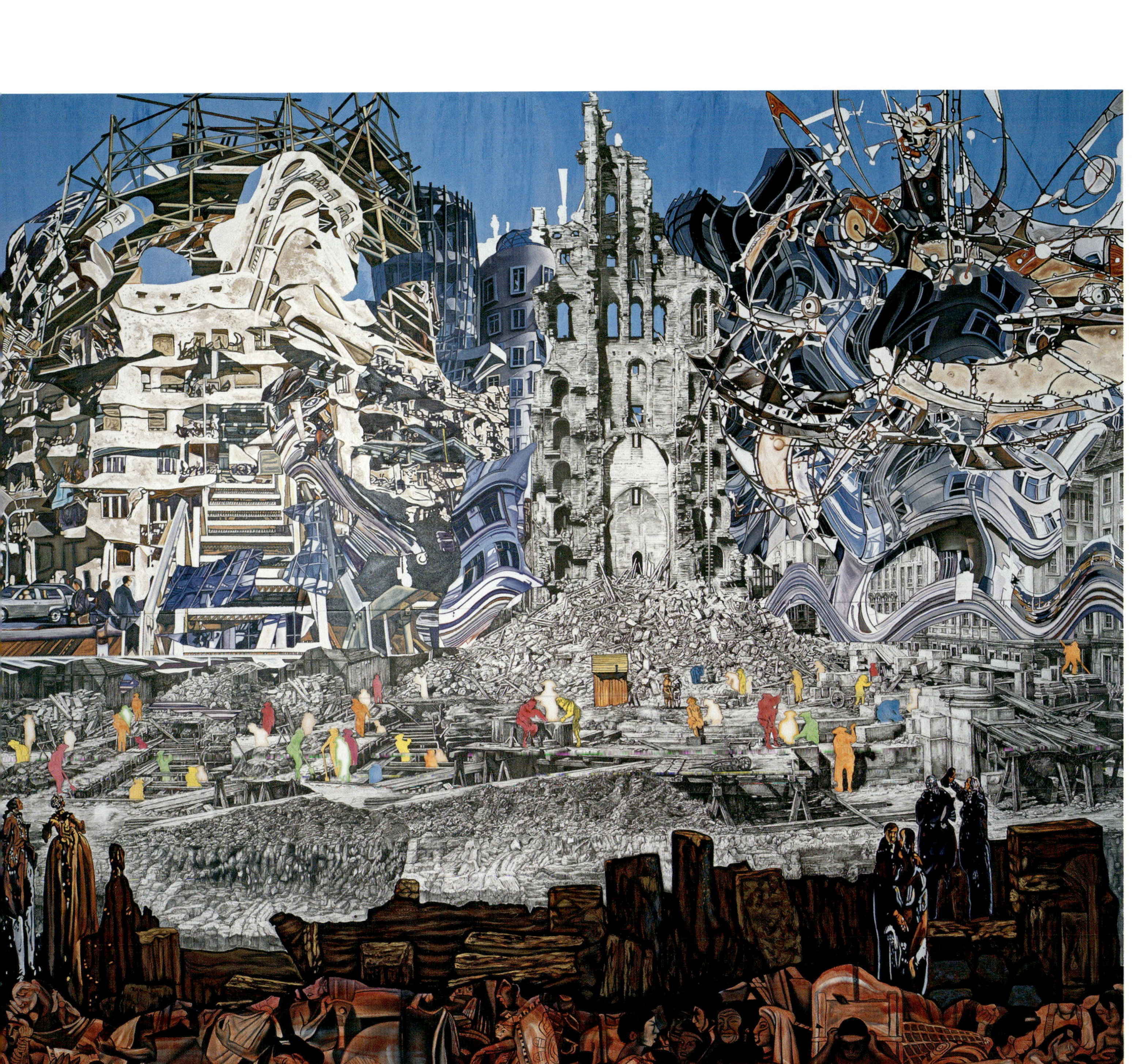

Fig. 94 **Tower**, 2005, oil, acrylic, and India ink on canvas, 139 x 144".
Ostrow Family Collection.

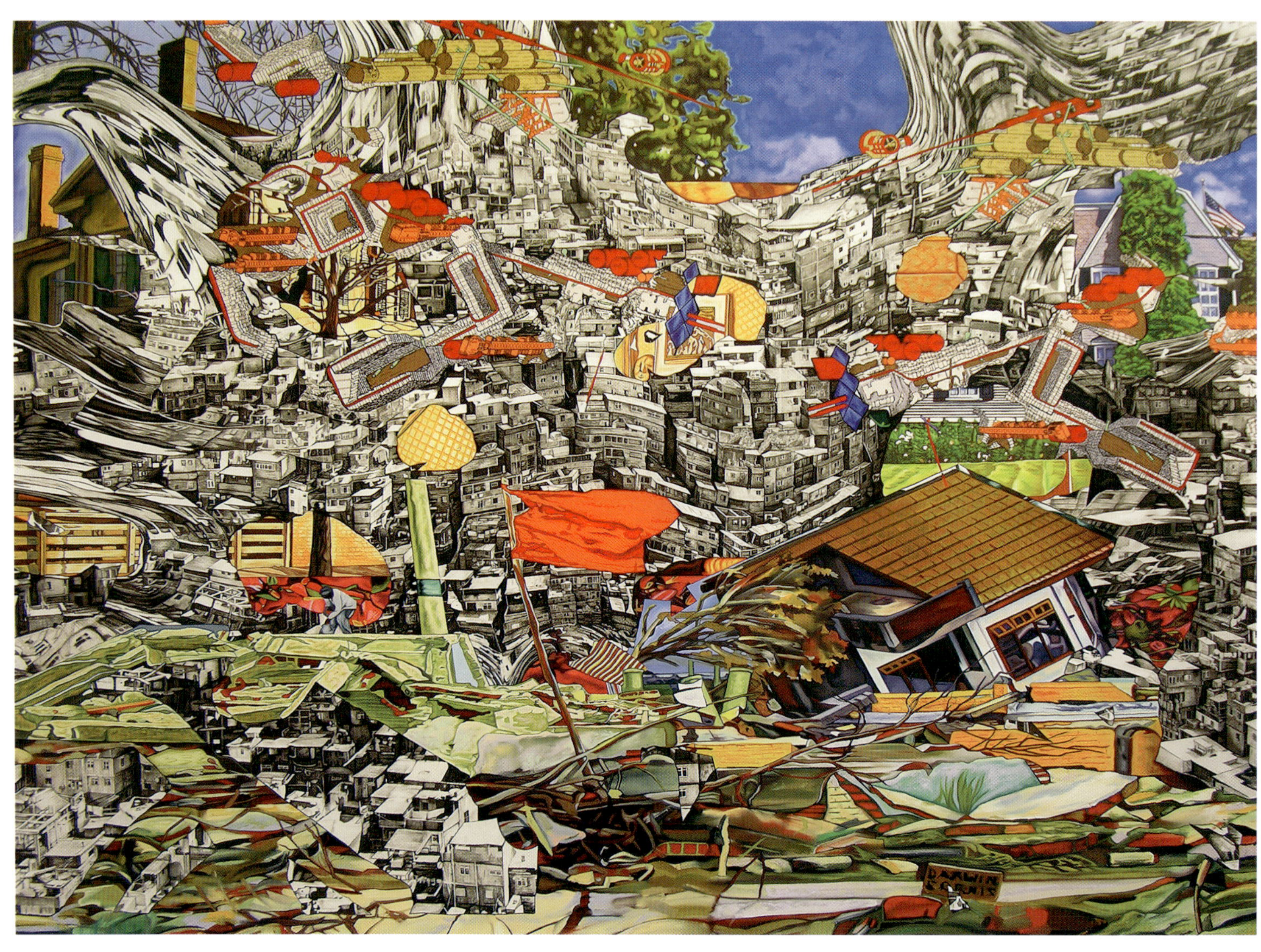

Fig. 95 **Landfall**, 2005, oil, acrylic, and India ink on canvas, 90 x 120".
Collection of Nicolas Rohatyn and Jeanne Greenberg Rohatyn.

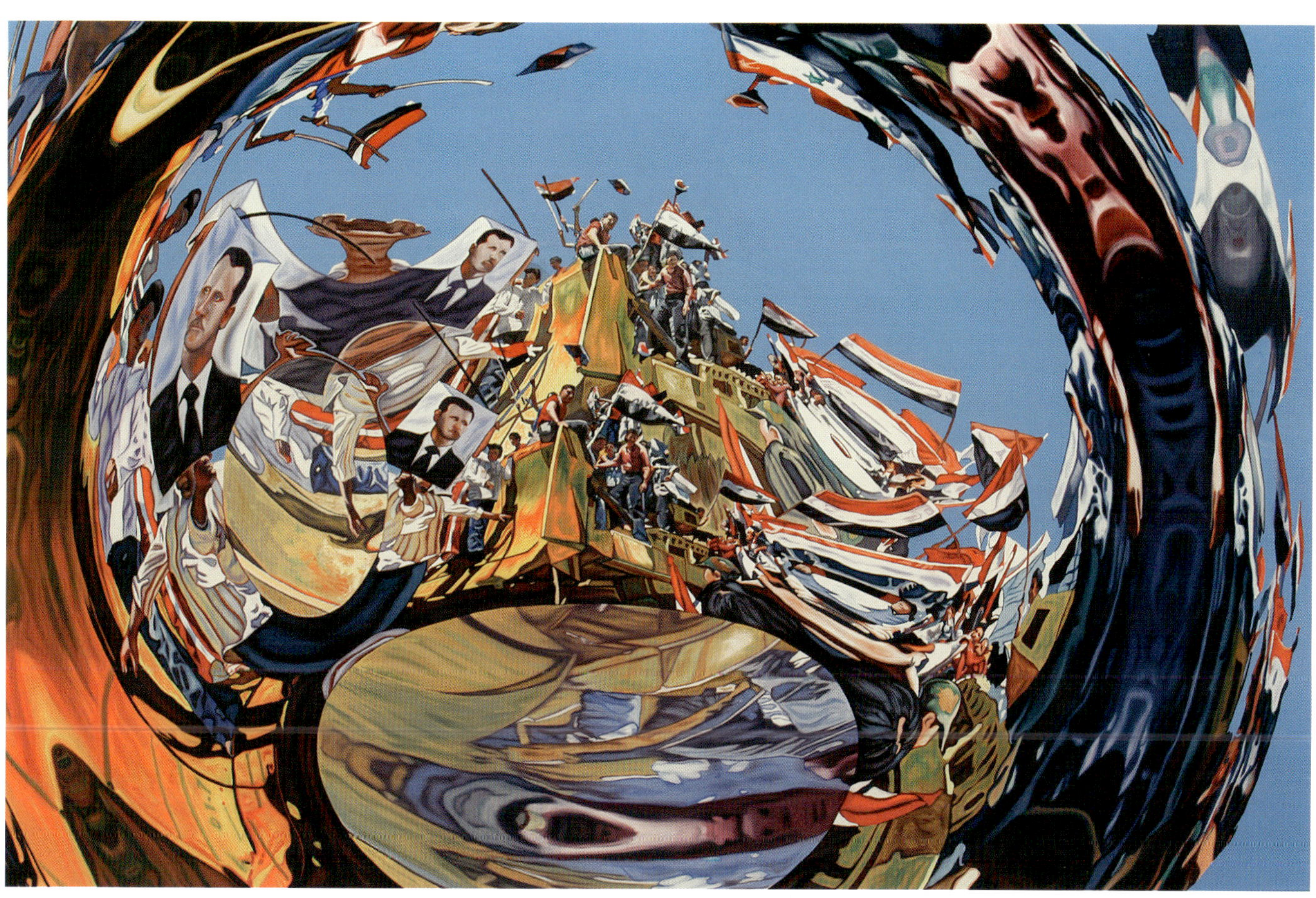

Fig. 96 **Norlevo**, 2005, oil and acrylic on canvas, 40 x 60".
Private Collection, Munich.

Fig. 97 **Untitled**, 2004, oil on panel, 30 x 30".
Collection of Carlos and Rosa de la Cruz.

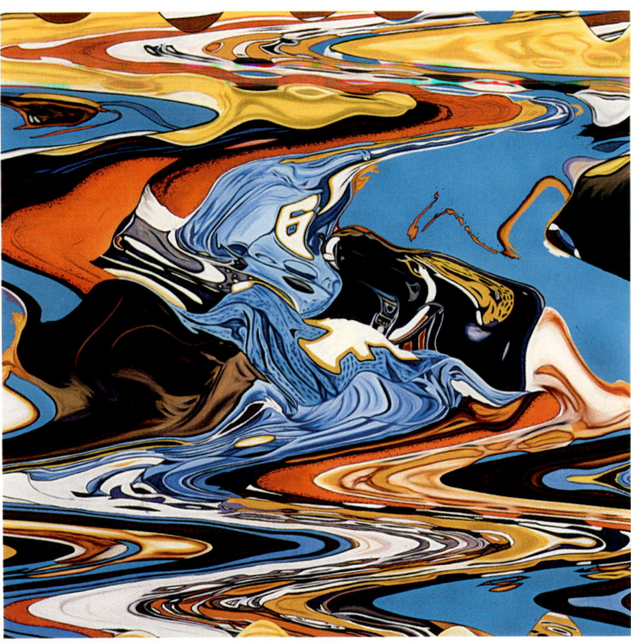

Fig. 98 **Bronx Science**, 2002, oil on board, 23 x 23".
Collection of Stavros Merjos and Honor Fraser.

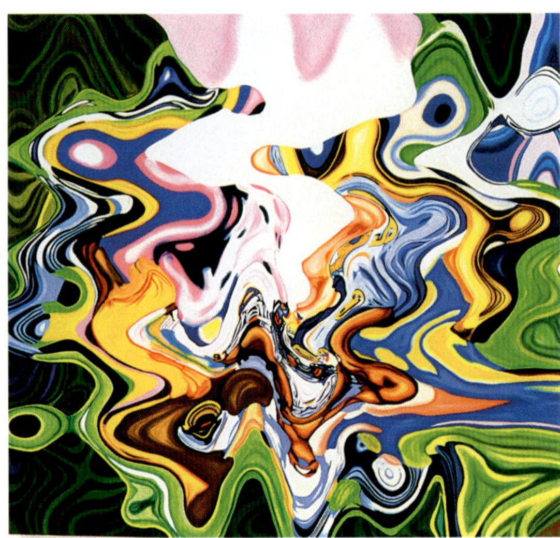

American sculptor Lee Bontecou, and
the young Berlin-based painter Daniel Richter.[1]
Peopled by eighteenth-century aristocrats,
day-glo construction workers, and contemporary urbanites, *Tower* seems almost too much
to take in—and it is. Nearly twelve feet tall,
the painting is frantically multi-referential, a
Tower of Babel that threatens at every moment
to come unhinged at the seams. The product
of a self-proclaimed "practicing visual junkie,"
Tower finds its match in Meyerson's own
biographic clash of cultures: Korean-born,
he is the adopted son of a Jewish New Yorker
and a Swedish Minnesotan.[2] His is the multi-
tasking, multi-cultural vision of the information
age, able to look toward the past, present,
and future at once.

Pictures compiled so densely from such
varied sources can be a challenge to make
sense of. Though his picture surfaces are unified
by a consistent, smooth facture, Meyerson's
battery of compositional tools otherwise
encourage destabilization and bewilderment.
The architectural fragments and foliage that
compose *Landfall*, 2005 (fig. 95), for instance,
seem to have been violently blown into place,
possibly by a hurricane, which gives no sign of
abating. Different spatial registers, from the
flatness of patterned elements to the illusionistic depth of a dense residential district,
negate the possibility of a unified point of view.
Elements abut one another in violent juxtapositions that echo the fast cuts of music
videos and advertising, but here layered into
a single plane that makes no obvious narrative
sense. Distortions abound, stretching,
squishing, or twisting photorealist depictions
into abstract ones. Sometimes the warping
takes a decidedly historic turn, as in *Norlevo*,
2005 (fig. 96), which offers a hallucinatory
glimpse of the world through mirror anamor-
phosis, a technique popularized in the Baroque
era whereby a cylindrical mirror placed over
a centrifugally dispersed picture makes
the distorted image legible. Of course, there's
no mirror here, and hence no resolution.

If Meyerson's recent paintings look to a web
of precise sources, in their moments of colorful
abstraction they seem to quote not from the
outside world but from his own earlier work,
in which kaleidoscopic effects dominate.
The web thickens, though, as even these earlier

Fig. 99 **Friendly Fire**, 2004, oil and acrylic on panel, 48 x 74".
The Saatchi Gallery, London.

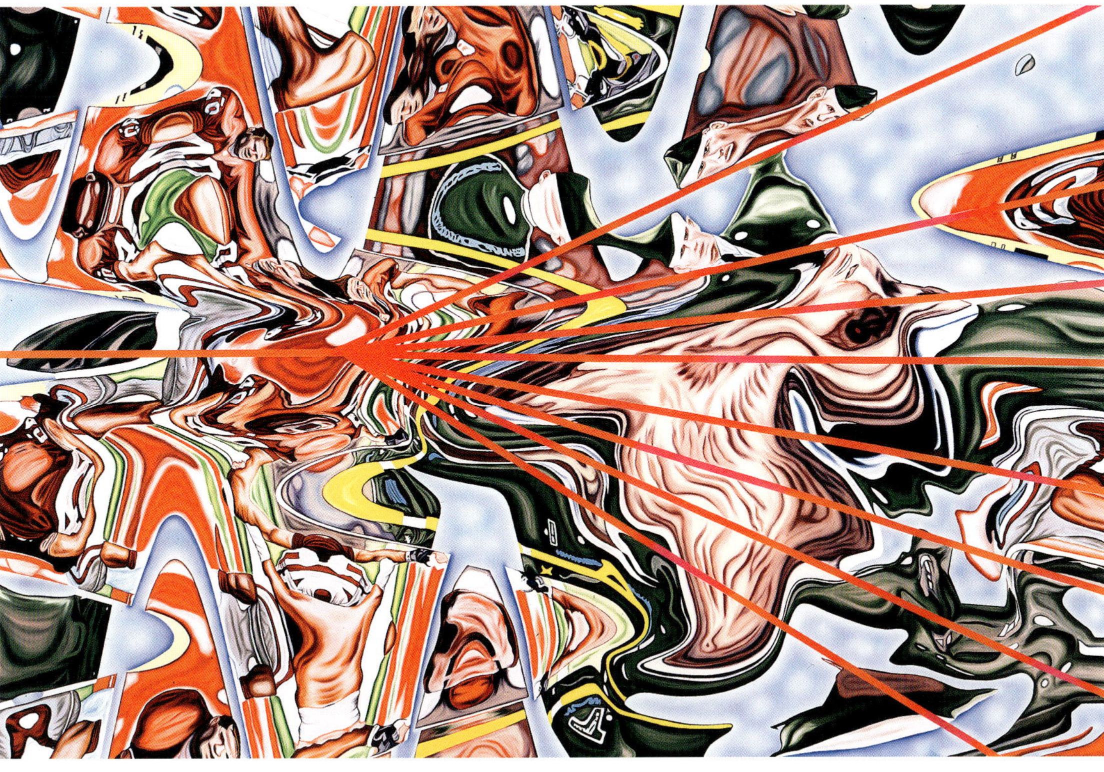

pictures derive from found visual material, however well masked through visual distortion. In *Untitled*, 2004 (fig. 97), for instance, waves of red, blue, white, and black undulate hypnotically like a reflection in a funhouse mirror, just barely revealing their origin in numbered football jerseys, helmets, and a pigskin. Previous works like *Bronx Science*, 2002 (fig. 98), and *Brooklyn Tech*, 2003, named for New York City public schools, eschew any pretense of legibility, using a psychedelic style and misleading titles to obfuscate the photographs of football games that were their starting point.[3] The effect is an all-out visual feast that pushes referentiality aside, but it's less hi-tech than it appears: though Meyerson now uses Photoshop to assemble his intricate collages, he obtained the warped morphology of these earlier works from repeatedly running his source imagery through a color copier and then painting from the results.[4]

Meyerson's trajectory from abstract to figurative modes of representation—in which optical illusion is replaced by distortion and fragmentation suggesting debris and destruction—makes us question how much distortion we can take and pushes the limits of our capacity for simultaneous looking. Which kind of image is most captivating? Is it one that obscures its subject matter, even when it is disturbing, as in *Friendly Fire*, 2004 (fig. 99), an abstract composition inspired by the death of an American soldier in Afghanistan? Or the one that puts it front and center, as do the more recent *Tower* and *Landfall*? Both strategies echo our contemporary hyper-mediated experience, where "truthiness" reigns over truth itself and too much information yields very little understanding. By progressively upping the ante at the level of both content and aesthetics, Jin Meyerson keeps us looking but also continually threatens to take that looking to the point of no return.
—LORI WAXMAN

1. Meyerson, conversation with the author, February 2, 2007; and Max Henry, "Jin Meyerson, 'High Cholesterol Moment'," *Time Out New York*, February 9–15, 2006, 70.

2. Meyerson, artist statement, March 31, 2003.

3. Meyerson, conversation with the author, February 2, 2007.

4. Ibid.

Collier Schorr

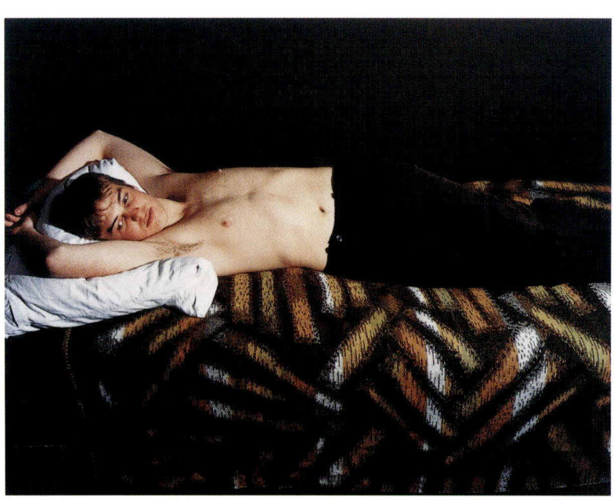

Fig. 100 **Forest Bed Blanket (Black Velvet)**, 2001, c-print, 35 x 44".

Fig. 101 **Bell Tower (H.T.)**, 2003, c-print, 44 3/4 x 33 3/4".

A beloved odalisque, topless and bathed in sunlight, emerges from the self-conscious pose of a soft-bodied boy. A teenage boy in American fatigues stands on a suburban street, which turns out to be in Germany, and the boy German. A verdant forest belies a landscape where helmets, buttons, and other Nazi insignia are buried. Neutrality holds no place in such pictures, only ambiguity. Gender flutters androgynously, nationality crisscrosses borders, time flows anachronistically, and history is retold in the telling. Photography, so dependent on fact yet so paradoxically well-suited to mixing it with fiction, finds an additional aptness here, a metaphorical one: just as the camera's object is seen through an adjustable lens, so Schorr pictures her many themes— masculinity, cultural memory, heroism, sexuality, to name a few—through shifting filters of desire, anxiety, fantasy, and difference.

Each of these filters must be understood expansively, such that desire, for one, retains its libidinous sense but also encompasses maternal, fraternal, and other connotations. The ongoing series "Jens F.," for instance (see fig. 100), for which Schorr has been photographing a German schoolboy in intimate, often feminine poses since 1999, revolves around desires, real and imagined, projected and assumed. Posed after the private pictures American painter Andrew Wyeth made of his neighbor Helga over the course of fifteen years, wherein Wyeth's every desire is embodied in his willing model, Schorr's "Jens F." disrupts the art-historical chain of desire built into depictions of women: the desire of the artist for the muse; the unknowable (yet often presumed) desires of the model; and the lust of the viewer to whom the images might appeal. Reversing the gender terms of Wyeth's project, as well as the historical artist-model relationship, radically tests but does not erase these

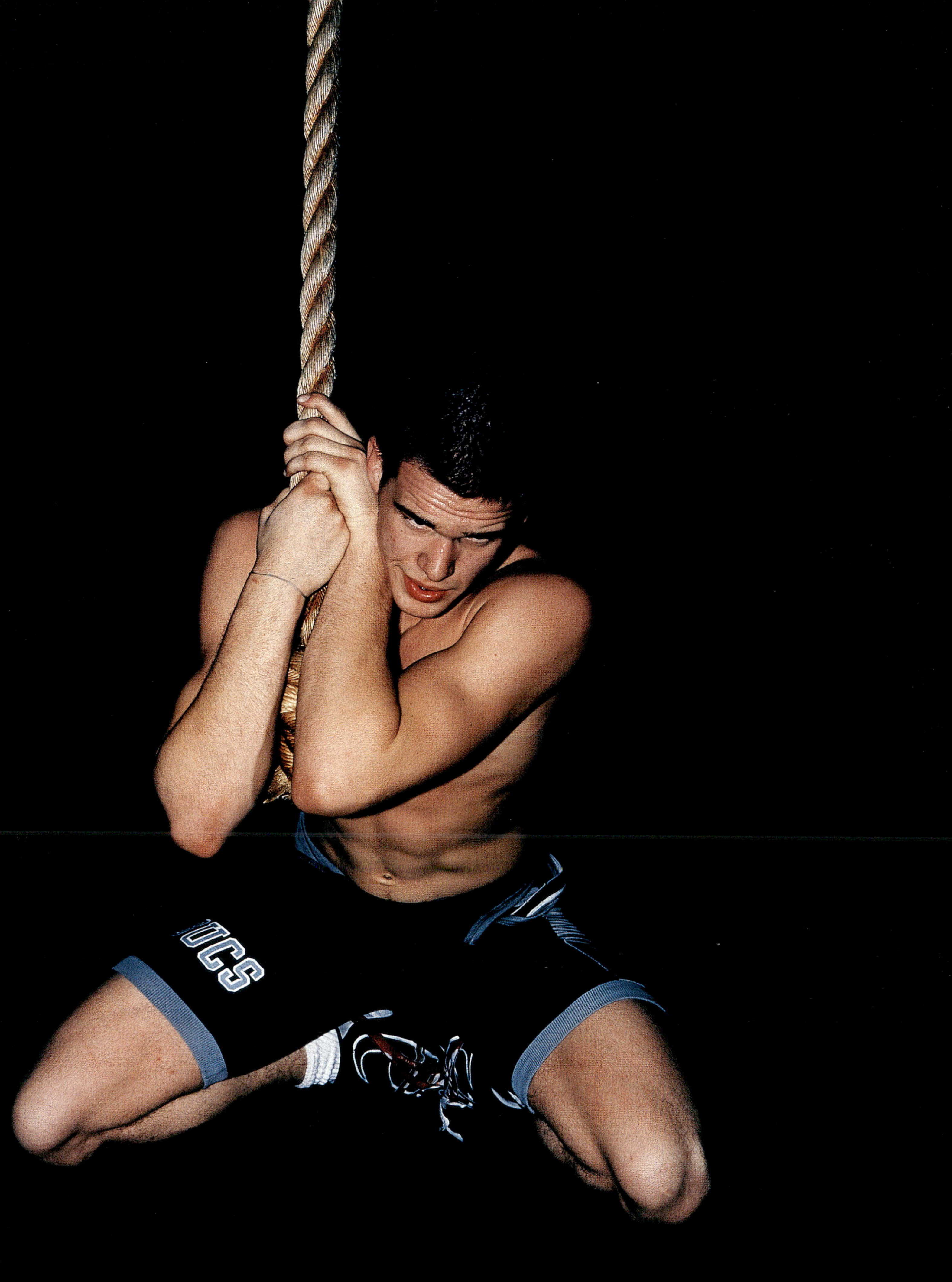
UCS

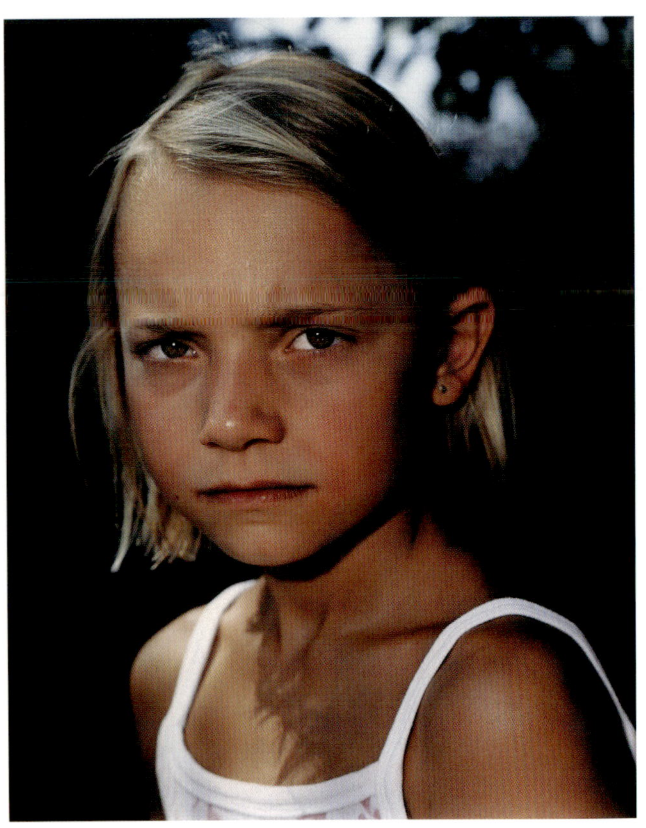

Fig. 102 **Laura**, 2004, c-print, 19 x 15".

Fig. 103 **Spielplatz (Lindenfeld)**, 1997, c-print, 20 x 28".

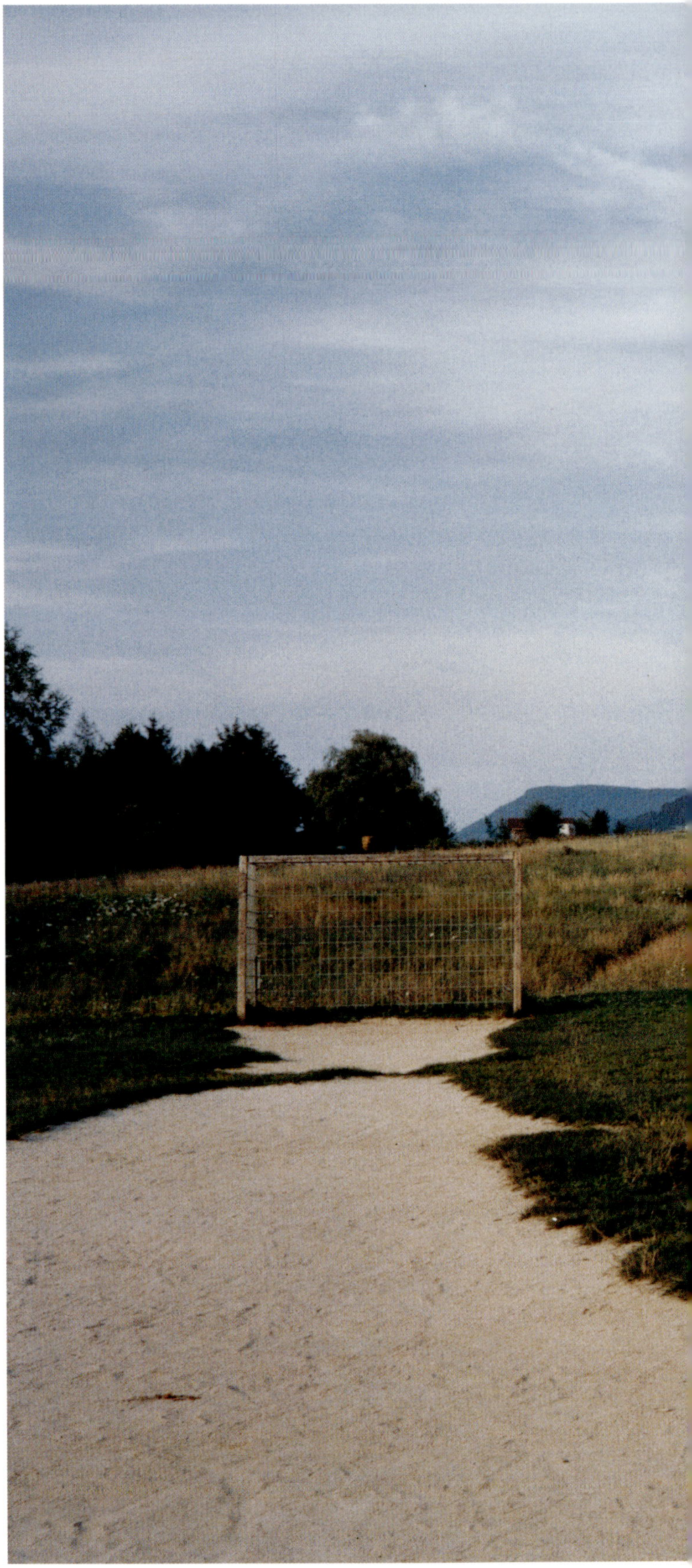

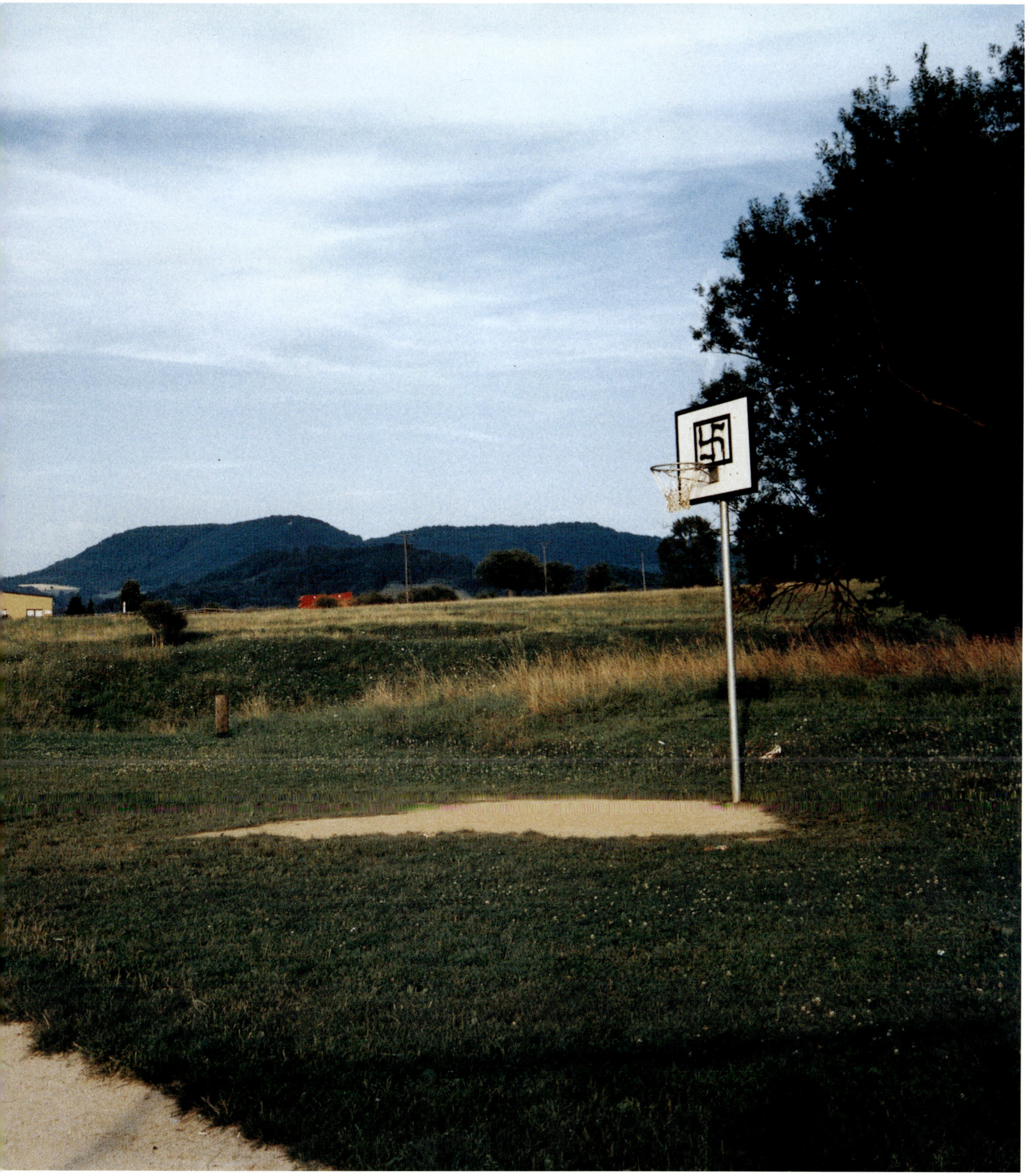

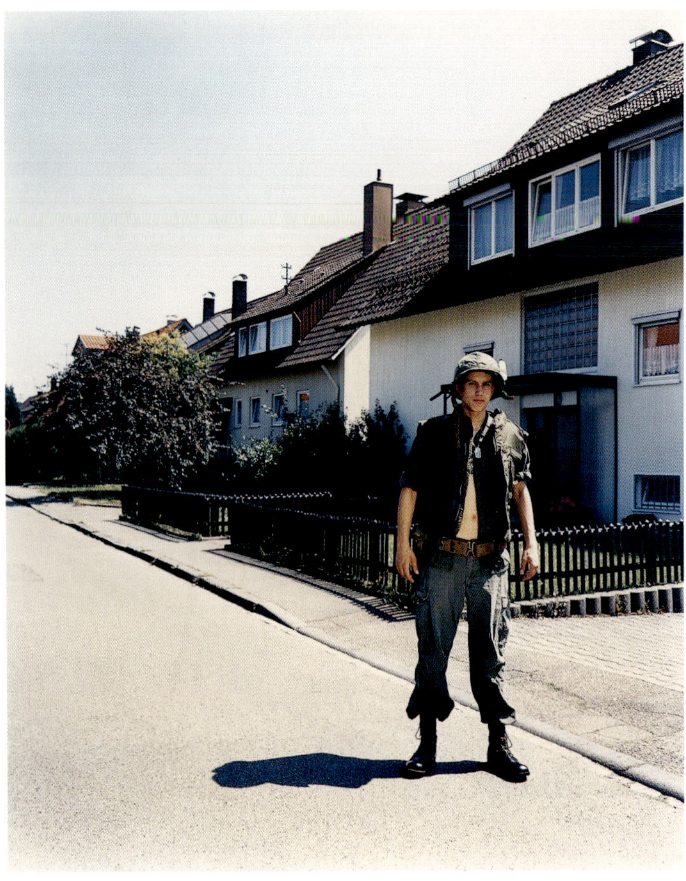

Fig. 104 **Matthew Occupation Barbarossastrasse**, 2001, c-print, 44 x 35".

Fig. 105 **Andreas POW (Every Good Soldier Was a Prisoner of War) Germany**, 2001, c-print, 39 x 28 ½".

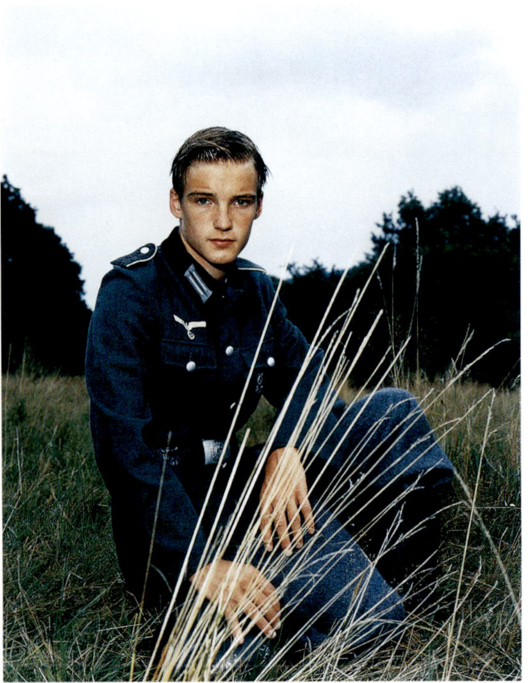

norms. Jens's body, soft when the series begins, changes and hardens over time, and Schorr's camera, on the surface at least, appears to study and possess it just as Wyeth's brush did Helga. In fact, the artist's intention was precisely to undercut the eroticism of the Helga images, as she notes: "I chose Jens F. because he looked like Helga and because he looked not like a typical erotic model. His body is probably the furthest thing from a typical pin-up or beauty shot. By picking such a model, I did not feel burdened by making images that were overly erotic or that granted objectification easily."[1]

Schorr's exploration of gender is joined by a deeper investigation of transformation in the group of pictures she has been making since 1998 of high school and collegiate wrestlers (see fig. 101). Working quickly at competitions and practices, Schorr orchestrates a chiaroscuro of shadow and light to isolate muscled, exhausted bodies into casually monumental poses that she associates with Catholic imagery like the Stations of the Cross.[2] The camera here chooses what it sees, intimately redrawing its vividly masculine object into a more nuanced, emotive, and sensual one, while also isolating and evoking the transcendental quality of ascetic religious practices in the punishing exercise, both mental and physical, in which the wrestlers engage.

The power to envision—to make visible—that which cannot otherwise be seen finds its fullest force in Schorr's images of young men emulating soldiers. For the past twelve summers the artist, who is a Brooklyn-born Jew, has been living in southern Germany, photographing a group of nephews and their friends as they try on and act out various militarized guises. The first of these finds the teenagers dressed in their own U.S. Army surplus (see fig. 104), a uniform to which Schorr later added yarmulkes to create what she calls hybrid American-Israeli soldiers. Fitted out as Americans, the German teenagers can play brave occupiers in a way that their own nation's historically compromised military garb does not allow. The pictures are not all heroic, however, and the more introspective ones begin to confront the myth of the Aryan soldier, a challenge Schorr met head on when in 2000 she gave the

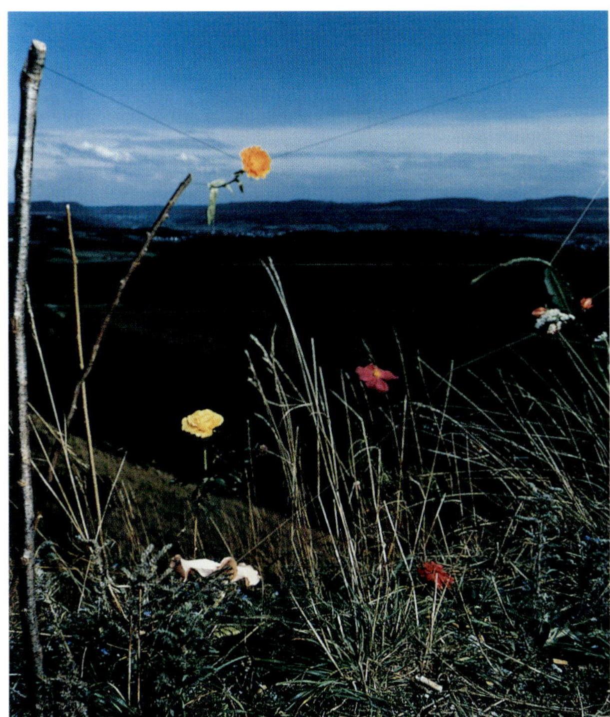

Fig. 106 **Arrangement #4 (Blumen)**, 2005, c-print, 38 5/8 x 31".

Fig. 107 **Hütte**, 2005, gelatin silver print, 34 x 44".

boys replica Nazi uniforms to wear. Dressed as the Wehrmacht, the boys pose in black-and-white and color images with attitudes that range from submissive to bucolic to confrontational. Schorr has said that in images such as *Andreas POW (Every Good Soldier Was a Prisoner of War) Germany*, 2001 (fig. 105), and *Steffen, Barbarostrasse, Garden*, 2001 (fig. 6), she was aiming "to create a vision of a German soldier that wasn't all powerful."[3] In so doing, however, her photographs perform a kind of double duty. They offer a means of emasculating what the artist has called "the Jewish girl's boogeyman,"[4] but they simultaneously recreate an effaced history, standing in for photographs that have disappeared from government halls and family photo albums, including, importantly, the boys' own. "They just never get to see this stuff," Schorr has said about the Wehrmacht costumes, "they only see it in movies."[5]

The ongoing series "Forests and Fields," begun in 1995, combines Schorr's photographs of soldiers, real and role-playing, with landscapes and portraits of her family and neighbors in Southern Germany (see figs. 102–107). Taken together, the series offers a partly fictional, partly documentary portrait of a small town and its past. Pictures of boys in Nazi costumes appear alongside those of young men newly conscripted into the Bundeswehr (the present-day federal forces), contradicting the widespread insistence that the German armies of World War II and today are thoroughly distinct. Juxtaposing these portraits with

landscapes, which seem idyllic but are often as not compromised by graffiti or manipulation, unsettles the lore of *Blut und Boden* (blood and soil), the traditional identification of Germans with their land that was exploited by the Third Reich. The inclusion of boys dressed in Vietnam-era American surplus also points to an unexpected shared history, as both Nazi soldiers and Vietnam vets returned home after their respective wars as something very far from heroes.

Time plays a peculiar role in many of the photographs from "Forests and Fields." Some seem pulled from the pages of history, others from a roll of film shot yesterday. Given that Schorr has worked with a core group of figures over many years, we see the boys grow older and their bodies and expressive repertoires mature. Something less obvious also happens, as many of Schorr's photographs of soldiers take on new resonance in the face of a changing world, where young boys in American uniforms—and German ones too— are now deployed around the globe in droves, unimaginably, once again.

—LORI WAXMAN

<hr>

1. Schorr, e-mail correspondence with Staci Boris, February 20, 2007.

2. Ibid.

3. Schorr, in Michael Wang, "An Interview With Collier Schorr," *Harvard Photography Journal* 9 (2006); online at www.hcs.harvard.edu/hpj/schorrinterview.htm.

4. Schorr, in "German Brutality and Roman Sensuality: Pictures of Soldiers in the Landscape," *Art:21* season 2, episode 6 (PBS); online at www.pbs.org/art21/artists/schorr/clip1.html.

5. Schorr, in Wang, "Interview."

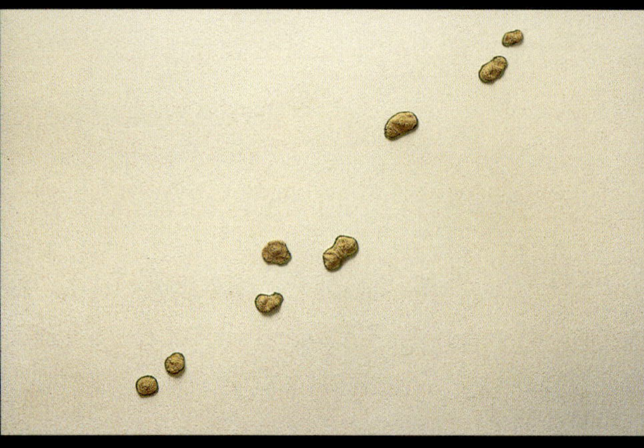

Fig. 108 **Islands**, 1996, cotton thread, approximately 1 x 1 1/2 x 1/2" each.

Fig. 109 **Islands** (detail), 1996.

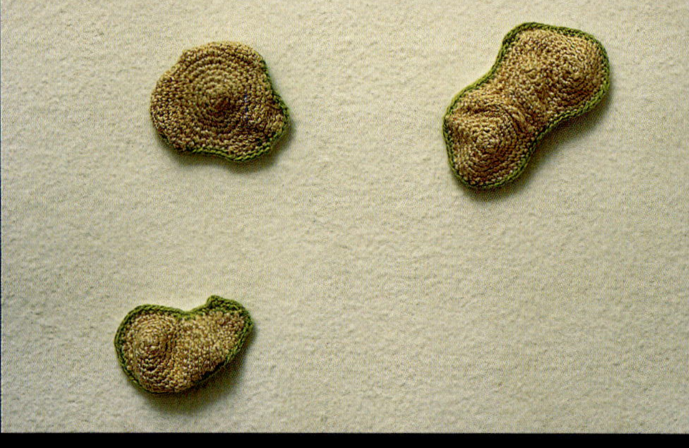

Her attention to process, materiality, and the handmade reflects an attitude toward art-making that refuses to distinguish between high and low, fine art and kitsch. By asking questions like "What does it mean to be able to weave a really good potholder or to make a really good key chain?"[1] Schwartz elevates items traditionally considered useless, insignificant, or inappropriate to a high art context. The artist's breadth of media and materials is equally egalitarian. Using sculpture, drawing, installation, performance, and video, Schwartz carries out darkly humorous investigations into the personal meaning objects acquire once they enter the home. Recalling Freudian notions of the uncanny (that which is "un-homely"), Schwartz's work examines how psychologically loaded these possessions can become.

Many of the sculptures Schwartz produced in the 1990s were inspired by memories of her youth. The origin of *Islands*, 1996 (figs. 108 and 109), for instance, lies in the artist's experience at Jewish summer camp in the 1970s, where she and her female friends were taught to crochet *kippot*, or skullcaps, for the boys. Hung in the formation of an archipelago, the misshapen kippot in *Islands* offer a feminist critique of "women's work," while implying that one can feel isolated, like an island, even within a group. Composed of the artist's weight in wax, *Self-Portrait as an Aromatherapy Candle*, 1999 (fig. 110), alludes to the type of do-it-yourself craft project Schwartz recalls undertaking at the kitchen table in her family's home in suburban Skokie, Illinois. The colorful layers of wax refer to the stripes that seemed to adorn everyone's bedroom walls but hers, speaking to a longing typical of teenage girls, namely the desire to fit in. The sculpture also suggests the passage of time, both in its formal resemblance to geological layers of rock and given the conceptual notion that, being a candle, it has a limited lifespan.

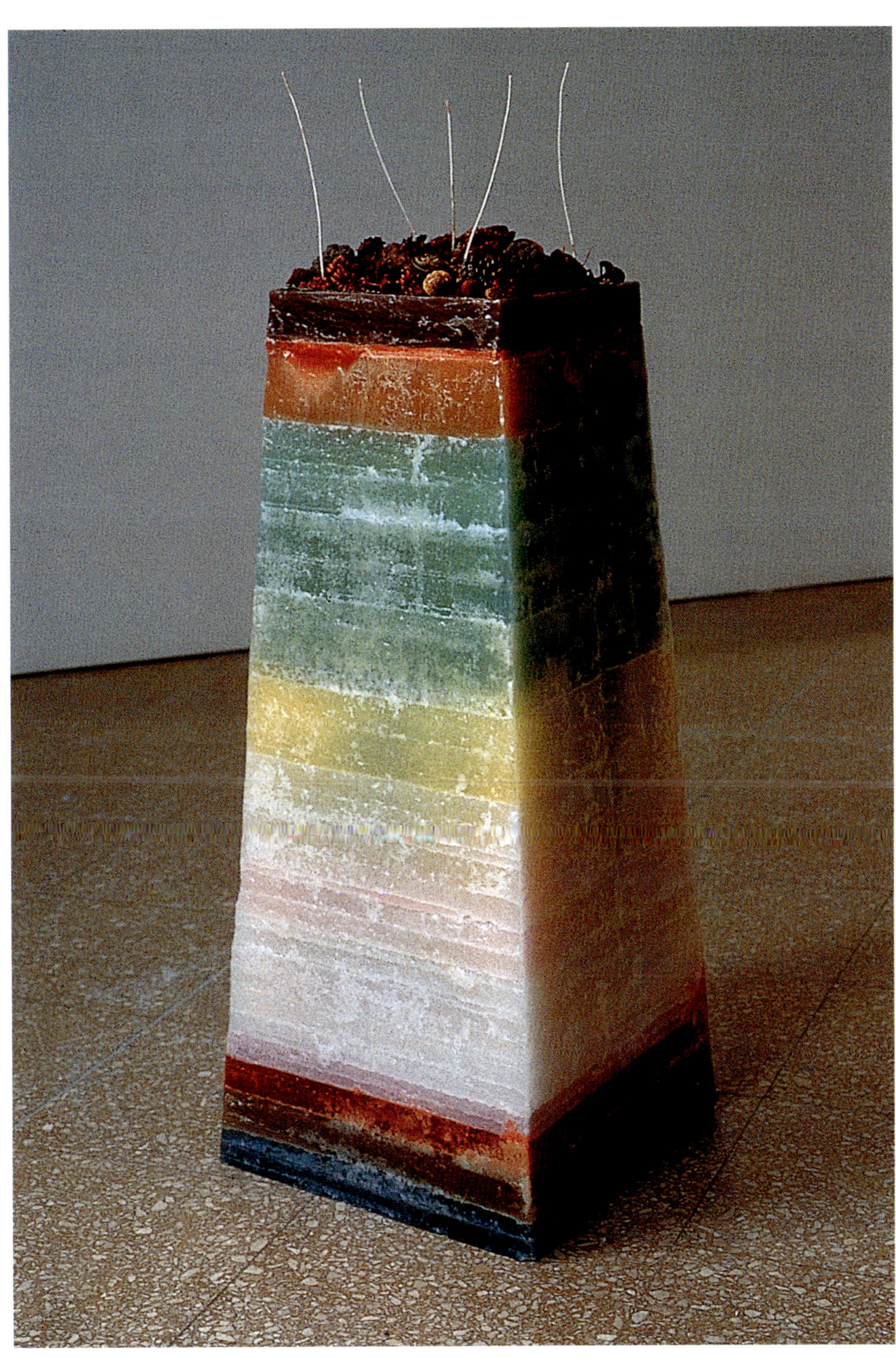

Fig. 110 **Self-Portrait as an Aromatherapy Candle**,
1999, artist's weight in wax, essential oils, potpourri, and wicks, 40 x 13 x 13".

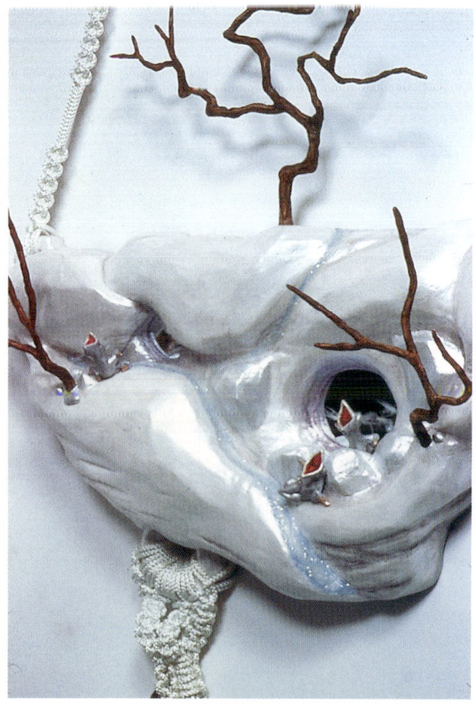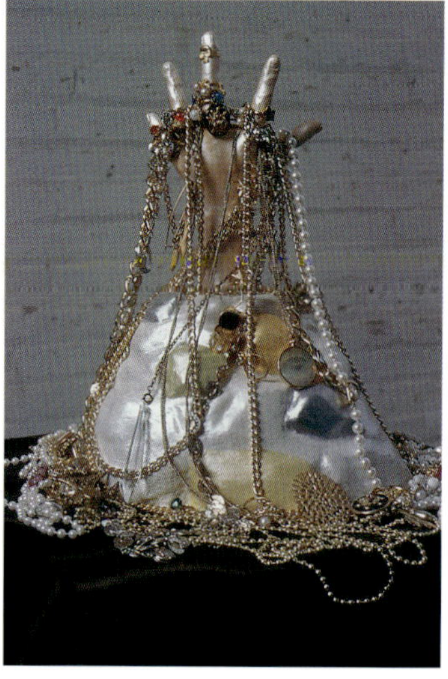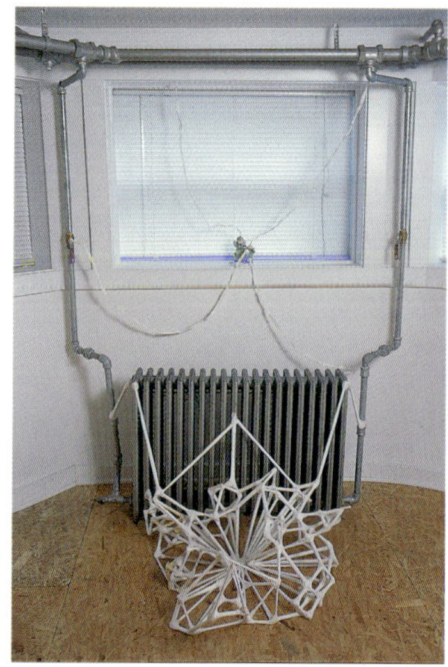

While the feelings these objects evoke are poignant, Schwartz's more recent work evinces darker threats and fantasies. *After Falling from Their Nest, Baby Birds Land on the Face of a Cliff. Confused and Weary, Their Lives Hang in the Balance*, 2004 (fig. 111), illustrates what the artist imagines happens when "the mundane objects in a domestic space [absorb] the emotional life and personal history of the people around them."[2] The opalescent sheen of the piece simulates the surface of porcelain collectibles, and the construction resembles that of the macramé plant holders commonly hung in 1970s living rooms. But creepy, bare branches rise from where one would expect to find a healthy plant, and a barren, rocky landscape exists where nutritious soil should be. Abandoned baby birds screaming to be fed complete the tableau, transforming an everyday object into a repository of dysfunction. *Zombie Hand with Treasure*, 2005 (fig. 112), represents "an excess, a distortion, or something formless that has attached itself to a memory."[3] In contrast to the delicate, passive, hand-shaped ring holder on which it was modeled, Schwartz's horror-movie version reaches up from a rocky grave, straining to grab whatever happens to cross its path. The greedy, disembodied form, restrained by its layers of plastic rings,

necklaces, and pendants, is reminiscent of a childhood dress-up fantasy gone awry.

Schwartz's site-specific installations convey an even more comprehensive inclination toward the anthropomorphic and the narrative. Capturing the spirit a child attaches to inanimate things, works like *Fairy*, 2005 (fig. 113), and *Macramé Intervention: Plant to Scratching Post to Ottoman*, 2006 (fig. 114), envision the life objects lead when no one is watching. In *Fairy*, a radiator, strewn with stretches of tape, seems to ponder abandoning its rigid metal shell to become as light and ever-expanding as the weblike tangle that sits before it. The tape streamers magically ensnare a dainty fairy figurine, maybe out of jealousy that the statuette can be carried anywhere in the house. Or perhaps it is the fairy who, out of boredom, has enchanted the radiator, prompting it to spawn a distorted, entangled version of itself. In *Macramé Intervention*, an unsatisfied macramé plant holder with imperialist leanings engulfs a series of helpless household objects resting nearby. The tension between the decorative floral design of the macramé rope and the sense of entrapment generated by its mutant extensions is palpable. Both works evoke a sort of ongoing, secret dissatisfaction that borders on malaise. The incorporation of

Fig. 111 **After Falling from Their Nest, Baby Birds Land on the Face of a Cliff. Confused and Weary, Their Lives Hang in the Balance** (detail), 2004, mixed media, 60 x 30 x 7".

Fig. 112 **Zombie Hand with Treasure**, 2005, wood, foam, resin, clay, and plastic jewelry, 16 x 10 x 9".

Fig. 113 **Fairy**, 2005, paper, tape, papier maché, and fairy collectible, dimensions variable. Installation view, Guest Room Project, Chicago, IL, 2005.

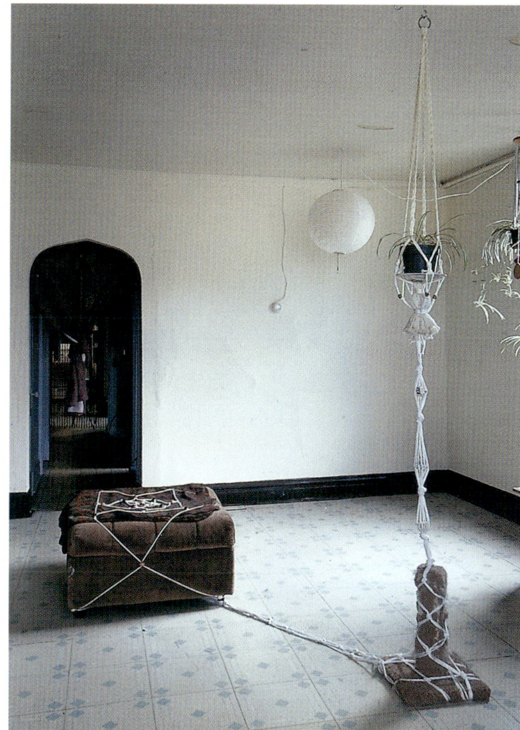

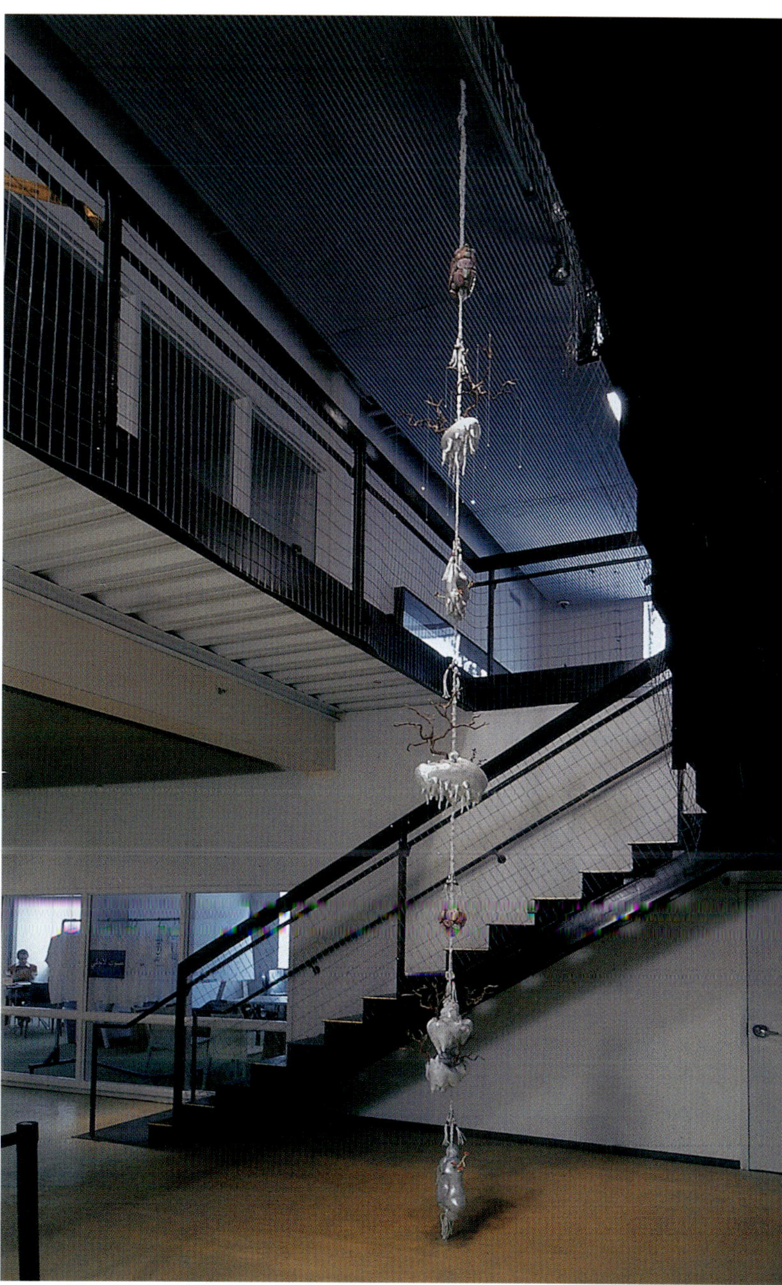

Fig. 114 **Macramé Intervention: Plant to Scratching Post to Ottoman**, 2006, mixed media, dimensions variable. Installation view, The California Occidental Museum of Art (COMA), Chicago, IL, 2006.

common, readymade objects into these pieces, atypical of the artist's oeuvre, suggests that any home can be infected.

Pushing Up the Daisies, 2006 (fig. 115), combines Schwartz's favorite themes, images, and processes into one foreboding yet humorous piece. Hung from the ceiling like a grand chandelier (albeit one that would adorn the *Addams Family* foyer), the work is made up of three sculpted frozen landscapes, two cutesy rose figurines, and two formations that resemble Chinese scholars' rocks, dispersed along a macraméd tendril of rope. Although the vertical format recalls Chinese landscape paintings, the mood is one of alarm and unease, rather than calm contemplation. The root structures of the trees are visible, as if the earth has been eroded by landslides or earthquakes. Crystal "tears" hang from barren tree branches. Red, bloodlike stains mysteriously mar the ground's milky iridescent patina. Against all odds, cartoonish flowers sprout from craggy rock formations. A hint of optimism or, as the title suggests, an indication that someone, or something, is buried beneath the permafrost? Schwartz leaves it up to the viewer's own overly active imagination.

—SARAH GILLER NELSON

Fig. 115 **Pushing Up the Daisies**, 2006, mixed media, 264 x 22 x 18". Installation view, Hyde Park Art Center, Chicago, IL, 2006.

---

1. Schwartz, in Phyllis Bramson, Deva Maitland, and Mindy Rose Schwartz, "Artists Trade Tape," *mouth to mouth* (Summer 2003), 19.

2. Schwartz, artist statement, 2006.

3. Schwartz, "Artists Trade Tape," 17.

Ludwig Schwarz

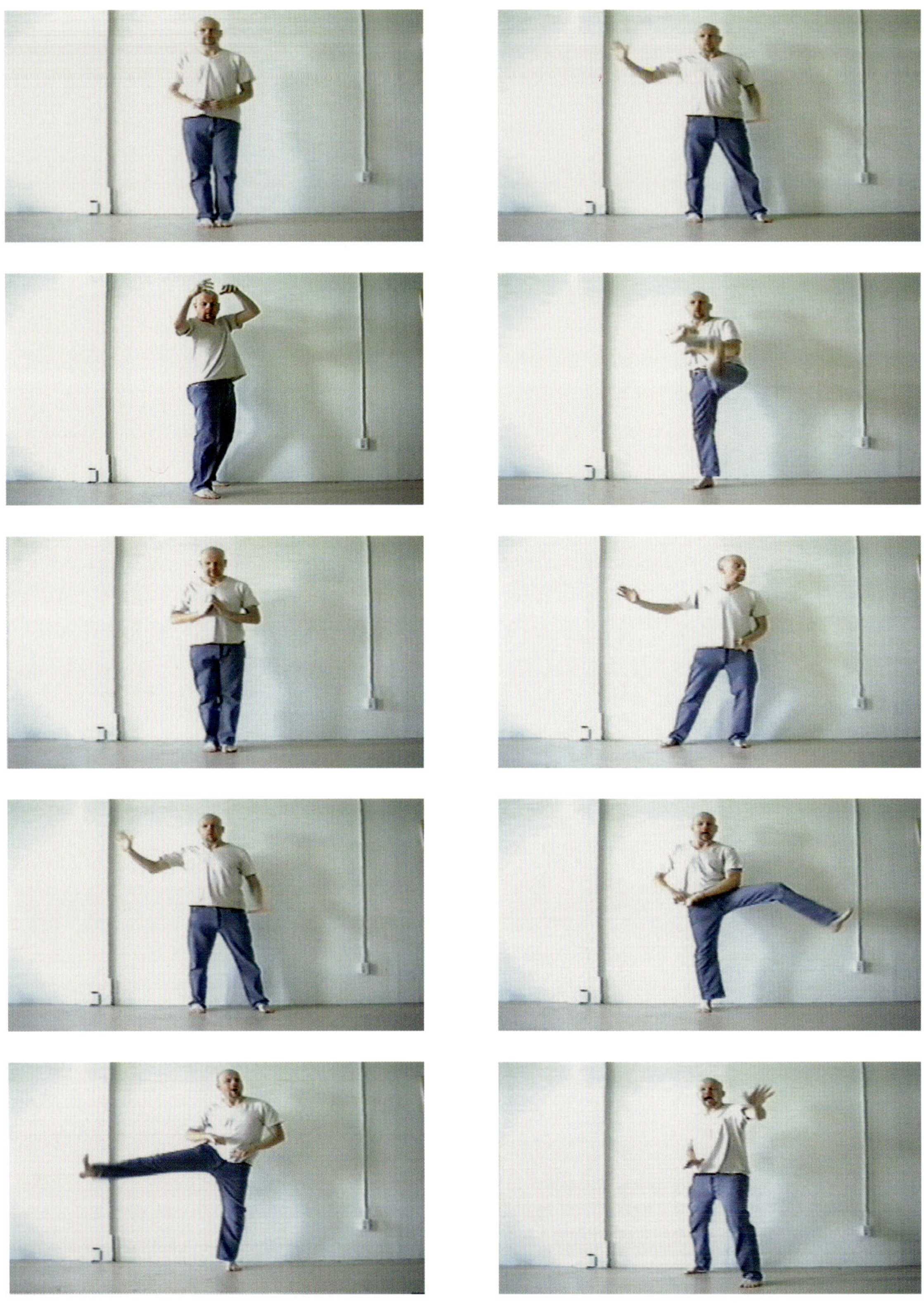

Fig. 116 **Great Moments in Painting Number Three**, 1999, stills from a video, 1:44 minutes.

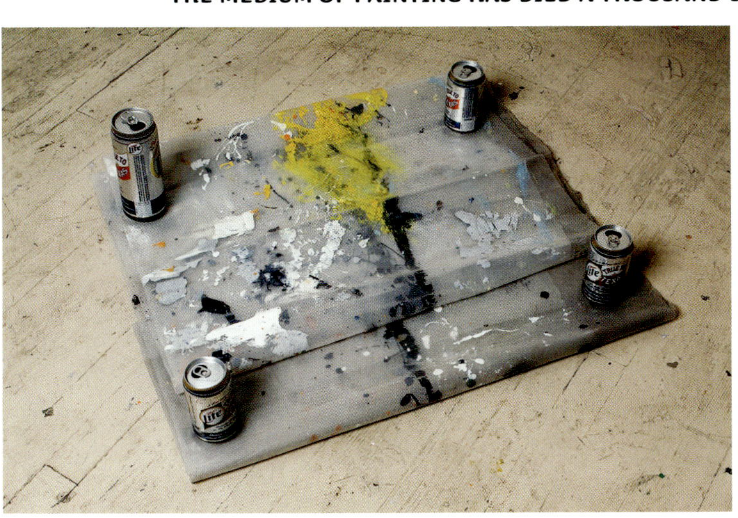

Fig. 117 **Great Moments in Painting Number Four**, 1999, plastic, paint, and beer cans, dimensions variable.

THE MEDIUM OF PAINTING HAS DIED A THOUSAND DEATHS. PHOTOGRAPHY AND FILM STRIPPED IT of its documentary primacy. The Russian Constructivists could find no place for it in a socialist society. The Mexican muralists deemed it antirevolutionary. Greenbergian modernism reduced it to an increasingly academic formalist endgame. And then 1980s poststructuralist theory dismissed it for being elitist and hand-made, among other complaints. Painting is perhaps the most fraught of contemporary artistic activities, a practice replete with the baggage of objecthood, commodification, decorativeness, preciousness, representation, and so on and so forth, ad infinitum. It's a quandary recognized by any critical painter working today, and artist Ludwig Schwarz is no exception. "I love to paint," he has said, "but painting is dead. Again."[1]

What's a painter to do? The body of work Schwarz has created over the past two decades features a variety of speculative situations meant to keep painting alive, if not always well. The series "Great Moments in Painting," 1996–1999, runs the gamut of these experiments. For *Great Moments in Painting Number Two,* 1996, he displayed six monochromes stacked one in front of the other, with only the outermost canvas visible; the remaining five could be viewed exclusively on an eponymous Web site, whose URL (www.greatmomentsinpaintingnumbertwo.com) was prominently printed on an adjacent wall. *Great Moments in Painting Number Three*, 1999 (fig. 116), consists of a video in which Schwarz attempts a succession of martial arts moves in a confined space meant to mimic the physical limits of the canvas surface and frame. Finally, *Great Moments in Painting Number Four*, 1999 (fig. 117), incorporates a paint-spattered plastic sheet, the kind used to line a studio floor, folded up on the ground and weighted down with beer cans on each of its four corners. Like the series title itself, these works mock the very

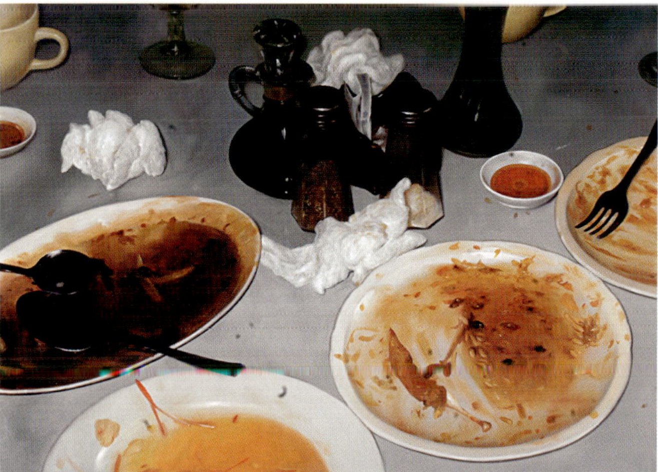

Fig. 119 **Untitled (Still Life With Chicken Wing)**, 2003, oil on canvas, edition 1/4 (painted in China), 52 x 72".

Fig. 120 **Untitled (Family Portrait)**, 2005, eight paintings, crates, two-channel video, TV monitor console, hand truck, found boxed sets, and miscellaneous documentation, dimensions variable. Installation view, Arthouse at the Jones Center, Austin, TX, 2005.

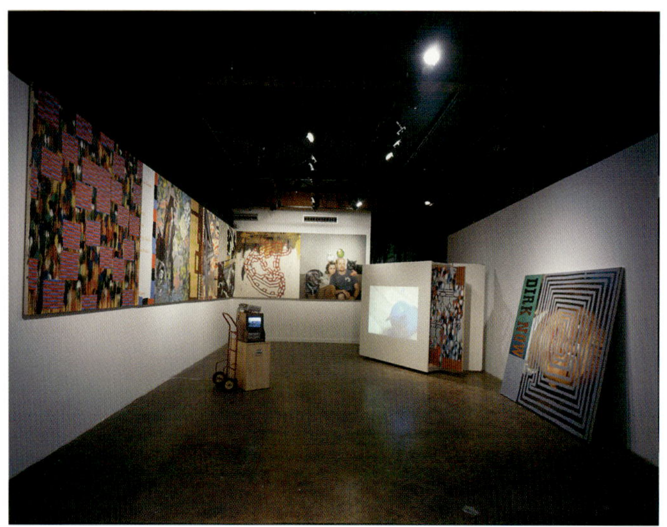

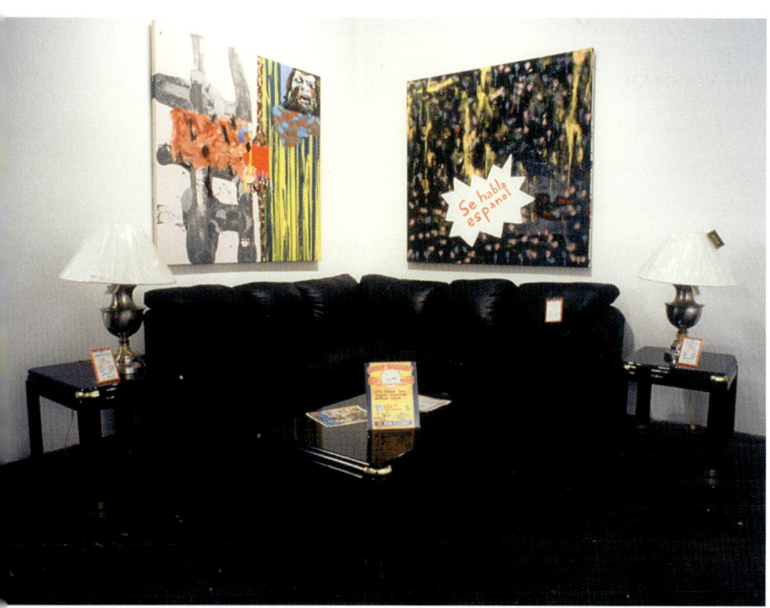

Fig. 121 **Rentown**, 2001, nine paintings and home furnishings, dimensions variable. Installation view, Angstrom Gallery, Dallas, TX, 2001.

Fig. 118 **Untitled (Middle of the Road)**, 2003, oil on canvas, edition 1/4 (painted in China), 72 x 72".

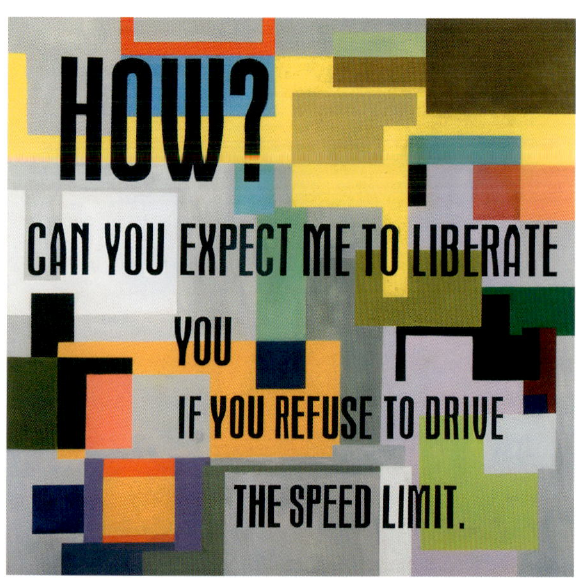

possibility of a great moment in painting while secretly hoping that they might, in fact, be it.

Another of Schwarz's strategies has involved the outsourcing of his production to China. Between 2002 and 2005, he sent JPEGs of artwork to the city of Shenzhen, where a burgeoning industry of skilled artists turn out cheap reproductions for the world market in an assembly-line version of individual craft. Schwarz has had a variety of images replicated, including digital collages and drawings like *Untitled (Middle of the Road)*, 2003 (fig. 118); photographs of his quotidian environment; altered photographs of his wife and pets, as in *Untitled (Wiggles #2)*, 2003 (fig. 1); and photographs of meals he has eaten, such as *Untitled (Still Life With Chicken Wing)*, 2003 (fig. 119). For *Untitled (Family Portrait)*, 2005 (fig. 120), he had eight of his own finished paintings reproduced at a reduced scale, in an edition of four, displaying all five versions at various locations throughout the country simultaneously. He even hawked one of the editions at a Dallas pawn shop, thereby netting a C-note and a de facto exhibition (alongside other wares for sale). These endeavors void painting of the authenticity and originality for which it has so long been valued, but what's surprising and significant is that they don't

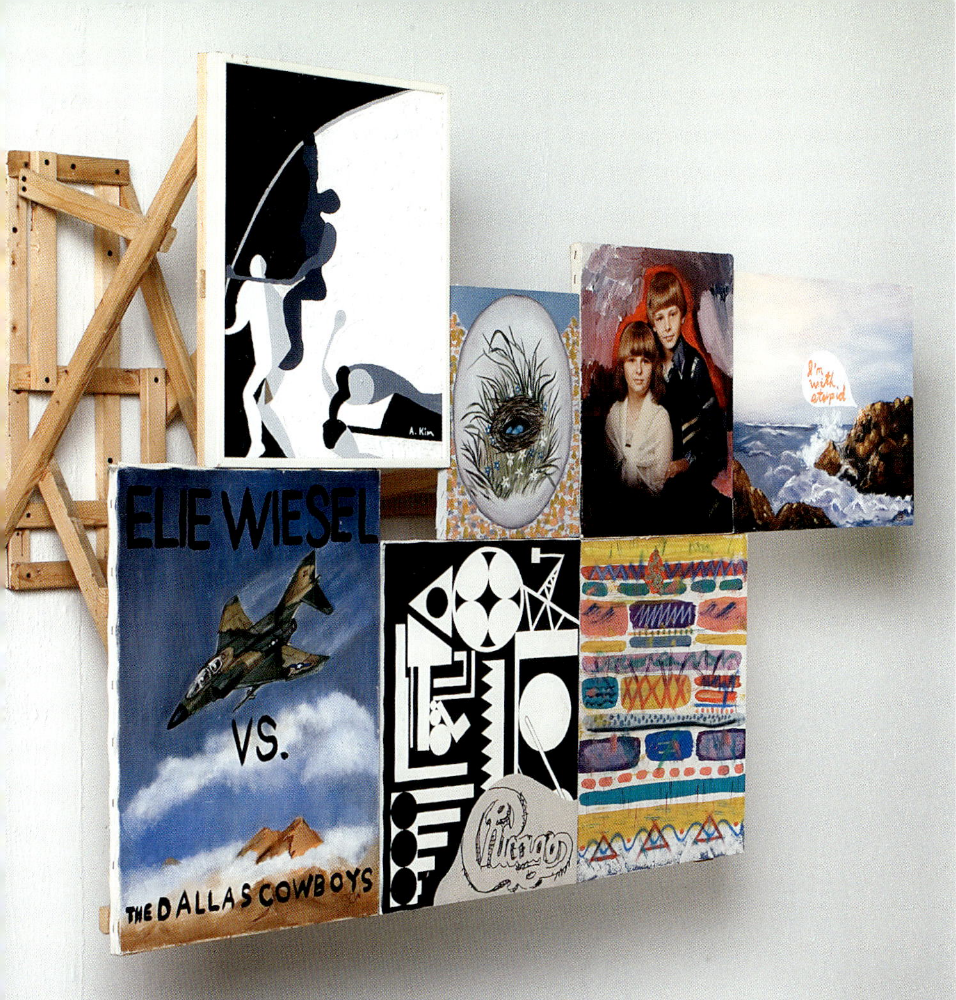

Fig. 122 **Untitled (Born to Be Mild)**, 2000, altered thrift store paintings, wood, and hardware, 44 x 68 x 19".

lead to a total depreciation; on the contrary, these paintings only grow weirder and more compelling through their proliferation.

Proliferation itself can be seen as a kind of gambit, one that Schwarz has engaged in stylistically as well as conceptually. Two decades of painting betray no consistency of style; if anything, his canvases are reliably inconsistent, ranging in references from gestural abstraction to color field to neo-geo to post-punk graffiti. Sometimes various styles crop up in one and the same installation, as they did in *Rentown*, 2001 (fig. 121), for which Schwarz temporarily transformed a gallery into a functioning outpost of Rent-a-Center. Sofas, dinettes, and entertainment units were available for cash purchase or rent-to-own alongside nine of the artist's paintings, the furnishings as mismatched as the art. As a tactic, this in-your-face stylistic pluralism finds an echo in the diversity of motifs reproduced in Schwarz's made-in-China paintings, as well as in an earlier assemblage. *Untitled (Born to Be Mild)*, 2000 (fig. 122), juxtaposes seven radically different thrift store pictures, each one slightly altered by the artist, such that a fighter jet gains the slogan "Elie Wiesel vs. The Dallas Cowboys" and a robin's nest becomes a Mondrian abstraction, circa 1914. Unexpected

and somewhat perverse, these various high-low juxtapositions—whether of tacky furniture and serious paintings, or of bad amateur pictures and clashing cultural references—question elitist presumptions about painting while also succeeding in being quite funny. Not funny ha-ha, of course, but funny strange. Painting, after all, is a serious, time-honored practice, one nearly impossible to tackle head on, but full of unforeseen possibilities when approached obliquely, as Ludwig Schwarz does, creeping up on it, both conceptually and literally, from the side or from behind.

—LORI WAXMAN

1. Schwarz, in Robert Faires, "The Final Four: The Artists up for the First Arthouse Texas Prize Talk about Their Work," *Austin Chronicle*, October 21, 2005.

Joel Tauber

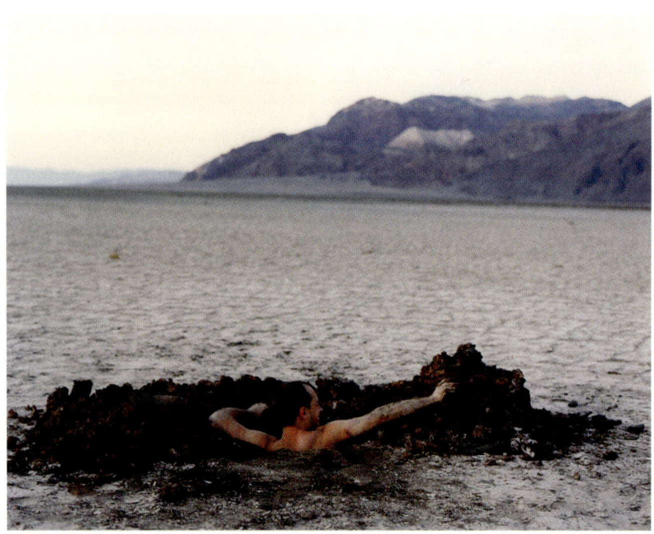

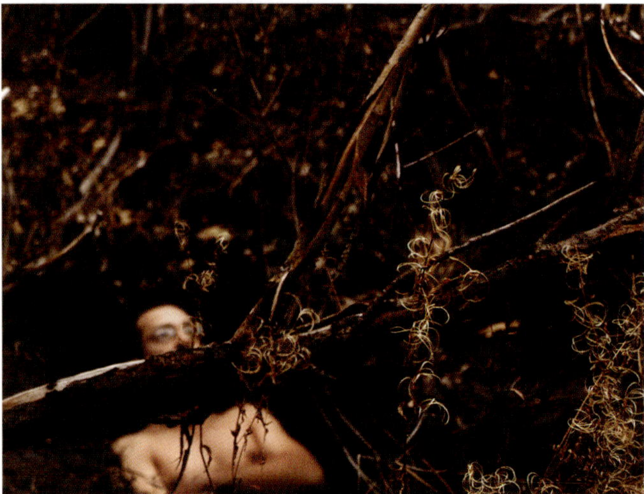

Fig. 123 **Untitled Image from Hole #1**, 2000, production still from *Seven Attempts to Make a Ritual*, 2000–2001, video, 24 minutes.

Fig. 124 **Untitled Image from Hole #2**, 2000, production still from *Seven Attempts to Make a Ritual*, 2000–2001, video, 24 minutes.

For Joel Tauber, this is not a rhetorical question. In each of the four video projects he has completed since 2000, the Los Angeles–based artist chronicles a different quixotic quest, each reflecting clear confidence that one can reach enlightenment through effortful action. The ambitious undertakings that become the subjects of the videos intertwine physical activity with mystical encounters and, more broadly, explore human relationships with nature and the divine.

Seven Attempts to Make a Ritual, 2000–2001 (see figs. 13, 123, and 124), for which the artist crawled into holes and caves in various sites near his home in southern California, mixes pantheistic beliefs with the traditional Orthodox Jewish view that a highly disciplined, ritualistic practice can lead to a connection with God. (While attending yeshiva as a boy, Tauber came to view the school's prohibition against art making as extremely restrictive.[2] Here he reclaims the validity of art as a personal spiritual pathway.) Having felt what he describes in the video's prologue as a "powerful intuition to place [himself] inside the Earth," the artist systematically established an unfiltered relationship between the landscape and his own body. The pre-set conditions for each immersive ritual varied: the twenty-four minute video follows Tauber as he struggles to either dig a hole large enough to accommodate his body or to climb as deeply as possible into a cave, then shows him sitting in the hole or cave, observing the landscape and meditating. In the final sequence, an exterior view of the cave fills the screen, and we hear the artist's disembodied voice talking about the state of heightened awareness he has been experiencing inside. The distinction between artist and earth has been erased.

Fig. 125 **Untitled**, 2003, light-jet print, 72 x 60". From *Searching for the Impossible: The Flying Project*, 2002–2003, video, 32 minutes.

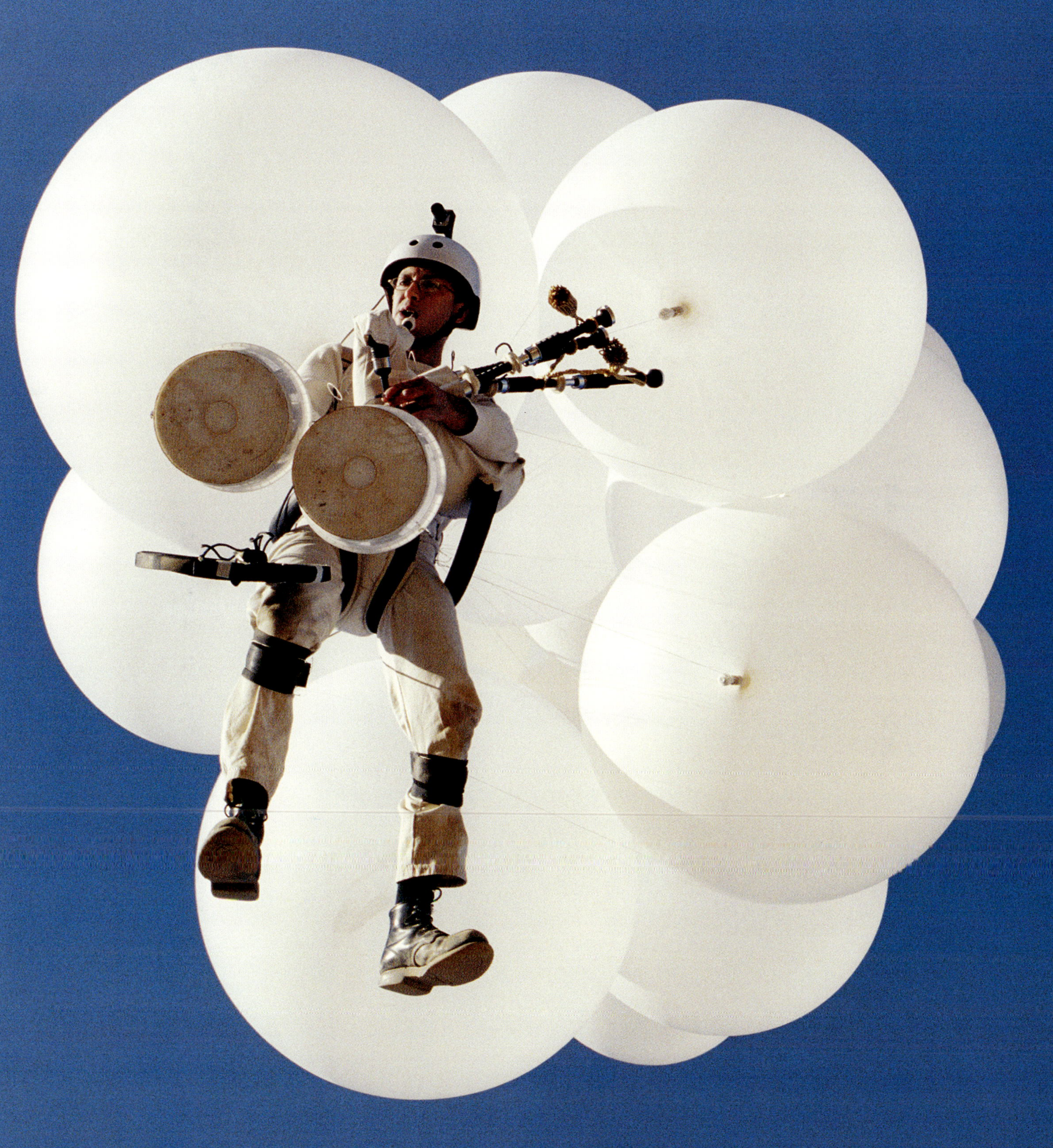

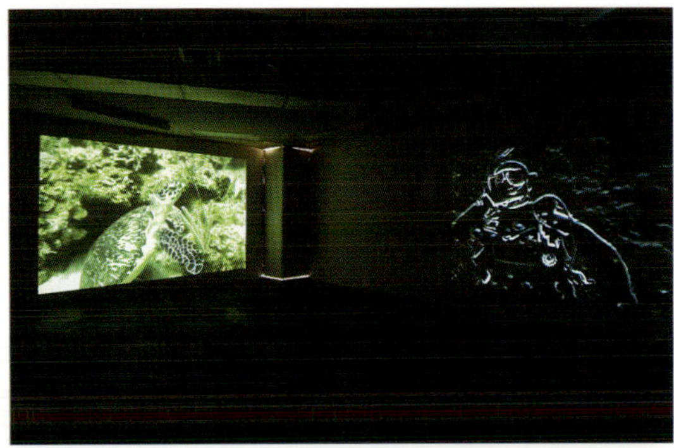

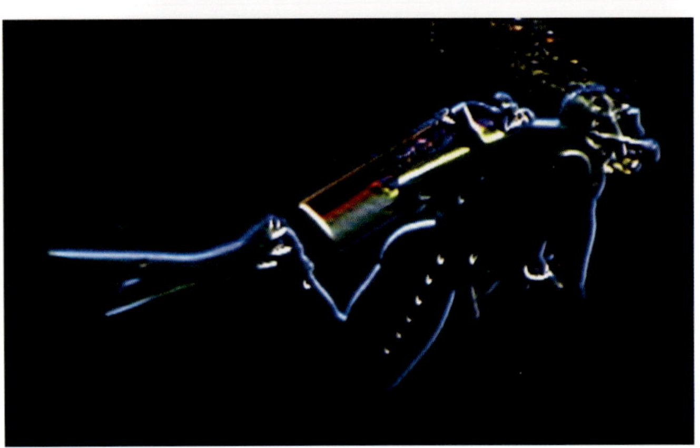

Fig. 126 **The Underwater Project: Turning Myself into Music**, 2003–2004, three-channel video installation, 51 minutes. Installation view, Susanne Vielmetter LA Projects, Los Angeles, CA, 2004.

Fig. 127 **The Underwater Project: Turning Myself into Music**, 2003–2004, still from a three-channel video installation, 51 minutes.

Fig. 128 **My Lonely Tree**, 2006, light-jet print, 56 x 72". ▶ From *Sick-Amour*, 2006–2007.

Tauber's journey continues in his next video, *Searching for the Impossible: The Flying Project*, 2002–2003 (see fig. 125), in which he depicts the art of flying as a spiritual experience rather than a Leonardo-like demonstration of scientific principles. Narrated by the artist, the thirty-two minute documentary begins with Tauber's efforts to fly without mechanical assistance. Inspired by Eilmer, an eleventh-century monk who believed that metaphysics was the key to flight, Tauber repeatedly stands at the edge of a large boulder, flaps his arms, breathes deeply, and jumps. Relying on "different mental preparations and flapping strategies," the artist never loses faith that, in that moment before take off, he can fly.[3] Positioning the camera so the viewer sees the launch but not the landing (on a crash mat below, it turns out) reflects this optimism. To the viewer, however, each attempt reinforces the senselessness of the task. After approximately one hundred tries at flying on his own, Tauber accepts the need for technological intervention. He takes up hang-gliding, but finds the apparatus too mechanical. A 1781 drawing by Pierre Blanchard of a flying ship powered by angels blowing into horns gives him a better idea. He creates his own music-driven flying contraption—a cluster of thirty-five six-foot latex balloons fastened by a custom-made parachute harness and powered, in part, by a bagpipe. Finally, he achieved the impossible: on a calm day in June 2002, Tauber climbed into his flight suit and floated 150 feet above a dry lake bed near Joshua Tree National Park—the proof is in the video. In its poetic demonstration of the power of determination *The Flying Project* suggests that it takes faith to achieve what no one else has. It also takes a bit of irrationality: Tauber is not reluctant to identify himself as "part of a continuum of fools" who blur the line between plausibility and absurdity.[4]

The premise of *The Underwater Project: Turning Myself into Music*, 2003–2004 (figs. 126 and 127), seems similarly preposterous. Encouraged by the flight and feelings of transcendence he gained through the power of sound, the artist next attempted to transform the corporeal (his body) into the ephemeral (music).[5] Having already communed with earth and sky, Tauber focused his energies on the sea. He first tracked his movements over the course of forty scuba-diving trips, then devised a method of translating the rhythm of his swimming body into melodies. In the three-channel video installation that reconstructs these endeavors, the viewer sees Tauber swim through the underwater landscape,

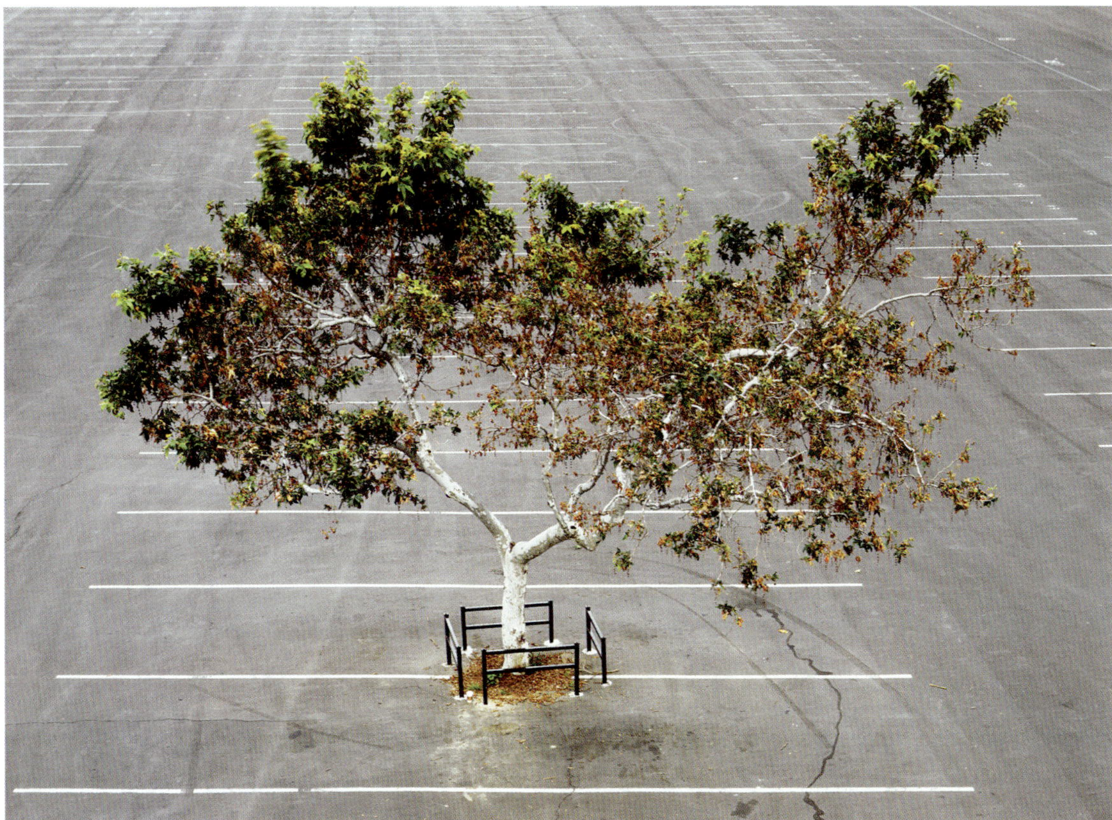

its "otherworldliness" emphasized by the image of his glowing, Photoshoped body projected onto one wall and extreme close-ups of exotic coral formations and sea creatures projected onto another. The third projection features a motion graph that displays the depth and duration of each dive.

Despite his best efforts, in *The Underwater Project* Tauber seems unable to fully engage with the natural world. In contrast to the serene images of him sitting in holes or floating in the air, here the images move across the ocean floor at a frenetic pace, as if the sea were more hostile than meditative. The notably synthetic-sounding music that accompanies the video reflects Tauber's sense that the underwater experience was more cybernetic than mystical.[6] Just as a turtle swims gracefully by, promising the artist the tranquility he seems to have been seeking, his oxygen supply runs low, and he is forced to cut short the dive.

Tauber's most recent project is back on dry land, bearing witness to his love for a tree. *Sick-Amour*, 2006–2007 (see fig. 128), a tripartite work comprising a documentary film, a video installation, and a permanent public artwork, chronicles the artist's very public crusade to save a dying California Sycamore stuck alone in the center of Rose Bowl Parking Lot K.

Like his earlier works, *Sick-Amour* examines the spiritual and ethical repercussions of seeking a profound connection with the natural world, but there's also a newly urgent engagement with politics and society at work here. Whether he is tending toward the absurd or the proactive, Tauber's endeavors are not at all futile. His conviction is contagious. If he can fly or turn himself into music, then why can't we all?
—SARAH GILLER NELSON

1. Tauber, artist statement, 2002.

2. See Hugh Hart, "Into It for the Shock of His Life," *Los Angeles Times*, December 24, 2004.

3. Tauber, conversation with the author, October 23, 2006.

4. Tauber, artist statement, 2003.

5. Tauber, in "FORMAT, Los Angeles 2005: Valdes, Ruben Ochoa, Lori Schindler, Joel Tauber, Kas Oshiro, Adria Julia," documentary produced by Swedish Television.

6. Tauber, conversation with the author, October 23, 2006.

Shoshanna Weinberger

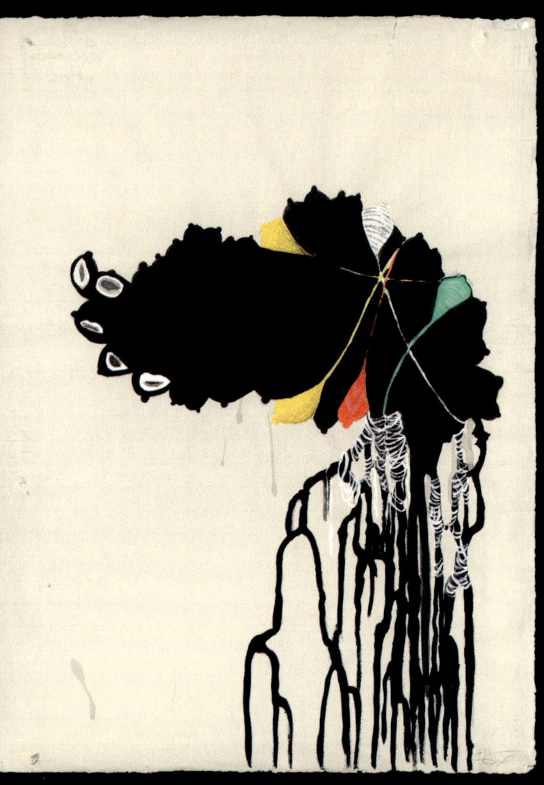

Fig. 129 **Pig Nose**, 2005, gouache on paper, 36 x 26".

RACE, GENDER, IDENTITY, AND SEXUALITY HAVE BEEN RICH SUBJECTS OF INVESTIGATION for several African American artists, notably Adrian Piper, Lorna Simpson, and Kara Walker. While these artists speak to the dualities of black/white, male/female, self/other, Shoshanna Weinberger, who is of Jewish and Caribbean descent, engages the in-between, expanding the inquiry to encompass her own cultural multiplicity. Weinberger's subversive distortions and transformations of the female form address hybridity, the fetishization of beauty, and power in a postcolonial world.

In the series "Hottentot Drawings," ongoing since 2005 (see figs. 129 and 130), for instance, the artist examines the construction and display of the non-white female body in Western society, connecting colonial spectacle to contemporary objectification. Reclaiming the derogatory name Dutch colonists gave to southern Africa's indigenous people, the "Hottentot Drawings" are inspired by images of Saartjie Baartman, a young Khoisan woman who was exhibited throughout England and France in the early nineteenth century. Popularly known as the "Hottentot Venus," Baartman became an object of intense fascination. She was often displayed caged and semi-nude, and her large buttocks were regarded as physical proof of what promotional materials called "the primitive sexual appetite" of the African female.

The "Hottentot Drawings" entwine Baartman-esque derrieres with thongs; taught lines representing overstretched, lacey G-string underwear criss-cross these "bodies," trans-forming a symbol of sexy, modern femininity into a sign of constriction. Weinberger's imagery reduces the female form to a flat composite of the body parts that men are said to love: ample breasts, perky nipples, rounded buttocks, long legs, and big, sexy hair. It connects the colonialist gaze to that of the con-temporary male, suggesting that the fantasy that Saartjie Baartman's physique represented

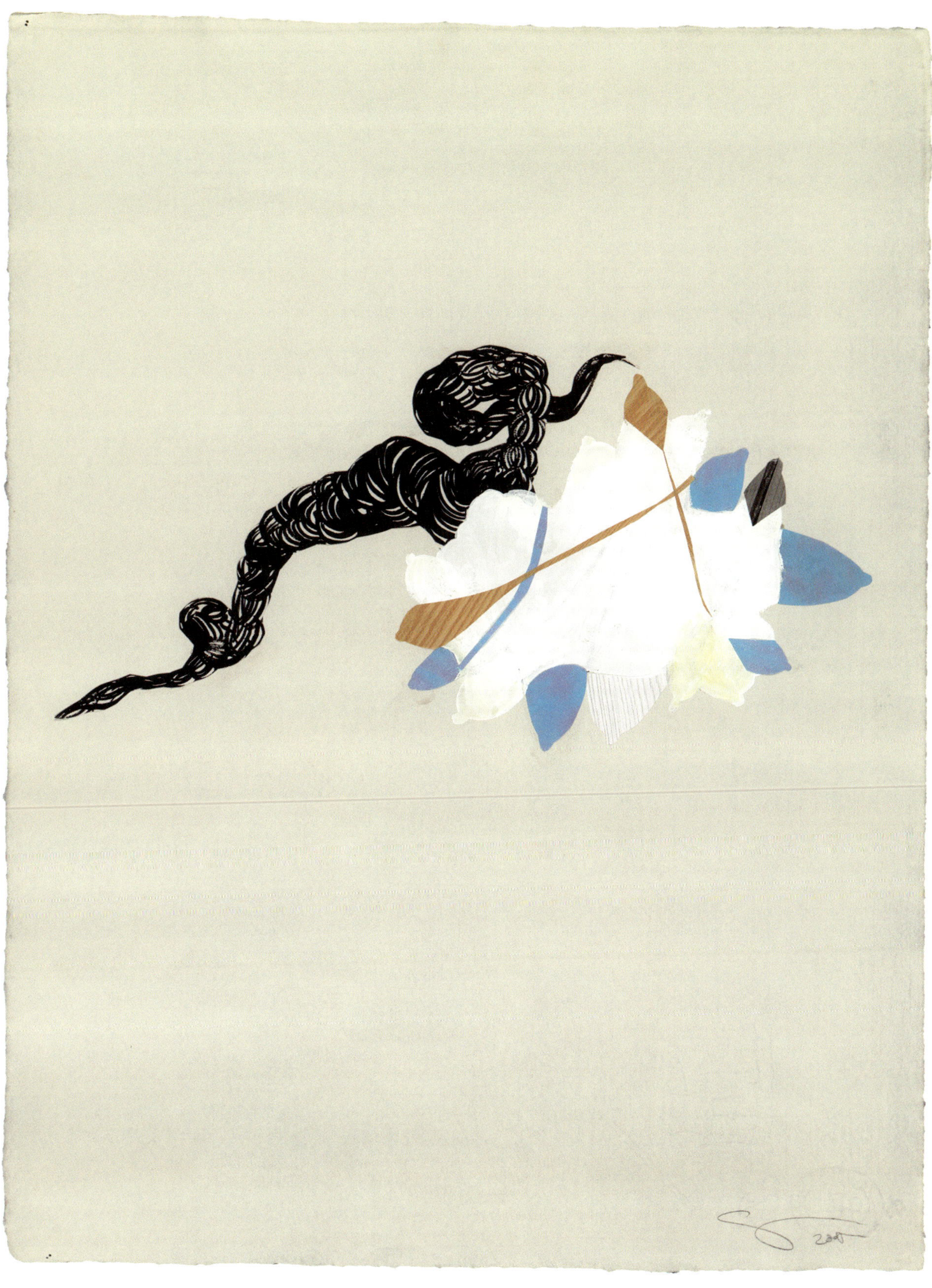

Fig. 130 **Hog Tied Again**, 2005, gouache and mixed media on paper, 23½ x 17¼".

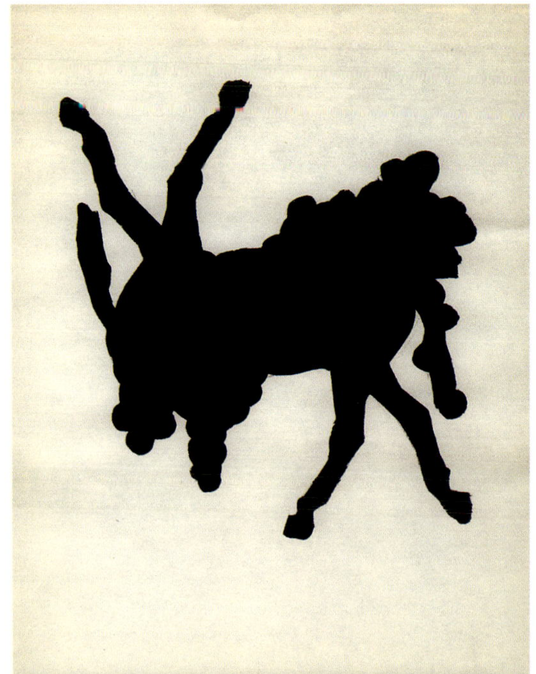

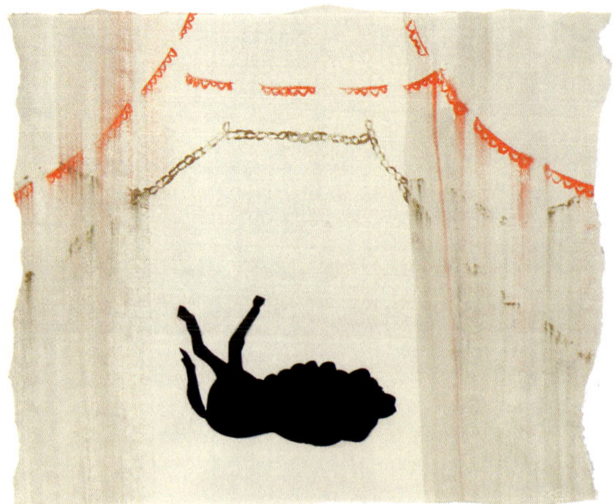

continues to pervade pop culture, influencing music, fashion, and standards of beauty, especially within the hip-hop community. "Hottentot Drawings" like *Strange Fruit*, 2005 (fig. 15), and *Pig Nose*, 2005 (fig. 129), take this fantasy to the extreme, exaggerating contemporary constructions of beauty in the form of impossibly long "legs" and a seemingly infinite number of breasts. That the body parts are interchangeable (the boobs double as butts which double as hair) reinforces just how disembodied the female form has become.

Whereas the "Hottentot Drawings" use visual synecdoche to represent the female form, the series "A Horse and Donkey Show: The Mulatto Diaries," 2005–2006, relies on metaphor for its associations. Spaniards colonizing the Americas labeled people of mixed race "mulattoes," a reference to the Spanish word for mule. Again reclaiming a derogatory term, Weinberger uses this multi-species animal as a metaphor for the multicultural female body, pairing the sexualized imagery of the "Hottentot Drawings" with mule legs, buttocks, and tails. (That "tail" is also slang for a desirable lady's rear should not go unnoticed.) The contorted, unadorned profiles of "The Mulatto Diaries" recall the silhouettes of Kara Walker, and function in a similar manner by equating the reductivism of the cut-out with the ignorance of the stereotype. Weinberger renders these figures in sexualized, supine positions, and her titles—*How Do You Want Me?* (fig. 131), *Just Got Paid* (fig. 132), and *Debut: She Is a Work in Progress*—evoke control and submission. *Wanti wanti na getti,*

getti getti na wanti, 2005 (fig. 134), in which the artist adds menacing claws and heaps of gold chains to the Frankensteinian form, functions as a modern-day *vanitas:* the title, roughly translated as "when you want it, you won't get it; when you get it, you won't want it," is a Jamaican proverb Weinberger's grandmother often utters as a warning against gluttony and jealousy.

Although as a self-described "visual anthropologist" Weinberger generally remains "an observer sitting on the periphery,"[1] she periodically forays into self-portraiture. Like Lorna Simpson, the artist depicts hair in her work to explore the way in which black women are identified, classified, and judged by their coiffures. *Zulu Jew*, 2004 (fig. 133), is clearly autobiographical. In it, an afro-like mane of hair resembling Weinberger's abundant tresses frames a black-and-white striped face, like curtains flanking a theatrical stage. The implication, it seems, is that race, ethnicity, and gender are performed, while identity is a costume. In *All of Me*, 2005 (fig. 135), the braided, beaded, and dreaded hair surrounds a costumeless (blank) place where the face would have been. This unnatural void reminds us of the ugliness that results when society defines a person as an amalgamation of parts. For Weinberger, identity is not about such piecemeal labeling, but about complex, lived experience.

—SARAH GILLER NELSON

---

1. Weinberger, e-mail correspondence with the author, September 18, 2006.

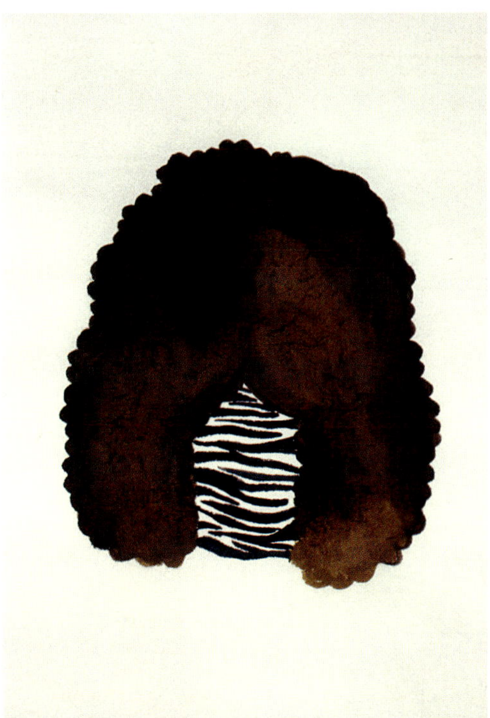

Fig. 133 **Zulu Jew**, 2004, gouache on paper, 10 x 8".

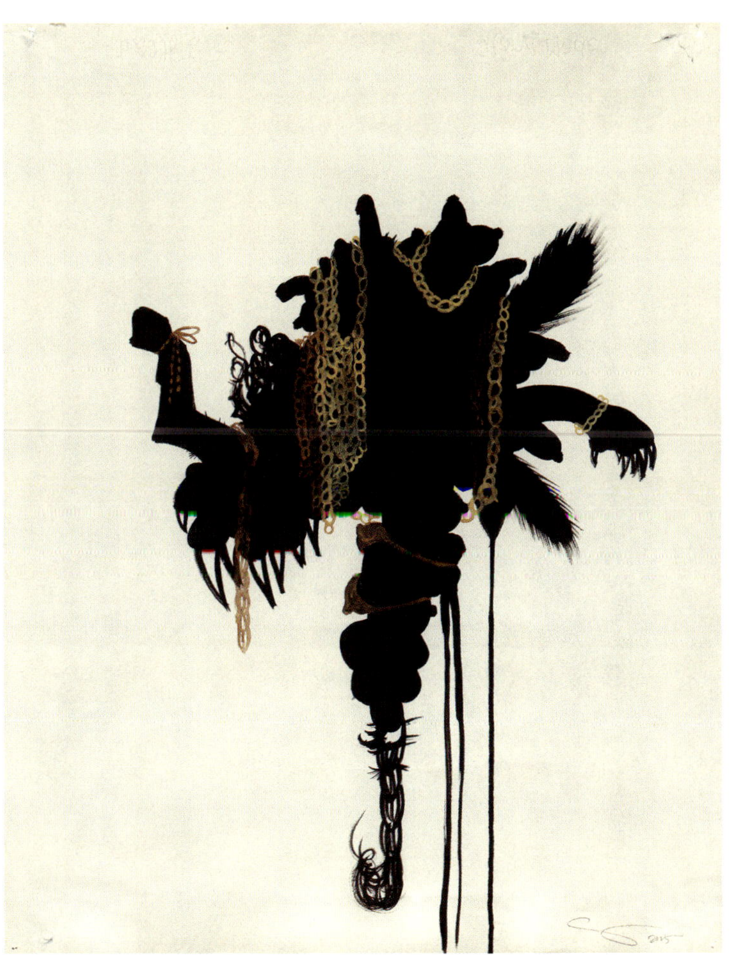

Fig. 134 **Wanti wanti na getti, getti getti na wanti**, 2005,
gouache and ink on paper, 23 1/2 x 18".

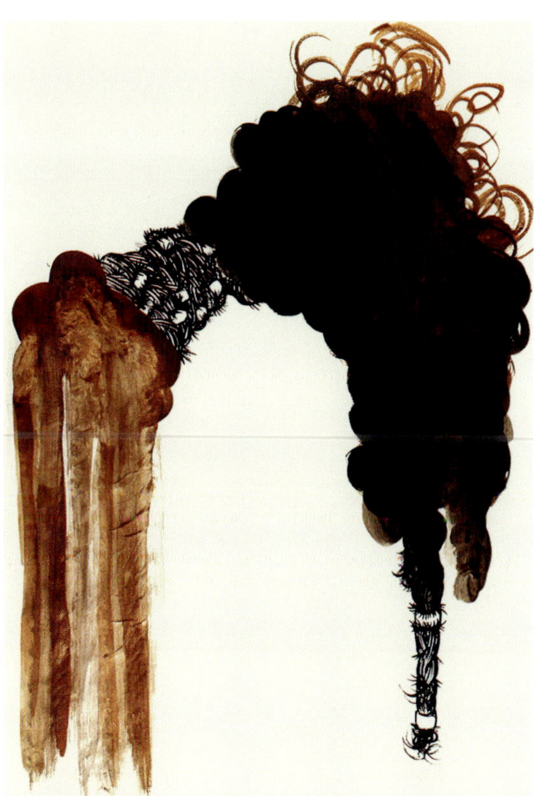

Fig. 135 **All of Me**, 2005, gouache and ink on paper, 21 x 16 1/2".

Jennifer Zackin

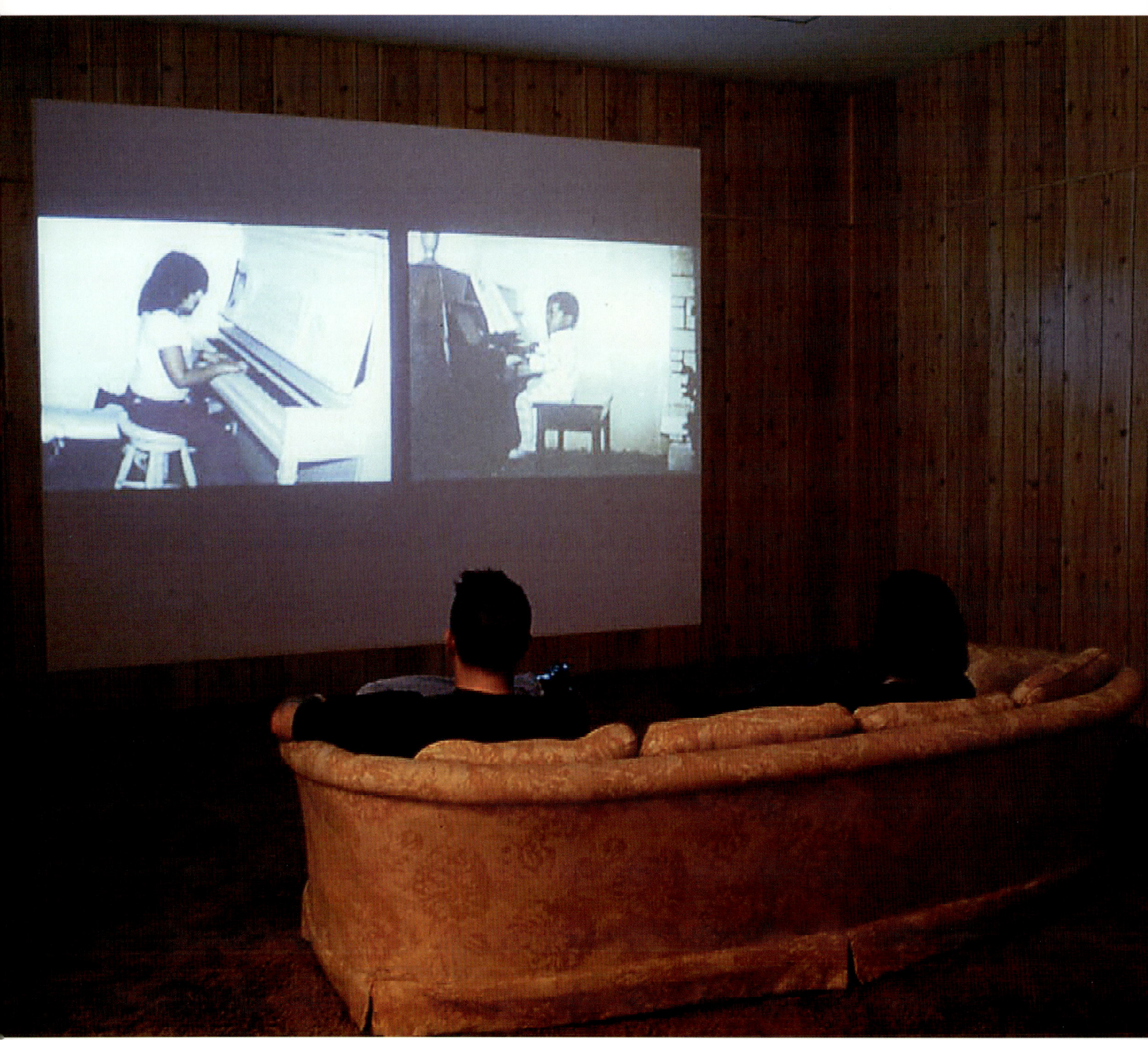

Fig. 136 Jennifer Zackin and Sanford Biggers, **a small world . . .**, 1999–2001, video installation, 5:30 minutes, dimensions variable. Installation view, Whitney Museum of American Art, New York, NY, 2002.

JENNIFER ZACKIN HAS WORKED WITH ROSE PETALS, LITTLE PLASTIC COWBOYS,

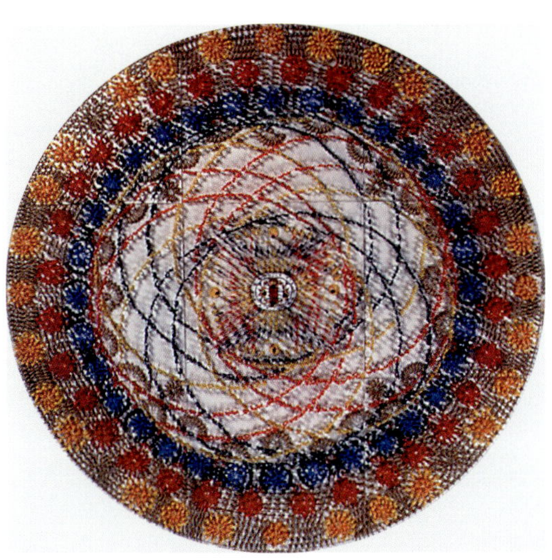

Fig. 137 **Wonder Woman Cosmos**, 2002, plastic toys and rubber, 108 x 108 x 29".

Fig. 138 **Wonder Woman Cosmos**, (detail), 2002.

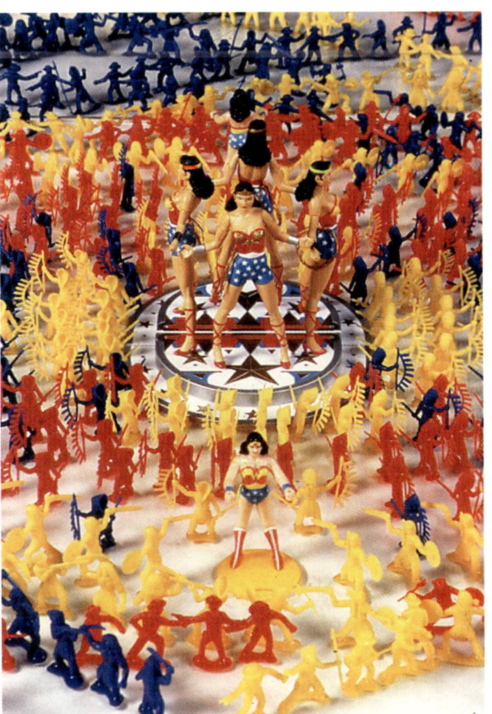

pre-Columbian bird symbols, bright handmade pom-poms, cheap mass-produced posters, coca leaves, and her grandfather's old Super-8 home movies. How she weaves them into rhythmic, often meditative forms depends in great part on the underlying patterns that she is able to detect and orchestrate among her diverse materials. Fervently pluralist, hers is a strategy that echoes the Pattern and Decoration movement of the 1970s, when artists like Miriam Schapiro, Joyce Kozloff, and Robert Kushner created a rich new vocabulary of line, motif, and undervalued materials. Zackin, too, has fashioned idiosyncratic, appropriative artworks in a multi-ethnic practice that incorporates influences from the arts and crafts of Western and non-Western cultures alike.

Before turning to the unfamiliar the artist explored the materials of home for signs of significant pattern. In the collaborative work *a small world . . .*, 1999–2001 (fig. 136), Zackin and artist Sanford Biggers project their respective home movies side by side, edited into a rhythmic montage of family birthday parties, holiday dinners, and vacations to Disneyland. While one family is East Coast Jewish, and the other West Coast African American, the footage is more or less interchangeable. As white family and black engage in look-alike versions of the American dream over and over again, a redundant pattern of middle-class sameness rather than racial or geographic difference emerges.

As if in response to the homogenizing vision of the world as a small place, Zackin has since worked in great part through immersing herself in foreign cultures. A self-declared "twenty-first-century xenophile,"[1] she has traveled extensively, weaving the vibrant threads of these experiences in and out of her work, forming an unexpected textile with the threads of her own American upbringing and home.

Fig. 139 **Rose Billboard**, 2004, digital print, dimensions variable.

Fig. 140 **I Have a Dream**, 2004, still from a single-channel video, 3:17 minutes.

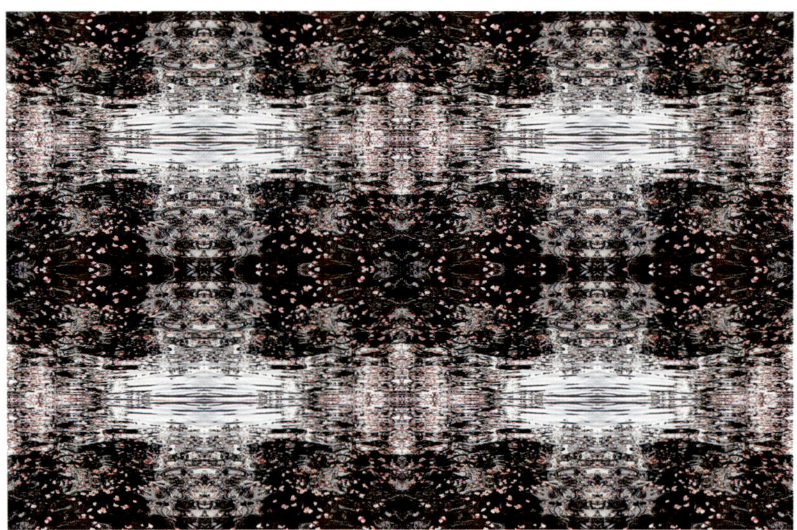

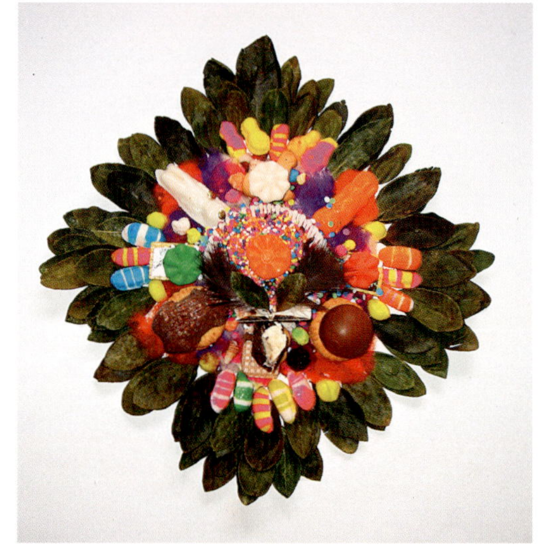

The resultant body of sculptures, videos, collages, and site-specific interventions provides a complicated and decidedly contemporary amalgamation of cross-cultural experience, exploring in particular how ritual practices can translate from one culture to another.

The mandala, a chart or geometric pattern used in both Buddhism and Hinduism to represent the cosmos, is one of the more recognizable ritual forms that recur in Zackin's work. Mandalas often serve as meditation devices. Typically circular and symmetrical in form, their center provides a focal point for practitioners' meditative gaze. Zackin's mandalas keep to these formal guidelines, but perform a humorous reinterpretation at the level of material. *Wonder Woman Cosmos*, 2002 (figs. 137 and 138), arranges concentric, color-coordinated circles of plastic Indians, firemen, and other "boy's" figurines around a central core of Wonder Woman dolls—conjuring the cosmos as understood by an American girl circa 1977. Zackin's juxtaposition of ancient diagram and mass-produced toys also enacts something more transcendent, transforming base into beautiful material through ritual patterning and revealing the hidden potential of lowly consumer goods.

This process of intuitively adapting traditional rituals found a unique expression in *Factory Direct*, 2004, a trio of performances plus print and video works made in collaboration with a fourth-generation family rose farm located in Connecticut. Given access to a generous supply of rose petals, Zackin set them adrift in both lake and ocean, where, she explains, they provide evidence of the water's rhythms, paying "homage to the inherent creative and destructive power of the natural world."[2] From these interventions Zackin created a series of meditative documents that intensify the results of her interactions with the environment. Prints like *Rose Billboard* (fig. 139) and *Rose Panel*, both 2004, composed from images of pink petals dappled across a lake, use repetition and cropping to suggest underlying natural patterns. *Lake Rescue*, 2007 (fig. 12), a newly edited version of similar footage, kaleidoscopically repeats the ebbing and flowing of waterborne petals to create a shimmering video mandala.

The reinvented offerings of *Factory Direct* were inspired by ceremonies Zackin partici-pated in during her visits with the Q'ero, an indigenous community who live to the east of Cusco, on the Amazonian side of the Andes.

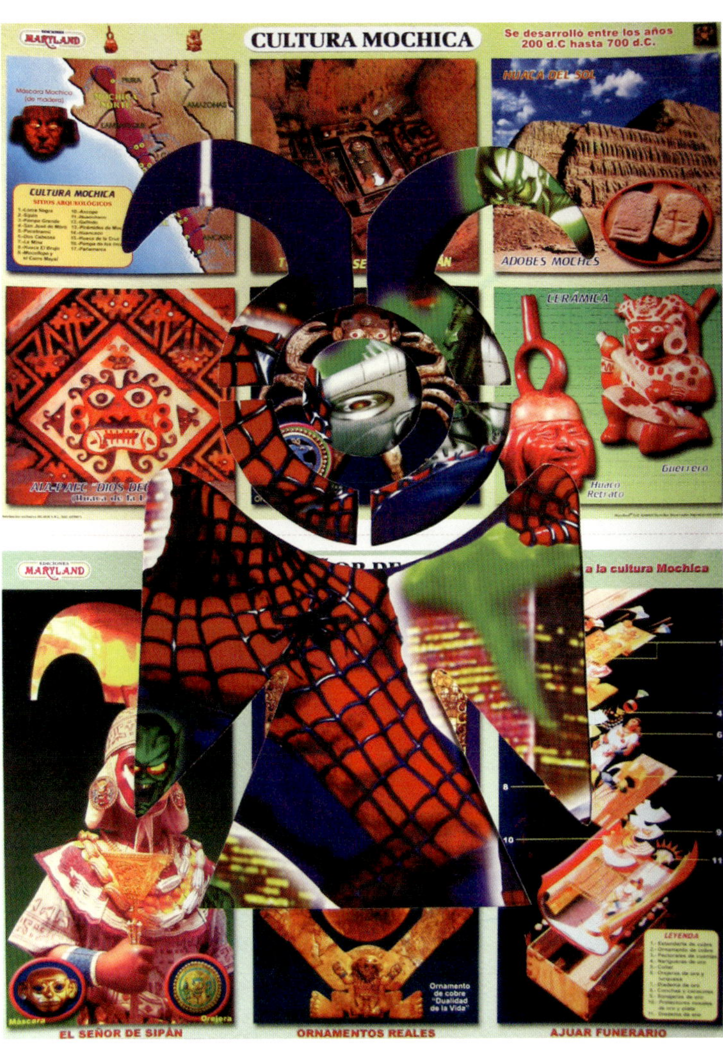

Fig. 141 **Nazca Over Spider-Man**, 2004, paper collage, 26 1/2 x 18 5/8".

Fig. 142 **Hanaqpacha Intiq Sombran (Heaven's Sun Shadow)** (detail), 2004, surplus U.S. military parachute and dyed cotton, dimensions variable. In collaboration with Nicholas Flores Apaza, Lorenzo Qhapaq Apaza, Mariano Quispe Flores, Benito Apaza Lunasco, and Santiago Quispe Qhapaq.

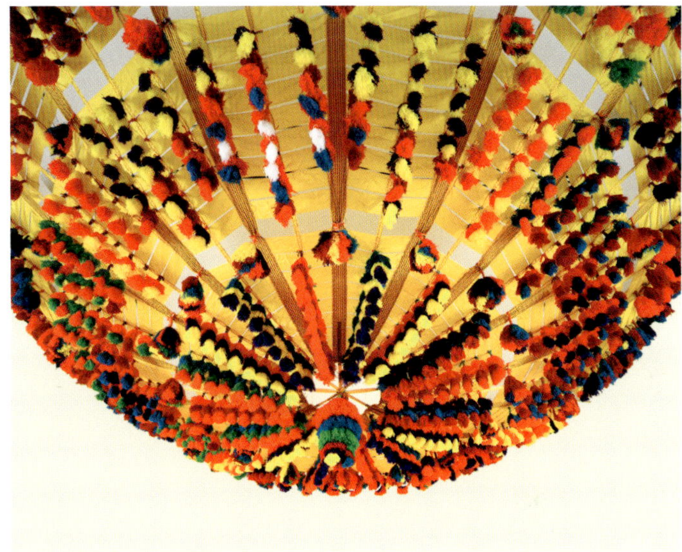

Various enterprises have resulted from her multiple stays in Peru, including *I Have a Dream*, 2004 (fig. 140), a video that layers the symbolic creation of a *despacho*, a traditional Andean oblation into which prayers can be blown, with another kind of wish: Martin Luther King Jr.'s "I have a dream" speech. A series of collages ensued from trips to Cusco's street markets, where Zackin found posters illustrating everything from Mochica culture to Peruvian presidents to Winnie-the-Pooh sold side by side. Layering pairs of posters and cutting through the top one in patterns inspired by Peruvian art, Zackin graphically elaborated the cultural mixing of the marketplace (see fig. 141). *Hanaqpacha Intiq Sombran (Heaven's Sun Shadow)*, 2004 (fig. 142), created in collaboration with five members of the Q'ero Nation, transforms a bright yellow parachute into a radiant, three-dimensional pattern piece through the addition of thirteen hundred pom-poms, inspired by the traditional *chu'llu* hat of the Q'ero.

Killamanta Kutismusaq—the title Zackin gave to a recent exhibition of the Peru projects—could be the motto for her entire body of work. Roughly translated from the ancient Quechua language of the Peruvian Andes, it means "to the moon and back," a fitting mantra for this peripatetic patterner of difference, one for whom the world is not so small after all.

—LORI WAXMAN

---

1. Zackin, artist statement, undated.

2. Zackin, artist statement, 2004.

Artist Biographies

DAVID ALTMEJD
Born 1974 in Montreal, Canada
Lives and works in New York, NY, and
London, England

EDUCATION

2001   MFA Columbia University, New York, NY

1998   BFA Université du Québec à Montréal,
Montreal, Canada

SELECTED SOLO EXHIBITIONS

2007   *David Altmejd: The Index*, Canadian Pavilion,
52nd Venice Biennale, Venice, Italy

David Altmejd: Métamorphose/Metamorphosis,
Galerie de l'UQAM, Montreal, Canada; traveled
to Oakville Galleries in Gairloch Gardens,
Oakville, Canada; Illingworth Kerr Gallery,
Alberta College of Art & Design, Calgary, Canada
(exh. cat.)

2006   Stuart Shave | Modern Art, London, England

2005   Xavier Hufkens, Brussels, Belgium

2004   Andrea Rosen Gallery, New York, NY

2003   *Sarah Altmejd*, Galerie SKOL, Montreal, Canada

2002   *Clear Structures for a New Generation*, Ten in
One Gallery, New York, NY

SELECTED GROUP EXHIBITIONS

2006   *Six Feet Under: Autopsy of our Dealing with the
Dead*, Kunstmuseum Bern, Bern, Switzerland

The Guggenheim Collection, Kunsthalle Bonn,
Bonn, Germany (exh. cat.)

A Brighter Day, James Cohan Gallery, New York,
NY (exh. cat.)

2005   *L'écho des limbes*, Galerie Leonard & Bina Ellen
Art Gallery, Montreal, Canada (exh. cat.)

*The Zine UnBound: Kults, Werewolves and
Sarcastic Hippies*, Yerba Buena Center for the
Arts, San Francisco, CA (exh. cat.)

*Ideal Worlds: New Romanticism in
Contemporary Art*, Schirn Kunsthalle Frankfurt,
Frankfurt, Germany

2004   *Noctambule*, Fondation Dosne—Bibliothèque
Thiers, Paris, France

Biennial Exhibition, Whitney Museum of
American Art, New York, NY (exh. cat.)

2003   8th Istanbul Biennial, Istanbul, Turkey

2002   *Demonclownmonkey*, Artists Space, New York, NY

2001   *Point de chute*, Galerie de l'UQAM, Montreal,
Canada; traveled to Centre d'Art Contemporain,
Brussels, Belgium (exh. cat.)

CHESELYN AMATO
Born 1958 in East Orange, NJ
Lives and works in Davis, CA

EDUCATION

1984   MFA Tyler School of Art, Temple University,
Philadelphia, PA

1980   BA Brown University, Providence, RI

1979   Tyler School of Art, Temple University in Rome,
Italy

SELECTED SOLO EXHIBITIONS

2006   *Vulnerability in the Presence of Love Is Heaven:
Revealed Treasure and Songs of Love*,
interactive performance ritual, artist's studio,
Evanston, IL

2004   *The Wild and The Tame & The Gestation of
Mature Love*, Pierro Gallery, South Orange, NJ

2003   *Apparitions in the Backyard*, Flatfile
Contemporary Gallery, Chicago, IL

2002   *The Manna Redemption*, Faculty Sabbatical
Exhibition, Betty Rymer Gallery, School of the
Art Institute of Chicago, Chicago, IL

Behold Your Treasure, Transmit Its Beauty,
interactive performance ritual, artist's studio,
Evanston, IL

2001   *Behold Shekinah: Her Indwelling Presence
Amongst Us*, interactive performance, artist's
studio, Evanston, IL

*Vocalizing the Song of Shekinah:
Improvisational Prayer, Visualizing The Tree of
Life*, and *Honoring Shekinah: Jewish Feminine
Voices*, performances at Studio Pardes,
Oak Park, IL

1996   *A Temple in Honor of Life Lived Everyday
An Unfinished Song of Love*, Chicago
Cultural Center, Chicago, IL

SELECTED GROUP EXHIBITIONS

2006   *Art from Chicago*, Studio 18 Gallery, New York, NY

2005   *The Hidden Garden: Three Artists Explore Kabbalah*,
The Borowsky Gallery, The Gershman Y,
Philadelphia, PA

2004   *Scanners*, Flatfile Contemporary Gallery,
Chicago, IL

Ner Tamid, Curators' Choice, Spertus Museum,
Chicago, IL

2002   *Piece Process*, ARC Gallery, Chicago, IL

I Love American, Unit B Gallery, Chicago, IL

Ragdale 25th Anniversary Exhibition, Fine Arts
Building Gallery Chicago, IL

2000   *Cleaning House*, Woman Made Gallery,
Chicago, IL

JOHANNA BRESNICK

Born 1973 in San Francisco, CA
Lives and works in New Haven, CT

EDUCATION

2001   MFA University of Illinois at Chicago, Chicago, IL

1995   BA Macalester College, St. Paul, MN
Studio Art Centers International, Italy

1990   Marie Walsh Sharpe Program, Colorado College,
Colorado Springs, CO

SELECTED SOLO EXHIBITIONS

2006   *Mamzer Loshen*, collaboration with Michael
Cloud, IPS Studio, New Haven, CT

SELECTED GROUP EXHIBITIONS

2007   *Connecticut Contemporary*, Wadsworth
Atheneum Museum of Art, Hartford, CT

Roadside Attractions, Small Space Gallery and
Kehler Liddell Gallery, New Haven, CT

2006   *The Everything and More Show*, The Nest,
Bridgeport, CT

2005   *In the Round*, Arts Council at John Slade Eli
House, New Haven, CT

Cultural Passages, Creative Arts Workshop,
New Haven, CT

2004   *Our Metaphors*, Starpin Gallery, Shelton, CT

2003   *Territories*, Galerie für Landschaftkunst,
Hamburg, Germany, and Artspace,
New Haven, CT

Group Show, 55 Mercer Gallery, New York, NY

where earth meets sky, Creative Arts Workshop,
New Haven, CT

2002   *Out of Place: Contemporary Art and the
Architectural Uncanny*, Museum of
Contemporary Art, Chicago, IL, and The Harn
Museum, Tallahassee, FL (exh. cat.)

2001   *Detourism*, The Renaissance Society, University
of Chicago, Chicago, IL (exh. cat.)

SHOSHANA DENTZ

Born 1968 in New York, NY
Lives and works in Brooklyn, NY

EDUCATION

2003   MFA Bard College, Annandale-on-Hudson, NY

1989   BA Brandeis University, Waltham, MA

1988   Parsons School of Design, Paris, France

SELECTED SOLO EXHIBITIONS

2006   *Portal please, please*, Triple Candie,
New York, NY

2005   *home lands*, Angles Gallery, Santa Monica, CA

home land 14e, Mixed Greens, New York, NY

2002   *Shoshana Dentz: Paintings*, Nicole Klagsbrun,
New York, NY

1998   *Shoshana Dentz*, White Columns, New York, NY

SELECTED GROUP EXHIBITIONS

2007   *Drawing, Thinking*, Von Lintel Gallery,
New York, NY

2006   *Human Rights Denied: Art Project*, Edinburgh
Festival, Edinburgh, Scotland

Up Against the Wall, Zilkha Gallery, Center for
the Arts, Wesleyan University, Middletown, CT
(exh. cat.)

Seeing Elsewhere, Education Alliance Gallery,
New York, NY (exh. cat.)

2005   *The Disasters of War: From Goya to Golub*,
Zilkha Gallery, Center for the Arts, Wesleyan
University, Middletown, CT (exh. cat.)

*Wall-to-Wall Drawings: Selections Summer
2005*, The Drawing Center, New York, NY

New Prints 2005/Spring, International Print
Center, New York, NY

2004   *Art and Impermanence*, Rubin Museum of Art,
New York, NY

2003   *After Matisse Picasso*, P.S.1 Contemporary Art
Center, Long Island City, NY

2000   *Fixations: The Obsessional in Contemporary Art*,
John Michael Kohler Arts Center, Sheboygan, WI
(exh. cat.)

LILAH FREEDLAND

Born 1971 in Ojai, CA
Lives and works in New York, NY

EDUCATION

1993   BA Bard College, Annandale-on-Hudson, NY

1991   Aegean Center for Art, Paros, Greece

SELECTED SOLO EXHIBITIONS

2007   *I'm gonna shit ourself*, collaboration with Mitch
Miller, Grizzly, ScopeBasel, Basel, Switzerland

SxSW: Brute Force and Daughter of Force,
Austin, TX

2006   *Sleepaway*, scopeNY, New York, NY

Undergod, collaboration with Alexis Hubshman,
Factor, ScopeLondon, London, England

2004   *The Clubhouse: Crowds and Power*, Carnegie Arts Center, Buffalo, NY

        Spell 06: Sellouthotel, scopeNY, New York, NY

SELECTED GROUP EXHIBITIONS

2006   *Will Boys Be Boys? Questioning Masculinity in Contemporary Art*, organized by Independent Curators International (iCI), New York, NY; traveled to Salina Art Center, Salina, KS; Museum of Contemporary Art, Denver, CO; Herbert F. Johnson Museum of Art, Ithaca, NY; and Indianapolis Museum of Art, Indianapolis, IN

2004   *Lore of the Trickster*, In The Kitchen, New York, NY

2003   *EAF03: Emerging Artist Fellowship Exhibition*, Socrates Sculpture Park, Long Island City, NY

        Low End Theory, Minnesota Center for Photography, Minneapolis, MN

2002   *Stupid Video*, Serpentine Gallery, London, England

        Proper Villains, Artspace, New Haven, CT

2001   *Purloined*, Artists Space, New York, NY

MATTHEW GIRSON

Born 1966 in Philadelphia, PA
Lives and works in Oak Park, IL

EDUCATION

1992   MFA University of Illinois at Chicago, Chicago, IL

1988   BFA University of the Arts, Philadelphia, PA

        Pennsylvania Certificate of Art Education, University of the Arts, Philadelphia, PA

SELECTED SOLO EXHIBITIONS

2007   Rowland Contemporary, Chicago, IL

2006   *. . . even in a room full of darkness*, Mary and Leigh Block Museum of Art, Northwestern University, Evanston, IL

        Dizzy Heights, Sonnenschein Gallery, Lake Forest College, Lake Forest, IL (exh. cat.)

1996   *Not a Forest*, Zolla/Lieberman Gallery, Chicago, IL

SELECTED GROUP EXHIBITIONS

2005   *Matthew Girson, Scott Short, Scott Stack*, Gahlberg Gallery, College of DuPage, Glen Ellyn, IL (exh. cat.)

        At the Limits of Representation, University of Texas, Dallas, TX

2002   *Tasty Dog*, LAC Exhibition Space, Krems, Austria

2000   *A Broad View: Landscape Painting and Photography*, University Art Gallery, Central Michigan University, Mt. Pleasant, MI

1998   *Chicago Hip*, Rocket Gallery, London, England

KARL HAENDEL

Born 1976 in New York, NY
Lives and works in Los Angeles, CA

EDUCATION

2003   MFA University of California, Los Angeles, Los Angeles, CA

2000   Skowhegan School of Painting and Sculpture, Skowhegan, ME

1999   Whitney Museum Independent Study Program, New York, NY

1998   BA Brown University, Providence, RI

SELECTED SOLO EXHIBITIONS

2007   *Last Fair Deal Gone Down*, Anna Helwing Gallery, Los Angeles, CA

        Harris Lieberman, New York, NY

2006   *MoCA Focus: Karl Haendel*, Museum of Contemporary Art, Los Angeles, CA (exh. cat.)

        Makes a Long Time Man Feel Bad, Sommer Contemporary Art, Tel Aviv, Israel

        Make Me Down a Pallet on Your Floor, Sorcha Dallas Contemporary Art, Glasgow, Scotland

2005   *Grits Ain't Groceries (All Around the World)*, Anna Helwing Gallery, Los Angeles, CA

2003   *You Can't Lose What You Ain't Never Had*, Anna Helwing Gallery, Los Angeles, CA

SELECTED GROUP EXHIBITIONS

2006   *Red Eye: Los Angeles Artists from the Rubell Family Collection*, The Rubell Family Collection, Miami, FL

        Transforming Chronologies: An Atlas of Drawings, Part Two, Museum of Modern Art, New York, NY

        Down by Law, curated by the Wrong Gallery, Biennial Exhibition, Whitney Museum of American Art, New York, NY

        A Brighter Day, James Cohan Gallery, New York, NY (exh. cat.)

2005   *Uncertain States of America: American Artists in the 3rd Millennium*, Astrup Fearnley Museet for Moderne Kunst, Oslo, Norway; traveled to Center for Curatorial Studies, Bard College, Annandale-on-Hudson, New York; Musée d'art moderne de la ville de Paris, Paris, France; Reykjavik Art Museum, Reykjavik, Iceland;

Serpentine Gallery, London; Herning Kunstmuseum, Herning, Denmark; The Centre for Contemporary Art, Ujazdowski Castle, Warsaw, Poland (exh. cat.)

Hunch and Flail, Artists Space, New York, NY

Rogue Wave, LA Louver, Venice, CA (exh. cat.)

2004 California Biennial, Orange County Museum of Contemporary Art, Newport Beach, CA (exh. cat.)

2003 *What do you see at night?*, Track 16, Santa Monica, CA

2002 *Emily Jacir, Karl Haendel, Kevin Hooyman*, La Panadería, Mexico City, Mexico

1999 *100 Drawings*, P.S.1 Contemporary Art Center, Long Island City, NY

LAURA KINA

Born 1973 in Riverside, CA
Lives and works in Chicago, IL

EDUCATION

2001 MFA University of Illinois at Chicago, Chicago, IL

1994 BFA School of the Art Institute of Chicago, Chicago, IL

SELECTED SOLO EXHIBITIONS

2007 *Aloha Dreams*, Diana Lowenstein Fine Arts, Miami, FL

2006 *Laura Kina: Loving*, Grand Projects, New Haven, CT

2003 *Hapa Soap Opera*, Diana Lowenstein Fine Arts, Miami, FL

Laura Kina: New Work, 55 Mercer Gallery, New York, NY

2002 *Laura Kina*, Union League Club of Chicago, Chicago, IL

SELECTED GROUP EXHIBITIONS

2006 *New ART as Universal LANGUAGE*, Art & Culture Center of Hollywood, Hollywood, FL

Hiddenvalleyranch, Diana Lowenstein Fine Arts, Miami, FL

2005 *Love Triangles: Asian Soap Opera Exhibition*, Asian Art Initiative, Philadelphia, PA

Top Choice: New Work by 5 Contemporary Artists, Korean Cultural Center, Los Angeles, CA

Semi-gloss: New Work by Laura Kina and Larry Lee, MN Gallery, Chicago, IL

2004 *Men and Boys*, Walkers Point Center for the Arts, Milwaukee, WI (exh. cat.)

Women in the Middle, Walkers Point Center for the Arts, Milwaukee, WI (exh. cat.)

2003 *Landmark Project*, Art-Link Ueno-Yanaka 2003, Tokyo, Japan

Mythical Nation, Artspace, New Haven, CT

FAWN KREIGER

Born 1975 in New York, NY
Lives and works in New York, NY

EDUCATION

2004 MFA Bard College, Annandale-on-Hudson, NY

1997 BFA Parsons School of Design, New York, NY

SELECTED SOLO EXHIBITIONS

2006 *ROOM*, collaboration with Tracy + the Plastics, The Moore Space, Miami, FL

Suspending Architecture, Tilt Gallery, Portland, OR

Stealing Home, PS122 Gallery, New York, NY

2005 Art in General, New York, NY

Treyf, Ohio University Art Gallery, Ohio University, Athens, OH

ROOM, collaboration with Tracy + the Plastics, The Kitchen, New York, NY

2004 *Treyf*, The Greenhouse Gallery / The James Beard House, New York, NY

SELECTED GROUP EXHIBITIONS

2007 *The Whole Fragment*, Sheppard Fine Arts Gallery, University of Nevada, Reno, NV (exh. cat.)

Animate Locate, Director's Lounge 2007, Berlin, Germany.

2006 *The New Baroque*, Nice & Fit Gallery, Berlin, Germany

Queens International 2006: Everything All At Once, Queens Museum of Art, Queens, NY

I may be some time…, James Nicholson Gallery, New York, NY

I can't quite place it…, Smack Mellon, Brooklyn, NY

escercizi #1, neon>campobase, Bologna, Italy

Il riflesso perplesso, neon>fdv, Milan, Italy

ad-vent, ArtCenter/SouthFlorida, Miami, FL

2005 *Systematic*, Vox Populi, Philadelphia, PA

no location relocation, Galleria d'Arte Contemporanea, Castel San Pietro, Italy (exh. cat.)

Craft Pathos, Maryland Art Place, Baltimore, MD (exh. cat.)

2002 *Matter As Protagonist*, Creative Arts Workshop, New Haven, CT

JIN MEYERSON

Born 1972 in Inchon City, South Korea
Lives and works in New York, NY

EDUCATION

1997 MFA Pennsylvania Academy of Fine Art, Philadelphia, PA

1995 BFA Minneapolis College of Art and Design, Minneapolis, MN

SOLO EXHIBITIONS

2006 *Accidental Tourist*, Galerie Emmanuel Perrotin, Paris, France

High Cholesterol Moment, Zach Feuer Gallery (LFL), New York, NY

2004 *More Than You Want, Less Than You Need*, LFL Gallery, New York, NY

Galerie Emmanuel Perrotin, Paris, France

GROUP EXHIBITIONS

2007 *Salon Nouveau*, Engholm Engelhorn Galerie, Vienna, Austria

More Is More—Maximalist Painting, Museum of Fine Arts, Florida State University, Tallahasse, FL

Vanhaerents Foundation, Torhout, Belgium

2006 *The Triumph of Painting*, The Saatchi Gallery, London, England (exh. cat.)

2004 *Surface Tension*, Chelsea Art Museum, New York, NY (exh. cat.)

2003 *Pantone*, Massimo Audiello Gallery, New York, NY

Tenth Anniversary, Frederieke Taylor Gallery, New York, NY

The Burnt Orange Heresy, Space 101, Brooklyn, NY

COLLIER SCHORR

Born 1963 in New York, NY
Lives and works in Brooklyn, NY

EDUCATION

1986 School of Visual Arts, New York, NY

SELECTED SOLO EXHIBITIONS

2007 Museum of Contemporary Art, Denver, CO

Badischer Kunstverein, Karlsruhe, Germany

2006 *Other Women*, Modern Art, London, England

2005 *Jens F.*, Roth, New York, NY

2004 Fotogalleriet, Oslo, Norway

303 Gallery, New York, NY

Modern Art, London, England

2002 Consorcio Salamanca, Salamanca, Spain

2000 Emily Tsingou Gallery, London, England

SELECTED GROUP EXHIBITIONS

2007 *Reality Bites: Making Avant-Garde Art in Post-Wall Germany*, Kemper Art Museum, Washington University, St. Louis, MO

2006 *Human Game*, Fondazione Pitti, Stazione Leopolda, Florence, Italy

Youth of Today, Schirn Kunsthalle Frankfurt, Frankfurt, Germany

2005 *Will Boys Be Boys? Questioning Masculinity in Contemporary Art*, organized by International Curators Incorporated (iCI), New York, NY; traveled to Salina Art Center, Salina, KS; Museum of Contemporary Art, Denver, CO; Herbert F. Johnson Museum of Art, Ithaca, NY; and Indianapolis Museum of Art, Indianapolis, IN

Seeing Double: Encounters with Warhol, The Andy Warhol Museum, Pittsburgh, PA

The Lost Paradise, Stiftung Opelvillen, Frankfurt, Germany

2004 *Opportunity and Regret*, Grazer, Kunstverein, Graz, Austria

Open House—Working in Brooklyn, Brooklyn Museum of Art, New York, NY

2003 *Terror Chic*, Spruth Magers, Munich, Germany

Strangers, Triennial of the International Center of Photography, New York, NY

Attack! Art and War in Times of the Media, Kunsthalle Wien, Vienna, Austria

2002 *Screen Memories*, Contemporary Art Center, Art Tower Mito, Japan

Biennial Exhibition, Whitney Museum of American Art, New York, NY

2001 *American Tableaux*, Walker Art Center, Minneapolis, MN

Uniform: Order and Disorder, P.S.1 Contemporary Art Center, New York, NY

Settings and Players: Theatrical Ambiguity in American Photography, White Cube, London, England

MINDY ROSE SCHWARTZ

Born in Chicago, IL
Lives and works in Chicago, IL

EDUCATION

1996   MFA University of Illinois at Chicago, Chicago, IL

1992   State of Illinois Art Teaching Certificate K-12,
        School of the Art Institute of Chicago,
        Chicago, IL

1985   BFA University of Illinois at Urbana-Champaign,
        Champaign, IL

SELECTED SOLO EXHIBITIONS

2002   Joymore Gallery, Chicago, IL

SELECTED GROUP EXHIBITIONS

2006   *Takeover*, Hyde Park Art Center, Chicago, IL

        COMA #1 and #5, California Occidental Museum
        of Art, Chicago, IL

        Strange Fictions, Northern Illinois University Art
        Museum Gallery, Chicago, IL

        Exposed: Envisioning the Invisible Body, McLean
        County Arts Center, Bloomington, IL

2005   *Nook*, The Guest Room Project, Chicago, IL

2004   *Portraits*, Highland Artworks Gallery,
        Portland, MN

        Cha Cha Cha, Worm-Hole Laboratory, Miami, FL

        Combine: Mixing Media, Lake Forest College,
        Lake Forest, IL

2002   *Watery Domestic*, The Renaissance Society,
        University of Chicago, Chicago, IL

2000   *Organic Produce*, International Museum of
        Surgical Science, Chicago, IL

        Blink, Interventions in the Salon, Northern
        Illinois University Art Museum Gallery,
        Chicago, IL

LUDWIG SCHWARZ

Born 1964 in Dallas, TX
Lives and works in Dallas, TX

EDUCATION

1990   MFA School of Visual Arts, New York, NY

1986   BFA Southern Methodist University, Dallas, TX

1984   School of the Art Institute of Chicago,
        Chicago, IL

SELECTED SOLO EXHIBITIONS

2007   *The Four Seasons (Season Premier)*, Sunday,
        New York, NY

2005   *Birdsongbird*, Sala Diaz, San Antonio, TX

        Untitled (Travelogue 8) Edition 1/4, 2/4, 3/4,
        FREIGHT+VOLUME, New York, NY; Q.E.D., Los
        Angeles, CA; Village Jewelry and Loan, Dallas, TX

2004   *Chronologic (Carry On)*, Three Walls,
        San Antonio, TX

        Schrempf 1000 (Carry On), South Side Gallery,
        Dallas, TX

2003   *Sound Chaser*, Angstrom Gallery, Dallas, TX

        The Jerk, Angstrom Gallery; Village Jewelry and
        Loan, Dallas, TX

2001   *RENTOWN*, Angstrom Gallery, Dallas, TX

        Thrillseeker(s), Lump, Raleigh, NC

2000   *True*, Angstrom Gallery, Dallas, TX

SELECTED GROUP EXHIBITIONS

2007   *The Audience Is Listening*, Road Agent,
        Dallas, TX

2006   *The Milwakee International*, Falcon Beer Hall
        Bowling Alley, Milwaukee, WI

2005   *Texas Prize*, Arthouse at the Jones Center,
        Austin, TX; Dallas Center For Contemporary Art,
        Dallas, TX; Galveston Arts Center, Galveston,
        TX (exh. cat.)

        Dirty Does It, Volume Gallery, New York, NY

        Parings, Dallas Center for Contemporary Art,
        Dallas, TX

2004   *Drunk vs. Stoned*, Gavin Brown at Passerby,
        New York, NY

        Twang, Art Museum of Southeast Texas,
        Beaumont, TX; McKinney Avenue Contemporary,
        Dallas, TX

        I Heart New York Texas, Allston Skirt Gallery,
        Boston, MA

2003   *False Emotion*, Kunstbunker Tumulka, Munich,
        Germany

2001   *Hand-Job*, University of Texas at Dallas,
        Richardson, TX (exh. cat.)

        Big as Texas, DiverseWorks, Houston, TX

        Herbert Heindl & Ludwig Schwarz, Homeroom,
        Munich, Germany

1997   *Post-Pop, Post-Pictures*, The Smart Museum of
        Art, University of Chicago, Chicago, IL (exh. cat.)

        Video Flash, Hohenthal und Bergen, Cologne,
        Germany

1996   *Fool's Rain*, Institute of Contemporary Art,
        London, England

JOEL TAUBER

Born 1972 in Boston, MA
Lives and works in Los Angeles, CA

EDUCATION

2002   MFA Art Center College of Design, Pasadena, CA

1997   MA Lesley University, Cambridge, MA

1995   BA Yale University, New Haven, CT

SELECTED SOLO EXHIBITIONS

2007   *Sick-Amour*, Susanne Vielmetter Los Angeles Projects, Culver City, CA; Adamski Gallery, Aachen, Germany

2006   *Searching for the Impossible: Digging, Flying and Diving*, Gallery Saintonge, Missoula, MT

2005   *Seven Attempts to Make a Ritual*, Susanne Vielmetter Los Angeles Projects, Culver City, CA

       The Underwater Project: Turning Myself Into Music, Helen Lindhurst Fine Arts Gallery, University of Southern California, Los Angeles, CA

2004   *Searching for the Impossible: The Flying Project*, Susanne Vielmetter Los Angeles Projects, Culver City, CA

2003   *Searching for the Impossible*, Adamski Gallery, Aachen, Germany

SELECTED GROUP EXHIBITIONS

2007   *Excess of Subjectivity*, Miki Wick Gallery, Zurich, Switzerland

2006   *Happy Believers*, 7th Werkleitz Biennial, Volkspark, Halle, Germany

       Eco Lux: Art in the Light of Ecology 1953–2006: Maya Lin, Samuel Yates, Kelly Poe, Rebecca Morales, Sharon Ryan, Yayoi Kusama, Brian Bress, Tia Pulitzer, Samantha Fields and Joel Tauber, Lightbox, Los Angeles, CA

       Good Bye Festival, CPH Kunsthalle, Copenhagen, Denmark (exh. cat.)

2005   *The Gravity in Art*, De Appel Centre for Contemporary Art, Amsterdam, Netherlands

       Still, Things Fall from the Sky, University of California Riverside/California Museum of Photography, Riverside, CA (exh. cat.)

2004   California Biennial, Orange County Museum of Art, Newport Beach, CA (exh. cat.)

2003   *Light and Spaced Out: 11 Artists From Los Angeles*, Loevenbruck Gallery, Paris, France; Centre d'Art Passerelle, Brest, France

2002   *Stuff From L.A. and Other Places*, Christine Konig Gallery, Vienna, Austria

       To Believe Much More Than That, Wight Gallery, UCLA, Los Angeles, CA

SHOSHANNA WEINBERGER

Born 1973 in Kingston, Jamaica
Lives and works in Newark, NJ

EDUCATION

2003   MFA Yale School of Art, New Haven, CT

1995   BFA School of the Art Institute of Chicago, Chicago, IL

SELECTED GROUP EXHIBITIONS

2006   *National Biennial Exhibition*, National Gallery of Jamaica, Kingston, Jamaica

       Working Title: The Group Show Exhibition, from the documentary film *Working Title*, Gallery 51, Montclair, NJ

2005   *First Annual Huron Pier Invitational*, Brooklyn, NY

2004   *5x7: On the Road*, Arthouse at the Jones Center for Contemporary Art, Austin, TX; Dunn and Brown Contemporary, Dallas, TX; The Old Jail Art Center, Albany, TX

2003   *New American Talent 18*, Arthouse at the Jones Center for Contemporary Art, Austin, TX (exh. cat.)

       Summer Jam, Roebling Hall Satellite Gallery, New York, NY

       Gilligan's Island, Ambrosino Gallery, Miami, FL

2001   *2001 Spaced Oddities*, Gallery 2, School of the Art Institute of Chicago, Chicago, IL

JENNIFER ZACKIN

Born 1970 in Waterbury, CT
Lives and works in New York, NY, and Middlebury, CT

EDUCATION

1999   MFA School of the Art Institute of Chicago, Chicago, IL

1998   Skowhegan School of Painting and Sculpture, Skowhegan, ME

1997   MA School of the Art Institute of Chicago, Chicago, IL

1992   BFA Parsons School of Design, New York, NY

1991   Studio Art Center International, Florence, Italy

SELECTED SOLO EXHIBITIONS

2006   *Killamanta Kutimusaq*, Aldrich Contemporary Art Museum, Ridgefield, CT

2005   *OM MY*, Public Art Project, Katonah Museum of Art, Katonah, NY

2004   *Mandala*, Alianza Francesa de Lima, Peru

        Pachamama Hanaqpacha K'anchay, Instituto
        Cultural Peruano Norteamericano, Cusco, Peru

2000   *TRANSPOSE*, Indigo Gallery, Kathmandu, Nepal

SELECTED GROUP EXHIBITIONS

2007   *From the Inside Out*, Dr. M.T. Geoffrey Yeh Art
        Gallery, St. John's University, Queens,
        NY (exh. cat.)

        Pretty Baby, Modern Art Museum of Fort Worth,
        Fort Worth, TX (exh. cat.)

        The Wild Bunch: Cowboys in Contemporary Art,
        The Arts Center, St. Petersburg, FL

2006   *Black Alphabet*, Zacheta National Art Gallery,
        Warsaw, Poland (exh. cat.)

        I ♥ the 'Burbs, Katonah Museum of Art, Katonah,
        NY (exh. cat.)

2005   *BROOKLinVIDEO*, Futura, Prague, Czech Republic

        Factory Direct, Artspace, New Haven,
        CT (exh. cat.)

        Set and Drift, Lower Manhattan Cultural
        Council, Governor's Island, NY

2004   *Social Studies: Eight Artists Address Brown v.
        Board of Education*, Krannert Art Museum,
        Champaign, IL; traveled to University of Kansas
        Spencer Museum of Art, Lawrence, KS (exh. cat.)

2003   *Splat Boom Pow*, Contemporary Arts Museum,
        Houston, TX; traveled to Institute of
        Contemporary Art, Boston, MA; Wexner Center
        for the Arts, Columbus, OH; Henie Onstad
        Kunstsenter, Høvikodden, Norway

        Somewhere Better Than This Place,
        Contemporary Art Center, Cincinnati, OH
        (exh. cat.)

        Family Ties, Peabody Essex Museum, Salem,
        MA (exh. cat.)

        Commodification of Buddhism, Bronx Museum
        of Art, Bronx, NY

        Contemporary Art/Recent Acquisitions,
        The Jewish Museum, New York, NY

2002   Biennial Exhibition, Whitney Museum of
        American Art, New York, NY (exh. cat.)

2001   *Freestyle*, The Studio Museum in Harlem,
        New York, NY (exh. cat.)

2000   *Culture of Class*, The Maryland Institute College
        of Art, Baltimore, MD

Works in the Exhibition

David Altmejd
The Settler, 2005
Wood, paint, Plexiglas, mirror, foam,
resin, synthetic hair, lighting system,
shoes, wire, beads, and glitter
40 x 46 3/8 x 90 5/8 in.
Courtesy of the artist and Andrea Rosen
Gallery, New York, NY

Cheselyn Amato
*Fabric Collage (Placemats, Napkins, &
Deathcamps)*, 2004/2007
From the series "Fabric and Textile
Collages," 2000–
Wall mural
Dimensions variable
Courtesy of the artist, Davis, CA

Johanna Bresnick
Ohne Lebensraum, 2004
Rug, mannequin, wood, foam, and
latex paint
40 x 92 x 140 in.
Courtesy of the artist, New Haven, CT

Shoshana Dentz
home lands #13, 2004
From the series "home lands," 2003–
Oil and gouache on canvas
70 x 140 in.
Courtesy of the artist, Brooklyn, NY, and
Angles Gallery, Santa Monica, CA

Lilah Freedland
dip ya karpas, 2001
From the series "Hebrew School Pin-Ups,"
2001–2005
C-print mounted on Sintra
20 x 24 in.
Courtesy of the artist, New York, NY

*dream as though you'll live forever, live as
though you'll die today*, 2003
C-print mounted on Sintra
24 x 20 in.
Courtesy of the artist, New York, NY

god bless video, 2002
Ink and acrylic on paper
14 x 11 in.
Courtesy of the artist, New York, NY

mass mitzvah, 2002
Ink and acrylic on paper
14 x 11 in.
Courtesy of the artist, New York, NY

next year in the holy land, 2002
From the series "Hebrew School Pin-Ups,"
2001–2005
C-print mounted on Sintra
20 x 24 in.
Courtesy of the artist, New York, NY

Matthew Girson
Dizzy Heights V, 2005
From the series "Dizzy Heights," 2005
Oil on canvas
20 x 20 in.
Courtesy of the artist, Oak Park, IL

Satellite view #2, 2006
From the series "Satellite View,"
2005–2006
Oil on canvas
63 x 63 in.
Courtesy of the artist, Oak Park, IL

Satellite view #3, 2006
From the series "Satellite View,"
2005–2006
Oil on canvas
63 x 63 in.
Courtesy of the artist, Oak Park, IL

*(blanc) a scent in ab·scent·ia by Matthew
Girson*, 2005
Materials related to perfume launch
Courtesy of the artist, Oak Park, IL

Karl Haendel*
F-16's, 2006
Pencil on paper
41 x 26 in.
Private Collection

Gay Republicans and Democratic Fetuses,
2006
Pencil on paper
51 x 79 in.
Courtesy of the artist and Anna Helwing
Gallery, Los Angeles, CA

Israel pulls out of Gaza, Gaza not Pregnant,
2006
Pencil on paper
22 x 30 in.
Courtesy of the artist and Anna Helwing
Gallery, Los Angeles, CA

List #4, 2007
Pencil on paper
39 x 52 in.
Courtesy of the artist and Anna Helwing
Gallery, Los Angeles, CA

Screaming Baby (negative), 2007
Unique c-print
80 x 52 in.
Courtesy of the artist and Anna Helwing
Gallery, Los Angeles, CA

Submarine, 2006
Pencil on paper
52 x 52 in.
Courtesy of the artist and Anna Helwing
Gallery, Los Angeles, CA

10th Question Mark, 2006
Pencil on paper
30 x 22 in.
Courtesy of the artist and Anna Helwing
Gallery, Los Angeles, CA

Untitled, 2007
Pencil on paper
90 x 70 in.
Courtesy of the artist, Los Angeles, CA,
and Harris Lieberman, New York, NY

Wasserlack #2 (Ghost Mirrored Version),
2006
Unique c-print
46 x 52 1/2 in.
Courtesy of the artist and Anna Helwing
Gallery, Los Angeles, CA

We Miss Clinton, 2006
Pencil on paper
74 x 51 in.
Courtesy of the artist and Anna Helwing
Gallery, Los Angeles, CA

* At the time of publication, some of the
loans for Karl Haendel's installation had
not been finalized.

Laura Kina
The Aronsons, 2001
Acrylic, pen, crayon, and pencil on canvas
70 x 36 1/2 in.
Courtesy of the artist, Chicago, IL

The Kina-Aronsons, 2001
Acrylic and collage on canvas
62 x 28 1/2 in.
Courtesy of the artist, Chicago, IL

The Rosenfelds, 2001
Acrylic on canvas
103 x 50 1/2 in.
Courtesy of the artist, Chicago, IL

Fawn Krieger
DAWNING 1, 2006
From the series "DAWNING," 2006
Fabric, stuffing, and thread with
wood base
69 1/2 x 28 x 4 in.
Courtesy of the artist and Envoy,
New York, NY

DAWNING 2, 2006
From the series "DAWNING," 2006
Fabric, stuffing, and thread with
wood base
66 1/2 x 26 x 4 in.
Courtesy of the artist and Envoy,
New York, NY

DAWNING 3, 2006
From the series "DAWNING," 2006
Fabric, stuffing, and thread with
wood base
68 x 25 x 4 in.
Courtesy of the artist and Envoy,
New York, NY

DAWNING 4, 2006
From the series "DAWNING," 2006
Fabric, stuffing, and thread with
wood base
63 1/2 x 20 x 4 in.
Courtesy of the artist and Envoy,
New York, NY

"TREYF," 2004
Series of 20 inkjet prints
Each 8 1/2 x 11 in.
Courtesy of the artist and Envoy,
New York, NY

Jin Meyerson
Tower, 2005
Oil and acrylic on canvas
139 x 144 in.
Ostrow Family Collection
(Spertus Museum only)

Landfall, 2005
Oil, acrylic, and India ink on canvas
90 x 120 in.
Collection of Nicolas Rohatyn and Jeanne
Greenberg Rohatyn
(The Rose Art Museum only)

Collier Schorr
Laura, 2004
From the series "Forests and Fields," 1995–
C-print
19 x 15 in.
Courtesy of the artist and 303 Gallery,
New York, NY

Spielplatz (Lindenfeld), 1997
From the series "Forests and Fields," 1995–
C-print
20 x 28 in.
Courtesy of the artist and 303 Gallery,
New York, NY

Steffen, Barbarostrasse, Garden, 2001
From the series "Forests and Fields," 1995–
Gelatin silver print
37 x 28 1/2 in.
Collection of Jay Dandy and Melissa
Weber, Chicago, IL

Mindy Rose Schwartz
Untitled (The River), 2007
Steel, rope, rocks, wood, foam, wire,
resin, crystals, plaster, paint, clay, glaze,
glue, pencil, ink, mulberry paper, fabric,
and artificial plants
Dimensions variable
Courtesy of the artist, Chicago, IL

Ludwig Schwarz
Untitled (Born to Be Mild), 2000
Altered thrift store paintings, wood,
and hardware
44 x 68 x 19 in.
Courtesy of the artist, Dallas, TX, and
Angstrom Gallery, Los Angeles, CA

Untitled (Wiggles #2), 2003
Oil on canvas
Edition 1/4 (painted in China)
60 x 84 in.
Private Collection

Joel Tauber
Seven Attempts to Make a Ritual,
2000–2001
Seven-channel video with sound
Courtesy of the artist and Susanne
Vielmetter Los Angeles Projects,
Los Angeles, CA

Shoshanna Weinberger
All of Me, 2005
From the series "Hair," 2003–2005
Gouache and ink on paper
21 x 16 1/2 in.
Courtesy of the artist, Newark, NJ

Hog Tied Again, 2005
From the series "Hottentot Drawings,"
2005–
Gouache and mixed media on paper
23 1/2 x 17 1/4 in.
Courtesy of the artist, Newark, NJ

How Do You Want Me?, 2006
From the series "A Horse and Donkey
Show: The Mulatto Diaries," 2005–2006
Ink on paper
10 x 8 in.
Courtesy of the artist, Newark, NJ

Just Got Paid, 2006
From the series "A Horse and Donkey
Show: The Mulatto Diaries," 2005–2006
Ink on paper
8 x 16 in.
Courtesy of the artist, Newark, NJ

Participant Cash Only, 2004
Gouache on paper
11 1/4 x 8 1/2 in.
Courtesy of the artist, Newark, NJ

Pig Nose, 2005
From the series "Hottentot Drawings,"
2005–
Gouache on paper
36 x 26 in.
Courtesy of the artist, Newark, NJ

Strange Fruit, 2005
From the series "Hottentot Drawings,"
2005–
Gouache and collage on paper
24 x 18 in.
Courtesy of the artist, Newark, NJ

Wanti wanti na getti, getti getti na wanti,
2005
From the series "A Horse and Donkey
Show: The Mulatto Diaries," 2005–2006
Gouache and ink on paper
23 1/2 x 18 in.
Courtesy of the artist, Newark, NJ

*Wonder Woman's Last Episode: My First
American Hero*, 2004
Gouache on paper
36 x 32 in.
Courtesy of the artist, Newark, NJ

Zulu Jew, 2004
From the series "Zebras," 2003–2005
Gouache on paper
10 x 8 in.
Courtesy of the artist, Newark, NJ

Jennifer Zackin
Lake Rescue, 2007
Single-channel video with sound and
archival inkjet prints
Dimensions variable
Courtesy of the artist, New York, NY,
and Middlebury, CT

Jennifer Zackin and
Sanford Biggers
a small world . . ., 1999–2001
Video installation
5:30 minutes
Courtesy of the artists, New York, NY,
and Middlebury, CT

Acknowledgments

Producing The New Authentics exhibition and publication was no small feat, and we would like to express our gratitude to those who have made this ambitious project possible. Our dramatic building, elegant galleries, and provocative programming would certainly not exist without the resolve and support of Spertus President Dr. Howard A. Sulkin. We greatly appreciate his efforts and his enthusiasm for our new mission.

To Jay Dandy and Melissa Weber; the Ostrow Family; Nicolas Rohatyn and Jeanne Greenberg Rohatyn; and others, we extend our sincere thanks for lending works from their collections to this exhibition and tour. We know how difficult it can be to part with art, even for a short while, and we appreciate their generosity.

We would also like to thank the following galleries for facilitating communication with artists as well as supplying research materials and images: Laura Mackall, Teneille Haggard, and Jeremy Lawson at Andrea Rosen Gallery; Anna Helwing and Morgan Satterfield at Anna Helwing Gallery; Zach Feuer and Grace Evans at Zach Feuer Gallery; Mariko Munro and Simon Greenberg at 303 Gallery; David Quadrini and John Ryan Moore at Angstrom Gallery; Susanne Vielmetter Los Angeles Projects; Jessie Washburne Harris at Harris Lieberman; and David McAuliffe at Angles Gallery.

We thank Ron Krueck, Mark Sexton, Tim Tracey, and others at Krueck & Sexton Architects for their elegant design of the exhibition. This project could not have happened without the hard work and sage advice of the Spertus museum and design staff: Arielle Weininger, Anne Bustamante, Tom Gengler, Susan Bass Marcus, Amanda Friedeman, Ilana Segal, Felicitas Heimann-Jelinek, Mark Akgulian, Sheila Cronin, Michael Miller, Tracy Kostenbader, Tony Doyle, and Robin Smith. Our thanks also go to Betsy Gomberg, Susan Baum, Mari Philipsborn, Emily Canham, Marv Cutler, and Beth Silverman for marketing and fundraising efforts.

This publication is the product of the combined efforts of many talented and dedicated individuals, including editor Jennifer Liese and designer Jason Pickleman of JNL Design. Dr. Stephen J. Whitfield, professor of American Studies at Brandeis University, contributed an insightful, lively, and wide-ranging essay. It is not often that Clifford Odets and Monica Lewinsky are united in prose. Lori Waxman wrote ten of the individual artist essays in record time. Her energetic and clever writing is a major contribution to the bibliographies of each artist. Craig Mandell provided expert legal advice and assisted on securing artwork reproductions. We extend our sincere thanks to them all.

This project is greatly indebted to Spertus Museum assistant curator Sarah Giller Nelson, who contributed six excellent essays on individual artists to this publication and also performed the immense task of coordinating the materials for both exhibition and catalogue, before and after the birth of her son, Jack. Sarah's work, both intellectual and organizational, is deeply appreciated.

We are thrilled that the exhibition will travel to The Rose Art Museum at Brandeis University in Waltham, MA, and thank Michael Rush, the Henry and Lois Foster Director, and Raphaela Platow, former chief curator, for their commitment to this project.

Along the way, many friends and colleagues have made constructive suggestions and offered valuable information and advice, for which our gratitude goes to Laura Stoland, Kay Rosen, Suzanne Weaver, Esther Bak, Hal Kugeler, Jennifer Draffen, Stephanie Smith, Michael Sittenfeld, Melissa Chiu, Shimon Felix, Ari Y. Kelman, Dan Sharon, and Michael Blaustein.

Our utmost appreciation is reserved for the "New Authentics" themselves, artists David Altmejd, Cheselyn Amato, Johanna Bresnick, Shoshana Dentz, Lilah Freedland, Matthew Girson, Karl Haendel, Laura Kina, Fawn Krieger, Jin Meyerson, Collier Schorr, Mindy Rose Schwartz, Ludwig Schwarz, Joel Tauber, Shoshanna Weinberger, and Jennifer Zackin. Each artist not only supplied us with compelling works to be included in the exhibition, but during the course of the exhibition's development, had a lot to say about art and Jewish, or post-Jewish, identity. These discussions inspired the direction of the exhibition, and it is for both their art and their challenging perspectives, not to mention their time, that we offer our profound thanks.

STACI BORIS, SPERTUS MUSEUM SENIOR CURATOR

RHODA ROSEN, SPERTUS MUSEUM DIRECTOR

Photography credits

All images provided by the artists unless otherwise noted.
Images in the Director's Foreword and in Stephen J. Whitfield's essay are credited in the captions.

David Altmejd: figs. 11, 24–29 courtesy of Andrea Rosen Gallery, New York, NY; fig. 11 photograph by Tom Powel
Shoshana Dentz: figs. 8, 46, 48 courtesy of Angles Gallery, Santa Monica, CA
Matthew Girson: figs. 3, 4, 61, 62, 65–67 photographs by Tom Van Eynde; fig. 60 photograph by Larry Kline
Karl Haendel: figs. 7, 68–76 courtesy of Anna Helwing Gallery, Los Angeles, CA; figs. 71–73 photographs by Joshua White;
figs. 74, 75 photographs by Karl Haendel
Laura Kina: figs. 17, 77–79, 81, 82 photographs by Jim Prinz; fig. 80 photograph by Saverio Truglia
Fawn Krieger: figs. 9, 83–88, 90–92 courtesy of Envoy, New York, NY; fig. 89 courtesy of Paula Court and The Kitchen,
New York, NY
Jin Meyerson: figs. 16, 93–99 courtesy of Zach Feuer Gallery, New York, NY
Collier Schorr: figs. 6, 100–107 courtesy of 303 Gallery, New York, NY
Ludwig Schwarz: figs. 1, 118, 119, 121, 122 courtesy of Angstrom Gallery, Los Angeles, CA
Joel Tauber: figs. 13, 123–128 courtesy of Suzanne Vielmetter Los Angeles Projects, Los Angeles, CA, and Adamski Gallery,
Aachen, Germany; figs. 13, 123, 124 photographs by Jason Mahanes; fig. 125 photograph by Michelle Coe;
fig. 128 photograph by Ian Hunter and Star Rosencrans.